PRIVATE GARDENS OF
LONDON
ARABELLA LENNOX-BOYD

PRIVATE GARDENS OF LONDON
ARABELLA LENNOX-BOYD
PHOTOGRAPHS BY JOHN MILLER

Weidenfeld & Nicolson

All plant names have been
checked with *The Plant Finder*.

page 1 Hostas growing in my own London garden
pages 2–3 from 'A Tropical Jungle in the East End'
page 4 One of a pair of Venetian herms from 'A Painter's Garden'

© text Arabella Lennox-Boyd 1990

© photographs and plans George Weidenfeld and Nicolson Ltd 1990

First published by George Weidenfeld and Nicolson Ltd
91 Clapham High Street, London SW4 7TA

Design by Lisa Tai
Plans by Andrew Wilson
Research by Barbara Mellor

All rights reserved. No part of this publication may be reproduced, stored in a retrieval system, or transmitted, in any form or by any means, electronic, mechanical, photocopying or otherwise, without the prior permission of the copyright owners.

British Library Cataloguing in Publication Data
Lennox-Boyd, Arabella
 Private gardens of London.
 1. London. Gardens to ca 1950
 I. Title II. Miller, John
 712.609421

ISBN 0–297–83025–2

Phototypeset by Keyspools Ltd, Golborne, Lancs
Colour separations by Newsele Litho Ltd
Printed in Italy by Printers Srl, Trento
Bound by L.E.G.O., Vicenza

For Patricia and Dominique

CONTENTS

Introduction

A GARDEN OF ROOMS IN TWICKENHAM 10

A PLANTSMAN'S GARDEN 18

A CORNISH COMBE IN PUTNEY 24

THE TRADESCANT GARDEN: A 'CABINET OF CURIOSITIES' 30

A GARDEN FOR ENTERTAINING 36

AMONG MINARETS IN CHELSEA 42

A BELGRAVIA BASEMENT 49

A GARDEN AFLOAT 51

LUTYENS REVISITED 54

BEHIND THE STUCCO: THREE GARDENS ON THE LADBROKE ESTATE 60

A VIEW TO THE HEATH 70

AN EMBROIDERER'S GARDEN 78

A ZEN GARDEN IN FULHAM 82

A STREET IN PECKHAM 89

WALPOLE HOUSE 94

A GARDEN OF THE UNEXPECTED 102

A MUSICIAN'S GARDEN 112

CHELSEA PHYSIC GARDEN 118

A PAINTER'S GARDEN 122

THE ULTIMATE ROOF GARDEN 126

A SMALL GARDEN IN BATTERSEA 132

A SECRET GARDEN 138

THE HILL, HAMPSTEAD: AN EDWARDIAN EXTRAVAGANZA 142

A VICTORIAN GARDEN 146

ON THE THAMES AT CHISWICK 152

THE VINEYARD 158

A TROPICAL JUNGLE IN THE EAST END 164

ECCLESTON SQUARE 170

COLOUR IN THE GARDEN 174

CANONBURY HOUSE 180

THE LANNING ROPER MEMORIAL GARDEN 184

MALVERN TERRACE, BARNSBURY 190

A LOW-MAINTENANCE GARDEN 192

A HIGHGATE GARDEN 197

A WHITE GARDEN 202

A FLORAL DECORATOR'S GARDEN 206

A POST-MODERN GARDEN 212

Further Reading
Index

INTRODUCTION

'As for our love of gardens, it is the last refuge of art in the minds and souls of many Englishmen: if we did not care for gardens, I hardly know in what way of beauty we should care for.' So wrote Sir Arthur Helps, encapsulating a truth as valid now as it was when he was writing, in the mid-nineteenth century. The English have a talent for cultivating their gardens, making them beautiful and interesting, just as they do for making their houses warm and welcoming; it is no coincidence that it was an Englishwoman who invented the idea of garden 'rooms'. And if English people in general cultivate their gardens with a passion, lavishing on them immense thought, devoted care and hours of work, Londoners are masters of the art. Buried deep in the psyche of the most inveterate city dweller there is frequently an innate love of the countryside, coupled with a desire to bring it into the city. Give them the smallest patch – be it a dark basement, an exposed rooftop or a tiny yard – and as often as not they will turn it into a luxuriant, flower-filled haven where they can observe the passing of the seasons and escape the noise and grime of the urban jungle.

As a garden designer living and working in London, I have for years been fascinated by the ingenuity, imagination and sheer variety of London's gardens, and was delighted to be given the opportunity to describe a few of them in the pages of this book. Readers will not find practical tips or technical discussions here, for I have concentrated instead on the individual nature of each garden, endeavouring to do justice to the elusive 'spirit of place': that personal quality that is unique to English gardens, I feel, and especially noticeable in London. For while all the gardens here enjoy the benefits of a favourable microclimate and amenable soil, enabling them to cultivate a wider variety of plants than almost anywhere in the world, they are equally subject to the inevitable disadvantages presented by an urban environment. Many of these gardens are hard-won triumphs against such adversity, and are the more cherished and fiercely personal for it.

Spoilt for choice, I have chosen almost forty gardens which I hope illustrate the remarkable variety of gardens to be found in London. There are historic gardens and botanical collections, communal squares and cottage gardens, grand formal designs and meadows of wild flowers, gardens perched on roofs and tucked into basements, painters' gardens and period gardens, a Japanese garden and a post-Modernist garden, a sub-tropical jungle and a vivid display on the roof of a narrowboat, and also I could not omit four of my own designs. Running like a thread through all of these gardens, uniting them in their tremendous variety, is the owners' great love of plants and the most strong feeling for design.

Many gardeners are only too happy to share their secrets and their plants, pressing cuttings and seedlings on fellow enthusiasts. This is particular to London gardeners, many of whom put hours of back-breaking work into cultivating a plot which may be enjoyed as much by passers by as by themselves, or club together to tend commonly-owned land, or willingly look after a neighbour's garden as well as their own for the sake of making the whole street look pretty. Many also open their gardens to the public once or twice a year under the National Gardens Scheme, often collecting considerable sums for charity. I too have been the beneficiary of this generosity, for on my visits to some of these gardens, a few rarities have now found their way into my garden in Lancashire.

I am most grateful to all the owners of all the gardens in this book for answering my questions and giving me access to their gardens with such kindness and patience. Researching and writing this book has been as instructive as

View from 'The Vineyard'

it has been pleasurable; my only regret is that space would not allow me to include more of the many lovely gardens I have seen, and from which I have learned so much.

Finally, I must express my warmest thanks to Barbara Mellor who is described Researcher, who did much research but also very much else besides, to make this book clear and readable.

A GARDEN OF ROOMS IN TWICKENHAM

There is a house in Twickenham which every May is a most remarkable sight; for it is then that the huge wisteria trained up Mr and Mrs Richard Raworth's Victorian villa comes into flower, covering the substantial façade with an avalanche of scented mauve racemes. It is not the only indication that this is home to two skilled and imaginative gardeners: above the neatly clipped privet hedge screening the street rises an arcade of pleached limes, attractive and unusual in spring and summer, when the leaves are fresh and light above the dense green of the privet, but perhaps even better in winter, when the low light throws into relief the architectural shapes and textures of the knotted branches. The same low light emphasizes the sculptured contours and feathery grey-green foliage of large mounds of rosemary (in flower at the same time as the wisteria) and 'Grappenhall' lavender, which produces its blue spikes later in the summer. Releasing their aromatic scents as you brush past them, they line the path to the entrance porch, splendidly Victorian still with its decorative tiles and stained glass, and flanked by two *Magnolia grandiflora*.

It was some sixteen years ago that the Raworths moved to this house, with its third of an acre of garden backing on to three acres of communal grounds shaded by mature trees. The garden was then laid out with open lawns surrounding rose beds and fruit trees, and dotted with some valuable mature trees and shrubs including skimmias and viburnums which must have been there since before the war, if not from Victorian times. These are all that now remains of the earlier design, which the Raworths decided to replace with a scheme that would provide more interest and variety, together with an element of surprise. They were also converts to the theory, paradoxical but undoubtedly true, that the way to make a space seem bigger is to divide it into a number of small compartments. Accordingly, with the help of garden designer Malcolm Hillier, they set out to devise a series of 'rooms' divided by hedges and traversed by the occasional vista.

The best and longest vista is to be had from the brick path that runs along the side of the house to the white picket gate leading into the communal area. At your feet as you stand at the front garden end of this path is a little sink garden, created recently to replace an imprac-

THE huge wisteria trained up the front of this Victorian villa, covered with an avalanche of scented mauve flowers, is a remarkable sight in early summer.

IN the front garden, a holly clipped in the shape of a giant ball backs a wide border planted with *Rosa* 'Maiden's Blush', *Rosa* 'Mme Pierre Oger', thalictrums, lilies and white foxgloves.

tical patch of lawn, where tiles and troughs of terracotta, stone and hypertufa are planted with mineral-coloured sempervivums and alpines, underplanted with bronze-green *Acaena microphylla* and arranged with Japanese precision. Before you stretches a narrow vista, past a silver border under an eleagnus hedge on the left and a magnificent conservatory on the right, through a gap in a yew hedge to a stately, tapering arch of *Thuja plicata*, where lavender, alchemilla and penstemons spill over the path, then up some shallow steps to the little gate and on into the green depths beyond.

Just before the gap in the yew hedge the path crosses a small brick courtyard just outside the kitchen door, which gives on to one of the most striking of the garden's rooms. It is extremely simple: a small brick courtyard, laid in a basketweave pattern and divided from the garden by a yew hedge, gives on to a rectangular space hedged all round with tall yew. A semicircular apse of yew at the far end provides the backdrop for a single white marble statue. Box-edged beds are filled with a monochrome planting of white annuals which varies from year to year, and terracotta pots hold balls and spirals of box and daisy bushes, silhouetted against the dark yew. Bay and helichrysum grown as standards add to the formality. This yew enclosure, now known as the Italian garden, demonstrates perfectly how a small space may generate a powerful atmosphere.

Through the yew hedge the mood changes dramatically, for here the garden opens out into a lawn surrounded by borders of shrubs and herbaceous plants, with an imposing brick and

As you pass through the gap in the yew hedge beyond the formal Italian garden the mood changes to one of very English informality. Cushions of white malva and rose-pink cistus fill the foreground of the view over a smooth lawn to deep herbaceous borders, while it is framed on one side by an apple tree underplanted with a pink hydrangea and clouds of *Campanula portenschlagiana*.

WISTERIAS are the most decorative of all climbers at all times. In early summer their scented drooping panicles of pea-like flowers smother the branches; these are followed by attractive pinnate leaves of the softest of greens which turn yellow in the autumn, leaving the beautiful gnarled shapes of the twisting trunk in winter.

cedar pergola at the northern end. This, until quite recently the vegetable garden, is now the garden's principal sitting area, paved with York stone and protected on three sides by tall hedges. Under the hedges are beds filled with pastel pink and white old-fashioned flowers: 'Mrs Sinkins', 'Laced Romeo', 'Prudence' and 'Margaret Curtis' pinks under old roses including China rose 'Sophie's Perpetual', 'Duchesse d'Angoulême', 'Duchesse de Montebello', 'Céleste' and 'Duc de Guiche', interspersed with regale lilies, *Nepeta nervosa*, *Diascia elegans* and *Geranium psilostemon*. Climbing up the brick pillars of the pergola are 'New Dawn' and 'Rambling Rector' roses, fragrant *Lonicera periclymenum* 'Belgica' and 'Serotina' and two white *Wisteria floribunda* 'Alba'. All these are eclipsed, however, by two *Solanum jasminoides* 'Album', planted in June 1987 as cuttings from a plant that had run riot in the conservatory, and within a year smothering the front and top of the pergola with their glossy green leaves and star-shaped white flowers. They now have to be thinned in late summer to let in the light, and in winter they are cut right back and well wrapped up against frost with hessian and straw.

From the pergola you look out over cushions of white malva, blue 'Hidcote' lavender and rose-pink cistus to the velvety lawn, flanked on its eastern side by the main shrub and herbaceous border. This is a densely planted bank of cottage-garden plants: clary and penstemons in pink, white and purple under an airy cloud of *Crambe cordifolia*; cistus and *Salvia uliginosa* under old roses; and pale foxgloves everywhere.

The path continues under the thuja arch

SIMPLICITY is the striking feature of this small formal garden surrounded by tall yew hedges. The statue, placed in the centre of the semicircular apse at the far end, gives it an Italian feel. Box-edged beds are filled with white annuals, and terracotta pots hold box balls and spirals and daisy bushes.

A GARDEN OF ROOMS IN TWICKENHAM

(planted and tended, like all the hedges, by Richard Raworth) and up some shallow steps. The Raworths soon began to realize that they were too inconspicuous and tended to trip people up. Resisting the notion of painting white lines along the edges of the steps, they copied an idea from Hidcote, gently emphasizing the risers with a strip of clipped *Cotoneaster thymifolium*. To the left is the herb garden, where a pretty, white-painted wrought-iron seat overlooks four geometrical beds edged with *Buxus sempervirens* 'Suffruticosa'. Gravel paths run between them, and a bird bath presided over by a mossy stone owl stands at the centre. At the centre of each bed is a box ball, surrounded by herbs which fill the air, especially on summer evenings, with their aromatic bouquet. This is where the family beehives stand, now empty, but in the past producing as much as 200 pounds of honey in a single summer.

Through the white gate is the communal garden, where the residents are allowed to look after the part immediately adjacent to their gardens. Here, on an area once choked with ivy, ground elder and hypericum, the Raworths are developing a wild garden, planting carefully nurtured seedlings rather than attempting to sow seed. Field scabious and poppies, purple loosestrife, betony and viper's bugloss should in time make a carpet of wild flowers. Already in early summer drifts of lacy cow parsley, nodding symphytum flowers and red and white campion spread under an old hawthorn tree, a white 'Seagull' rose threading through its branches.

As you walk back to the house you are struck by the size and the profuse planting of the conservatory, the garden's *pièce de résistance*. The land where it stands, against the north side of the house, was a waste land after the Raworths demolished an ugly addition to the house and a row of concrete garages. They intended to build a conservatory, and persevered in the face of a chorus of disapproval from all the books and virtually every expert, in whose view a north-facing conservatory was virtually a waste of time and space. All sorts of problems, financial and practical, had to be overcome before the conservatory was finally completed. Largely Richard Raworth's own work, it now stands finished, furnished and planted: thirty feet long and fourteen feet wide, it is a splendid vindication of the Raworths' determination.

On one wall is a cascade of mauve-pink pelargonium flowers, grown on a single plant which in two years grew to a size of fourteen by ten feet from a six-inch cutting. Beside it, also planted in the beds that run round the walls, is a *Jasminum polyanthum*, now a huge column of delicate leaves and fragrant white flowers, its intoxicating scent only rivalled by a vigorous *Trachelospermum jasminoides*, which fills a corner with its pendulous white flowers from June to September. *Clematis florida* 'Plena', *Billiardiera*, *Cassia obtusa*, *Jasminum suavissimum* and *Mimulus longifolia* are among the other climbers smothering the walls, and the beds below are filled with a forest of ferns, myrtle and ivies, with mimulus, fuchsias, lilies and pelargoniums for summer colour. Streptocarpus, *Campanula pyramidalis*, *Anisodontea capensis* and *Lantana sellowiana* grow in pots, whilst two ball-shaped standard *Helichrysum petiolatum* add formality to the central marble table.

A MOSSY stone owl with a slightly surprised air sits in the bird bath at the centre of the herb garden. Four geometrical box-edged beds, each with a box ball in the middle, are filled with a variety of aromatic herbs which scent the air on summer evenings.

PRIVATE GARDENS OF LONDON

THE roots of the spectacular wisteria are buried under a drift of soft planting in the front garden. After the Raworth's moved in some sixteen years ago, Richard Raworth decided the neglected and aged climber needed close attention: detaching it from the wall he laid it out over the front garden and carefully untangled it, branch by branch and tendril by tendril, before rearranging it over the façade of the house.

A GARDEN OF ROOMS IN TWICKENHAM

Curiously the conservatory's north-facing position seems to suit a great number of tender plants with only a very little heating in winter. A little direct sun in the morning and a good spell in the afternoon in summer is enough to raise the temperature inside without necessitating complicated shading arrangements, and four roof ventilators keep the atmosphere buoyant. In these conditions a number of rareties thrive, including a *Lapageria rosea*, with lovely bell-shaped waxy flowers; *Jasminum sambac*, the Arabian jasmine, with its tight clusters of fragrant white flowers; *Rhodochiton atrosanguineum*, brought from Sissinghurst, which throughout the summer bears tubular deep purple flowers enclosed in a pink corolla; *Pandorea jasminoides*, with panicles of lovely white tubular flowers stained with crimson; and *Eccremocarpus scaber*, hung with racemes of scarlet tubular flowers throughout the summer and autumn.

The generosity of planting in the conservatory and garden alike are largely due to Richard Raworth's interest in propagating. Behind the eleagnus hedge is the 'working' part of the garden, the final room, containing a modest-sized greenhouse equipped with a semi-professional mist propagator. The greenhouse and the gravel outside are crammed with cuttings and seedlings: the Raworths estimate that between them they produce some six hundred plants a year. There is no shortage of plants, energy or ideas in this garden; the only thing lacking, Mrs Raworth observes, is the space to make more of the garden rooms for which she and her husband have such a talent.

THIS path runs along the side of the house and up a few steps, which have *Cotoneaster thymifolius* grown along the risers, towards a thuja arch and a white picket gate which leads to the communal garden. Here a wild garden is being developed. The narrow opening between the two yew hedges in the foreground through which you get a tantalizing view of the next garden is an invitation to go further.

THE conservatory is the garden's *pièce de résistance*. Largely Richard Raworth's own work, it is mostly filled with plants grown from their own seeds. The pelargonium on the left grew to a size of fourteen feet by ten from a six-inch cutting in two years.

17

A PLANTSMAN'S GARDEN

As you step out of the back door of this pretty early Victorian house in Barnsbury and stroll down the garden path, it is agreeable to reflect that it is more than two centuries since the first pleasure gardens were laid out on the site. Ripplevale Grove's original – and more robust – name, Albion Grove, gives a clue to the story, for it was one Thomas Albion Oldfield who in the 1780s was the proprietor of the pleasure grounds, aristocratic cricket ground, dairy and chinoiserie teahouse to which crowds of Londoners flocked at holiday and fair times. The cricket subsequently moved to Lord's, and the teahouse became a public house, which still stands at the end of Ripplevale Grove.

Near to the source of the White Conduit, which watered the fields here, stood White Conduit House, a tavern which in 1754 was advertised as serving coffee and tea with fresh milk from the dairy and hot loaves. Pleasure grounds were laid out with a fishpond, a 'shrubby maze' and secluded arbours; City apprentices diverted themselves here with what became known as the 'White Conduit House method of introduction'. The technique, according to a contemporary, 'was for the gallant 'prentice to tread on the lady's train, to apologise profusely, and finally to suggest an adjournment for tea in one of the arbours'. Young ladies and their beaux were able to saunter through 'pleasing walks, prettily disposed' to 'genteel boxes for company, curiously cut into hedges', and to enjoy the fine prospect to the sound of a chime of bells hung in a miniature steeple. Paintings adorned the boxes, and a *trompe l'oeil* tableau depicting more such attractions was placed at the end of the gardens so as to increase their apparent length.

In the early nineteenth century, however, such innocent pleasures were overtaken by entertainments which were considered more vulgar, and which appealed to a rowdier clientele. Balloon ascents and fire-eaters were among the more spectacular of these, but it was the rather *risqué* shows which cost White Conduit House its licence. By then the buildings of Thomas Cubitt's Barnsbury development were encroaching and blocking out the views, and in a few more years the pleasure grounds had disappeared under new streets of trim villas such as Albion Grove.

It is twenty-five years since the owner moved here, when, he says, the house was 'a slum' and the garden 'a rubbish dump with not a single plant'. He did most of the construction, design and planting of the garden, only latterly enlisting the help of designer friends (John McKeon with construction, Myles Challis with less usual plants). On a long thin site he has made a meandering path bordered with dense planting and opening out at intervals into a series of clearings. With his preference for 'layer upon layer upon layer of planting, then climbers through that', he has made a secluded and intimate garden, always interesting and full of things to discover. His gardening is of the *laissez-faire* school which – effortless as the results may appear – depends on a profound knowledge and understanding of the individual plants and their habits. A walk down the garden is punctuated with reminiscences of who gave which plants to him and when,

A THICKET of trees and shrubs screen the rest of the garden from view. A magnolia casts its shade over clumps of ferns and *Trachystemon orientalis*. This plant is useful as it likes dry dense shade, and is ornamental in spring, when it sends up delightful spikes of blue flowers.

where they came from and why, for he remembers the individual history of each with affection. One of the beguiling aspects of this garden is that you can be quite sure that it would be viewed with deep suspicion by gardeners of the 'no-nonsense' school, who cleave to manicured lawns and neatly drilled flower beds, such as the immortal R. Clipston Sturgis, who at the beginning of this century stoutly declared: 'The making of surprise, such as the sudden revealing of unsuspected features in the garden scene, must always be considered as evidence of debased taste, the prostituting of a beautiful art, for the sake of securing a momentary exclamation of astonishment.'

The garden door leads you directly on to a brick terrace, where a *Solanum jasminoides* 'Album', smothered with highly fragrant white flowers from July to October, clambers up one side of the house. On the other side are a *Clematis armandii* – another evergreen with strongly scented flowers – and *Rosa* 'Old Blush China', with loose pink blooms, an early cross with the original China rose. Dotted around the terrace are pots of various sizes, one of them holding a deceptively delicate-looking *Fuchsia magellanica* 'Alba', which bears dainty palest pink flowers from July to October. Magellanicas, despite appearances, are the hardiest of the fuchsias, and in country areas of Ireland are often used for hedgerows. Even if they are cut down by frost they will usually recover.

In the shady part of the terrace a pond was dug and at first puddled with Bentonite, a form of Fuller's Earth from Woburn Sands. Sadly it was not proof against the proddings of tree roots, however, and here the roots of a neighbouring *Platanus orientalis* penetrated the layer of clay and damaged the membrane. As puddling is an expensive business nowadays, when it came to repairs a semi-rigid polythene liner was used, and the black edges of the plastic were skilfully hidden by clever planting. Now ferns, *Alchemilla mollis* and *Soleirolia soleirolii* virtually obscure it completely.

Overhung by trees and shrubs, notably *Clematis* 'Contessa Lavinia Maggi', the little pond has an air of mystery about it. The great rough leaves of *Trachystemon orientalis* – useful as it loves dry, dense shade, and very ornamental in spring, when it sends up delightful spikes of blue flowers – make interesting shapes in combination with the large, round, purple-backed leaves of *Ligularia dentata* 'Desdemona', which bears orange-red flowers in July and August. Meanwhile *Osmunda regalis*, the regal fern, which likes its feet to be nearly touching the water, casts graceful shadows over the pond.

Behind the pond a thicket of trees and shrubs screens the rest of the garden from view. Large camellias, such as rose-pink, semi-double 'Leonard Messel' and single white 'Francis Hanger', the gaunt, Japanese-looking *Rhus typhina* and velvet-leaved *Hydrangea sargentiana* all flourish here, while the ground beneath them is smothered with lamiums, hostas and autumn-flowering cyclamen. A *Fatsia japonica* grown from seed (it grows like mustard and cress according to the owner), adds to the splendid leaf contrasts in this area, where two aucubas, throw-outs from somebody's window box, have grown to full size above a thick underplanting of trachystemon. Nearby a *Forsythia suspensa* throws out its far-reaching shoots and is clustered with pale yellow flowers in February and March. This is the prettiest of

THIS small pond is in a shady part of the garden where *Soleirolia soleirolii* obscures the edges completely, giving it a natural look. *Alchemilla mollis*, which welcomes damp conditions, particularly in London's dry gardens, thrives here and has seeded itself all over. *Aponogeton distachyos*, the water hawthorn, grows happily in the water and flowers throughout the spring and summer.

the forsythias, for the branches are less stiff and the flowers less yellow than in other species. But it is the *Mahonia japonica* that is the owner's favourite, as it flowers all winter and the scent of the yellow flower clusters is breathtaking. He has trained it against the wall as a climber, encouraging the huge rosettes of leaves to fall forward, so bringing the flower spikes to eye (and nose) level. Mahonia has the added advantage of being easy to propagate: if its head is put into a pot and covered with a cloche it will readily root.

Hidden behind this thicket is an open area, where clusters of sun-loving plants surround a sunken patch of York stone, and everything seeds itself everywhere. *Camellia japonica* 'Adolphe Audusson' is deliberately hidden behind *Rosa* 'Bloomfield Abundance', as its brilliant crimson flowers, while marvellous for picking, are too bright for the owner's taste. He prefers them to 'burn away in the background'. A black form of the purple phormium is planted next to a *Bupleurum fruticosum* with an *Acanthus spinosus* behind, all of them contrasting with an old rosemary bush in a successful combination of foliage. Potentillas are underplanted with masses of primroses, and a large white *Cistus crispus* has a self-sown, blue-green-leaved *Euphorbia characias wulfenii* growing through it. *Rosa* 'Little White Pet' is planted in front, with a variety of geranium which sprawls over the stones and into the cracks. Nearby *Hebe* 'Blue Clouds', bred by Mr Hutchins of County Park Nurseries in Essex is covered with blue flowers in summer and turns beetroot-red in winter.

Rambling through a useless London lilac into the next-door garden is an enormous *Rosa* 'Bobbie James', its thousands of highly scented white flowers making a spectacular sight in early summer. Later a golden hop threads its endless branches through it and over it, the yellow vine-like leaves and green flowers adding extra colour to the mass of twining branches as the summer wears on. Also wound through the rose is a *Clematis redheriana*, which gives a last show of cowslip-scented flowers in October. *Rosa* 'Bloomfield Abundance' now

grows in an ample bed which provides it with all the space this large rose needs, having been moved from a small central bed, where it was planted in a case of mistaken identity. The owner thought it was 'Cécile Brunner', much smaller but otherwise hard to distinguish, and thought it would look well in the central bed with a juniper. Now *R.* 'Bloomfield Abundance', covered every year with masses of miniature pale pink opening to darker pink blooms of perfect form, is so vigorous that it has to be chopped down every now and then. The juniper, meanwhile, also outgrew its space – a timely reminder that sometimes even the best gardeners can be caught out by plants' rate of growth and the size they ultimately reach. Now the juniper stands by the wall, its dark branches wound round with the pink Bourbon rose 'Zéphirine Drouhin'. A specimen of *Phlomis chrysophylla* from Great Dixter is very much in evidence here, conspicuous because of its beautiful silvery white leaves. Grown for the bright tones of its foliage, which are an asset to a border, rather than for its flowers, it also takes cuttings quite easily. Through all this a red rose casually threads its way. Most of the roses in this garden are old-fashioned, the best being *R.* 'Mousseline', with its intensely fragrant pale pink moss rose blooms.

Seeded all over are more geraniums, *Erigeron*

THE carpet of *Soleirolia soleirolii* around the pool has spread under a neighbouring seat, which is surrounded by ivies, fuchsias, hostas, euphorbias, acanthus and other shade-tolerant plants.

RAMBLING into the next door garden, and next to *Pyrus salicifolia* 'Pendula', is *Rosa* 'Bobbie James', its thousands of scented white flowers making a spectacular sight in the summer. On the terrace below are a riot of different flowers and shrubs: *Hebe* 'Blue Clouds', a self-seeded euphorbia in front of a rosemary bush and *Artemisia* 'Powis Castle' next to *Phlomis chrysophylla*.

karvinskianus (*the* daisy, according to the owner's family) and *Erica lusitanica*, which bears beautiful long racemes of grey-white flowers until May or sometimes later. Here some steps, cleverly designed and built by John McKeon with a brick pillar to either side, lead to another hidden part of the garden at the very end. A *Cornus alternifolia* 'Argentea' is positioned to show off its elegant tiered branches studded with exquisitely variegated leaves in green and white. To the left of the brick pillars is *Camellia* 'Cornish Snow', one of the prettiest camellias, with delicate inch-wide pure white flowers unfolding in late December in mild winters. An enormous cotoneaster stands next to an eight-foot *Pieris* 'Forest Flame' which, according to the owner, who has kept a record of the cost of all the plants from the beginning, cost the princely sum of one pound twelve shillings and sixpence (£1.62). It is a shrub of great value, for with its lily-of-the-valley buds which it keeps all winter opening to honey-scented flowers, its bright green leaves throughout the year and its scarlet and pink new growth in spring, it is unsurpassable. *Polygonum sachalinense* planted against the sun is another favourite, its variegated leaves making such a pretty contrast with the large *Arbutus unedo* at the end of the garden that its rather unhappy habit of spreading a little too enthusiastically is soon forgotten.

This is a garden which, as well as having a delightful atmosphere for sitting and walking, invites and rewards close attention, for its combinations of plants are not only pretty but also interesting. Subtle associations and bold contrasts of leaf shape and colour have been chosen with great care and discrimination. The choice of cultivars is also extremely learned, and the garden's complement of trees and shrubs is a plantsman's selection. But this is far from being a botanical garden, for it is the manner in which the plants are combined and tactfully allowed their proper space to grow which gives rise to the sense of casual ease and informal lushness which are so characteristic here. It is as if the owner were following Gertrude Jekyll's injunction: 'In garden arrangement, one has not only to acquire a knowledge of what to do, but also to gain some wisdom in perceiving what it is well to let alone.'

OVERHUNG with trees and shrubs, the little pond has an air of mystery about it. Different leaves make interesting combinations, the large rounded leaves of *Ligularia dentata* 'Desdemona', which bears orange-red flowers in July and August, casts its shadow into the water.

22

A CORNISH COMBE IN PUTNEY

As you look out of Marigold Assinder's drawing room window, down the steep narrow garden and towards the river at the bottom, you might imagine that you were at the head of one of those combes sheltering in the lee of the hills of southern Cornwall, where great plantsmen have for centuries cultivated the vast collections of trees and shrubs gathered on their travels. Mrs Assinder comes herself from a family of Cornish gardeners, of whom her brother Nigel Holman is one of the most distinguished. In the garden of the house where she was brought up were several Himalayan magnolias and a vast collection of other rare trees and plants. It comes as no great surprise that it should be a Cornishwoman who has had the vision to transform this typical long, thin London garden into something altogether different. Taking full advantage of the London climate, which in its mildness resembles the warm conditions of the south-west, she has created a garden which in its planting, its disposition and its atmosphere bears an unmistakable resemblance to a Cornish one.

She could not resist planting a *Magnolia campbellii mollicomata*, which she chose because unlike its relation, the great Himalayan tulip tree which takes up to thirty years to flower,

THE handsome spherical flowers of *Echinops ritro* are silhouetted against the trellised boundary fence. The thistle-like deep grey-green leaves are very ornamental, and unlike the ones in other species, they are without spines. The globular flowers are steel-blue and are at their best in July/August.

THE foreground of the view from the window is taken up by the huge pink flowers that stud the bare branches of *Magnolia campbellii* var. *mollicomata*. This giant Himalayan pink tulip tree thrives in the warmer counties where early March frosts will not spoil the enormous goblet-like flowers which resemble waterlilies. When in flower it is unforgettable.

PRIVATE GARDENS OF LONDON

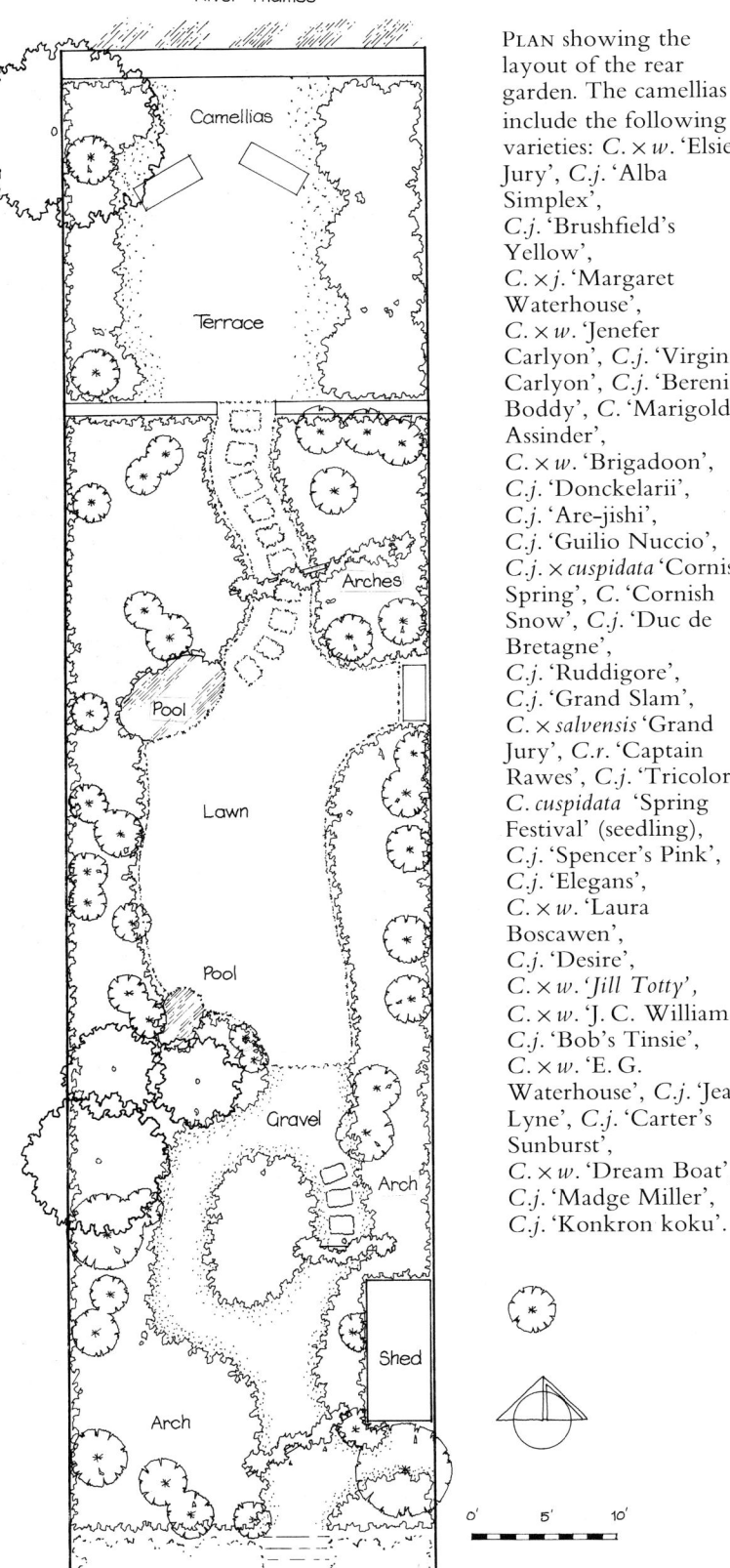

PLAN showing the layout of the rear garden. The camellias include the following varieties: *C.* × *w.* 'Elsie Jury', *C.j.* 'Alba Simplex', *C.j.* 'Brushfield's Yellow', *C.* × *j.* 'Margaret Waterhouse', *C.* × *w.* 'Jenefer Carlyon', *C.j.* 'Virginia Carlyon', *C.j.* 'Berenice Boddy', *C.* 'Marigold Assinder', *C.* × *w.* 'Brigadoon', *C.j.* 'Donckelarii', *C.j.* 'Are-jishi', *C.j.* 'Guilio Nuccio', *C.j.* × *cuspidata* 'Cornish Spring', *C.* 'Cornish Snow', *C.j.* 'Duc de Bretagne', *C.j.* 'Ruddigore', *C.j.* 'Grand Slam', *C.* × *salvensis* 'Grand Jury', *C.r.* 'Captain Rawes', *C.j.* 'Tricolor', *C. cuspidata* 'Spring Festival' (seedling), *C.j.* 'Spencer's Pink', *C.j.* 'Elegans', *C.* × *w.* 'Laura Boscawen', *C.j.* 'Desire', *C.* × *w.* 'Jill Totty', *C.* × *w.* 'J. C. Williams', *C.j.* 'Bob's Tinsie', *C.* × *w.* 'E. G. Waterhouse', *C.j.* 'Jean Lyne', *C.j.* 'Carter's Sunburst', *C.* × *w.* 'Dream Boat', *C.j.* 'Madge Miller', *C.j.* 'Konkron koku'.

this one flowers within ten to fifteen years. She placed it below the house so that in February and March, now that the tree has reached flowering age, the foreground of the view out of the window is taken up with the huge pink flowers that stud its bare branches. Goblet-shaped at first as they emerge from their hairy calyces, the enormous blooms soon open their petals wide to resemble water lilies, displaying the paler pink of their inner petals. Smothered with their exotic blooms, these mighty trees are a familiar sight to connoisseurs of Cornish gardens, but in the thin grey light of London, which seems to lend them an even more ethereal air, they are an extremely unusual sight.

Moreover, Marigold Assinder must be one of the few people in London who can stroll down the garden to visit her namesake. 'Marigold Assinder' is one of her extensive collection of camellias, another Cornish favourite, which came from her brother in Cornwall as a seedling. The garden, which contains some seventy varieties of camellias, with which Mrs Assinder regularly wins prizes at Royal Horticultural Society shows, is that of a true plantswoman. Broadening the purist Cornish tradition of planting, which limits itself rather rigorously to rhododendrons, camellias and trees, she has introduced a variety of different plants, both rare and ordinary, to extend the flowering season and create interesting leaf associations. Never static, always changing, the design is in a constant state of flux as plants that have outgrown their space are transplanted or removed, while Mrs Assinder seizes with relish the opportunity to make new plans. Her latest project is the replanting of the space left by a thirty-year-old mulberry, which, with some sadness and after a great deal of deliberation, has recently been felled.

The strip of garden, 139 feet long and 25 wide, slopes gradually down to the Thames from south to north, with the Edwardian house overlooking it from the top of a steep bank at the southern end. As the ground falls away so steeply at the back of the house, a pretty wrought-iron spiral staircase links it with the

A CORNISH COMBE IN PUTNEY

A TENDRIL of ivy winds around the neck of a sculpture by Mrs Assinder's husband, Peter Assinder, while a lacecap hydrangea flowers overhead.

THE architectural shapes of *Acanthus mollis* are undeniably an asset in any garden. It is not a rapid spreader and it does not mind which soil it grows in. The arching, shining dark green leaves are broadly lobed and the tall prickly stems of foxglove-like flowers emerge with elegance.

garden, where a flight of steep brick steps leads down the bank. At the bottom of this is the first of a series of rose and clematis arches that lead you through the garden, with camellias to either side of it. A *Rosa* 'Schneezwerg' with small double fragrant white flowers is encouraged to grow up one side of the arch with the vivid mauve-pink *Clematis* 'Comtesse de Bouchaud', while on the other side *R*. 'Blanc Double de Coubert', a very beautiful white rugosa, twines in with the rampant, evergreen *C. armandii*, which bears its white flowers in April.

Beyond, against the constant background of camellias of all colours, a meandering gravel path surrounds a bed planted with the delicate *Buddleia alternifolia*, the sweet-scented *Daphne blagayana*, which bears its clusters of creamy white flowers in April and May, and *B.* × *weyeriana*, an unusual hybrid with orange ball-shaped flowers borne in long slender panicles. In spring and summer the dramatic blooms of the camellias, waxy and flawless, weigh down the sinewy branches and flood the garden with vivid colour.

Among Mrs Assinder's particular treasures is the deep pink *C. reticulata* 'Captain Rawes', introduced by Rawes himself in 1820, and regarded as the original *C. reticulata* until the collector George Forrest discovered the wild form in west China in 1912. Considered by many to be one of the most beautiful of flowering shrubs, *C. reticulata* is the parent of a large number of interesting but tender camellias. Another magnificent camellia here is 'Cornish Spring', developed in the 1960s and flowering from December. The majority of the other camellias in the garden are *C. japonica* or × *williamsii*. The wild species of *C. japonica* is a native of Japan and Korea, introduced in 1739, and later followed by various cultivars from China and, again, Japan. Japonicas here include 'Alba Simplex', one of the best of the whites, 'Konkron koku', a marvellous dark red, free-flowering and very hardy, blood-red semi-double 'Adolphe Audusson', light-pink, anemone-shaped 'C. M. Wilson', 'Contessa Lavinia Maggi', white with broad rose-cerise stripes, rose-red, peony-shaped 'Are-jishi', and 'Guilio Nuccio', with very large, semi-double

THE garden is in a constant state of flux as plants that have outgrown their space are transplanted or removed. Despite the sadness of losing old favourites, Mrs Assinder always welcomes the opportunity of making new plans. A stone seat overhung by a *Buddleia alternifolia* now fills the space left by a thirty-year-old mulberry, cut down after this photograph was taken.

THE blooms of *Camellia × reticulata* 'Dr Clifford Parks' may reach over six inches across, and are unusual in both form and colour. Usually semi-double, they may vary on the same plant from loose peony to full peony or even anemone form. This beautiful hybrid is a cross between *C. reticulata* 'Crimson Robe' and *C. japonica* 'Kramer's Supreme'.

coral-pink blooms. *C. × williamsii* hybrids, developed by J. C. Williams at Caerhays Castle in Cornwall in about 1925, are generally held to be possibly the best for general planting in Britain, for they are exceptionally free-flowering and bear their extremely beautiful flowers over a long season, sometimes from November to May. 'J. C. Williams', with single blush-pink flowers, was one of the first clones of *C. × williamsii* to be named, and is one of the loveliest of all camellias. Not surprisingly it is one of Mrs Assinder's favourites, together with the semi-double 'Margaret Waterhouse', another *C. × williamsii*.

During the months of the year when they are not in flower the camellias' dark and glossy evergreen leaves form a dense background which throws into high relief the different leaf colours and shapes of a collection of variegated and silver foliage plants. Variegated *Rhamnus alaternus* 'Argenteovariegata', *Pittosporum tenuifolium* 'Variegatum', *Cornus alba* 'Variegata' and *Weigela* 'Florida variegata' look especially good here, as do the silver leaves of a whitebeam, *Eucalyptus gunnii*, Brachyglottis 'Sunshine' and *Rosa glauca*. This mass of foliage makes the perfect setting for delicate rose blooms: creamy white 'Nevada', strongly scented clear pink 'Sarah van Fleet', fragrant crimson-purple 'Roseraie de l'Haÿ' and, most beautiful of all, delicate blush-pink 'Fantin-Latour'. A single rhododendron, meanwhile, the slightly tender *R. Cilpinense*, bears its flowers early in the year, a mass of pink against the pleasing mid-green of its leaves, which are less heavy and dark than those of most other rhododendrons.

As its meanders past the central bed the gravel path passes under another rose arch, this time clothed with white 'Iceberg' roses, fragrant white jasmine and *Vitis pulchra*, before opening out on to a token patch of grass, which so far has escaped Mrs Assinder's urge (largely, one suspects, for the sake of her dog, Borage) to fill every available space with yet more treasures. At each end is a little pool edged with pebbles and planted with water irises, and to one side is the space where the mulberry used to stand, framed by a newly planted *Ceanothus impressus*, *Azara microphylla* and various large camellias, which will now form the framework for the new planting scheme.

Beyond the second pool stepping stones wind down towards a terrace overlooking the river, passing under one of a pair of arches engulfed by shrub roses and climbers: white 'Boule de Neige' and palest pink 'New Dawn' roses with the nodding white flowers of *Clematis alpina sibirica* and carmine-pink *C.* 'Ville de Lyon' on one; and on the other rampant *Clematis montana* and *Rosa banksiae*.

Throughout the garden, under the camellias and other shrubs, are quantities of geraniums, including the tender *G. maderense*, particularly fine in combination with *Clematis* 'Ville de Lyon', and lilac-grey *G. phaeum lividum*, set off by *Rosa* 'Roseraie de l'Haÿ'. In the low planting of the front garden's sunny borders more geraniums come into their own. Here a magnificent *Prunus* 'Tai-haku' with the ornamental vine 'Brant' growing through it takes centre stage, filling the almost square space with its dazzling white blossom in spring. The sophistication of the low planting in the front of the borders – a profusion of subtle woodland flowers such as symphytums, primulas, pulmonaria, campanulas, violas, dicentras, irises and of course geraniums – confirms Mrs Assinder's great knowledge of and taste in plants. Taller shrubs – roses, hydrangeas, cistus, weigelas,

A CORNISH COMBE IN PUTNEY

pieris, pittosporums and the ubiquitous camellias – are planted against the street wall and the front of the house. There are some particularly successful associations here, for example *Weigela* 'Florida variegata' with the deep burgundy *Pittosporum* 'Irene Patterson' and *Clematis* 'Gipsy Queen', set against *Pieris japonica* 'Variegata' and *Fuchsia magellanica* 'Versicolor'. The delicate mauve-blue blooms of *Clematis alpina* 'Frances Rivis' frame the red brick of the porch, and over the side gate to the garden is an arch anticipating the rose arches of the back garden, wreathed with *Rosa* 'Golden Showers', *Lonicera japonica* 'Halliana' and *Clematis × durandii*.

Despite the disadvantages of poor soil (overcome by importing large quantities of peat) and a lack of sun on the rear garden in the winter months, this garden is extremely fortunate in that it benefits from the single-minded attention and enthusiasm of a serious plantswoman and avid collector, who has both access to choice and unusual plants and an encyclopedic knowledge of them. Add to these Mrs Assinder's innate ability to create compositions of considerable beauty and subtlety, and you have an unusually fine garden.

Prunus 'Tai-haku', with the ornamental *Vitis* 'Brant' growing through it, stands in the middle of the front garden. In the borders are symphytums, primulas, campanulas and geraniums. The delicate mauve-blue flowers of *Clematis alpina* 'Frances Rivis' frame the brick porch.

Clematis and rose arches are a feature of the garden: these two at the bottom of the garden are covered early in the year with *Clematis alpina* and *C. montana*, followed later on by *C.* 'Ville de Lyon' and *Rosa* 'Boule de Neige', 'New Dawn' and *R. banksia*.

THE TRADESCANT GARDEN: A 'CABINET OF CURIOSITIES'

On the south bank of the Thames, opposite the Palace of Westminster and next to Lambeth Palace, stands the church of St Mary-at-Lambeth. Its tower has been a landmark for Londoners since the fourteenth century, when Lambeth was a village and royal deer parks stretched from Vauxhall to Kennington, and a church has stood on this site for over 900 years, for a predecessor of the present building was mentioned in the Domesday Survey. Now it rises from among the sea of office blocks, flats and arterial roads which is present-day Lambeth, a monument to the indomitable determination and dedication of four people, divided in time by three centuries, but united in spirit by their love of plants and gardening.

The first pair of this remarkable quartet now lie in the churchyard, under a sarcophagus carved with strange and exotic beasts, plants and buildings and inscribed:

'Know stranger, ere thou pass, beneath this stone
Lie John Tradescant grandsire, father, son;
The last dy'd in his spring: the other two
Liv'd till they had travell'd Art and Nature
   through;
As by their choice Collections may appear,
Of what is rare in land, in sea, in air,
Whilst they (as Homer's Iliad in a nut)
A world of wonders in one closet shut.'

This tomb was to be their link with the second pair, Rosemary and John Nicholson, who in 1976 discovered it, blackened with soot and age and enveloped by long grass and litter. The church, which had not been used for worship since 1972, was derelict and vandalized, the subject of a demolition order, and the churchyard, piled high with rubbish, had become a shelter for the vagrant and destitute. The Nicholsons' fascination with the enterprise and courage of these extraordinary men and their love of gardens and gardening history had drawn them to this spot, and their disappointment soon gave way to a determination to restore the church and plant the churchyard as a tribute to the Tradescants. 1977 was the year of the Queen's Silver Jubilee, and the abandoned church would be the first sight to meet the eyes of tourists crossing Lambeth Bridge as they followed the proposed Jubilee walkway along the Embankment. Moreover two royal gardeners lay in the churchyard. Nothing would deter the Nicholsons from pursuing their engagingly eccentric and – in the eyes of the world at least – hopelessly unrealistic dream.

THE way to the Tradescant Garden lies through the ancient church of St Mary-at-Lambeth, for centuries the parish church of Lambeth and now converted into a museum of garden history. Only fifteen years ago both church and churchyard lay derelict.

ROSEMARY, Solomon's seal and other plants the Tradescants would have known now surround the tombs in the garden; the crumbling stone and soft planting combine to create a pleasurable melancholy.

SEATS surrounded by sweet-smelling flowers and herbs are an encouragement to linger and enjoy the peace of the garden. Within these walls it is surprisingly easy to forget the traffic that thunders along the embankment, and to let your mind drift back over the centuries.

John Tradescant the Elder, born in about 1570, was one of those men of boundless enterprise, energy and curiosity, one of those explorers and scientists, collectors and travellers who earned for the Elizabethan era the soubriquet of the 'Age of Discovery'. Eventually to become gardener to Charles I and one of the first great plant collectors, Tradescant was introduced to horticulture in 1609, when he was engaged by Robert Cecil, Chancellor to Elizabeth I and one of the richest and most powerful of her courtiers, to help with the design, laying out and planting of the gardens of the great mansion he had built at Hatfield. Tradescant the adventurer and fearless traveller was despatched to the Continent in quest of rare blooms, shrubs and trees to embellish this most magnificent of estates. He returned with roses and cherry trees, mulberries and redcurrants, quinces and medlars, cypresses and myrtles, gillyflowers, fritillaries and 'flowers called anemones', as well as many rare shrubs which were the gift of Jean Robin, Keeper of the Jardin des Plantes in Paris (and who gave his name to the beautiful *Robinia pseudoacacia*).

Thus was Tradescant set on his plant-hunting course, and henceforth, as a contemporary noted, he 'wonderfully laboured to obtain all the rarest fruit he can hear of in any place in Christendom, Turkey yea or the whole world'. From Russia came the first-ever botanical inventory of native flora, and from the coast of Algeria (where his quarry was nominally some troublesome pirates) the Algerian apricot. In his middle age he settled in Lambeth, a mere stone's throw from the parish church, and found material reward in his appointment as gardener to Charles I. Now he had the leisure to develop his 'closett of rarities', a cornucopia of things rare and strange, 'a world of wonders', as their epitaph records, 'in one closet shut'. From far and near people came to wonder at Tradescant's Ark, as it became known, among them Izaak Walton, who in *The Compleat Angler* noted breathlessly, 'You may see there the hog-fish, the dog-fish . . . the salamander . . .

The intricate design of the knot divides the square into a jigsaw of large and small beds. Artemisias, gladiolus, *Salvia officinalis* 'Tricolor', *Cardamine pratensis*, and *Rosa gallica* 'Versicolor' are amongst the great number of plants of Tudor origin flowering in the summer.

and the bird of paradise; such sorts of snakes, and such birds' nests, and of so various forms and so wonderfully made, as may beget wonder and amazement in any beholder.' The collection, which also included the mantle of Pocahontas's father, Chief Powhatan, and Guy Fawkes' lamp, extended into the sixty-acre garden, which an employee of the East India Company described as 'a little garden filled with divers outlandish herbs and flowers, whereof some that I had not seen elsewhere but in India'. Fruit trees seem to have been a speciality: to no fewer than fifty-seven varieties of plum were added forty-nine each of apple and pear, twenty-four cherries, and numerous apricots, quinces, cherries, nectarines and vines.

John Tradescant the Younger inherited not only his father's Ark, his physic garden and his position as royal gardener, but also his unquenchable curiosity and thirst for travel. Where the father had explored the Old World the son set out to discover the curiosities of the New, visiting the young colony of Virginia three times, bringing back among other plant treasures specimens of the tulip tree (*Liriodendron tulipifera*), the plane tree and the red maple, *Aquilegia canadensis* and *Yucca filamentosa*. In an age when the journey to America took two or three months, during which time plant specimens, stored on deck in slatted containers, had to endure dramatic fluctuations of temperature, irregular watering and periodic drenchings with sea spray, lack of light and the depredations of rats, this was no mean achievement. Tradescant also brought back the border perennial then known as spiderwort, which Linnaeus christened *Tradescantia virginiana*. This, with the ubiquitous houseplant *Tradescantia fluminensis*, was for many years virtually the Tradescants' sole memorial. After their death even their celebrated Ark ceased to commemorate their name, despite the fact that it became the nucleus of England's first museum, the Ashmolean Collection, via a bequest to Elias Ashmole.

The Nicholsons were determined that the

name of the Tradescants should no longer be forgotten. They set themselves the herculean task of saving the church from demolition and refurbishing it to house a museum of garden history, of which the *pièce de résistance* would be a garden in the churchyard, designed in Elizabethan style and filled with plants collected or known by the Tradescants. The shady, windy site was cleared by volunteers, and a design for a knot garden was drawn up by Lady Salisbury, descendant of the first Lord Salisbury for whom John Tradescant had laid out the gardens of Hatfield House some three centuries earlier. A typical Tudor knot garden was a small rectangular or square bed containing a geometrical pattern – the more intricate the better – laid out in dwarf box, rosemary or sometimes thrift. Sometimes the gaps in between would be filled with different coloured gravels or crushed stone, sometimes with flowers chosen for their colour, their scent or their evergreen foliage. The Tradescant garden is a faithful reincarnation of such a garden, 'fitted', like the knots at Hatfield in a seventeenth-century description, 'for the growth of choice flowers, bordered with box in the points, angles, squares and roundlets'.

The knot lies in the middle of the churchyard, under the high, machicolated, ivy-clad wall that separates it from the grounds of Lambeth Palace, seat of the Archbishops of Canterbury. A square outlined in dwarf box (*Buxus sempervirens* 'Suffruticosa') encloses a circle of equal diameter, which in turn encloses another, smaller square. Four ellipses meeting at the larger square's corners and intersecting at its centre cut the pattern again, making an intricate jigsaw of beds. *Santolina chamaecyparissus* adds variety to the hedging, and the centre is marked by *Ilex aquifolium* 'Silver Queen'.

In spring the beds come alive with a variety of bulbs and corms, among them *Muscari comosum* 'Plumosum', *Erythronium dens canis*, cyclamen and *Tulipa sylvestris*, followed by fritillaries and narcissi. The little *Viola septentrionalis* shares a tiny gap with *Primula auricula*, and later drifts of dianthus fill the air with their delicate scent. In summer old roses hold the stage – *Rosa gallica* 'Versicolor' (Rosa Mundi) and *R. g. officinalis*, the exquisite *R.* 'De Meaux' (*R. centifolia pomponia*), *R.* 'Burgundiaca' and *R. acicularis nipponensis*. Shrubs and herbaceous plants such as *Daphne mezereum*, cheiranthus and quantities of salvias, lavenders, artemisias, teucriums, campanulas and – of course – tradescantias crowd the beds, above a ground cover of oregano and thyme. As the seasons pass more plants come into their own: glorious madonna and martagon lilies, and the tall carmine spikes of *Gladiolus communis byzantinus* in iridescent combination with *Artemisia absinthium* and the deep blue flowers of the willow gentian, *Gentiana asclepiadea*, borne on slender arching stems.

The garden is bordered by 'boscages' of taller shrubs and trees, with here and there a stone seat for quiet contemplation, interspersed with clumps of fragrant rosemary and lavender, old-fashioned pinks and silvery, aromatic hedges of briar roses. A broad brick path inset with centuries-old gravestones leads to the grandiose sarcophagus of Vice-Admiral William Bligh (himself a plantsman, who was returning from Tahiti with specimens of the breadfruit tree when he had his notorious altercation with his crew), his wife and, most poignantly, his twin one-day-old sons. Beside it stands the tomb of three generations of Tradescant.

To enter this garden is to travel back through the centuries: the thundering of the traffic on the Embankment and the exhaust fumes seem miraculously to disappear as you stand by the Tradescants' tomb, immersed in the sights and scents of the plants they knew so well. If the spirits of the Tradescants were to see the delightful garden that now commemorates them they might well imagine that the epitaph inscribed on their tomb had come true:

'*These famous Antiquarians that had been
Both Gardiners to the Rose and Lily Queen
Transplanted now themselves sleep here, and when
Angels shall with their trumpets waken men
And fire shall purge the world, these hence shall rise,
And change this Garden for a Paradise.*'

THE grandiose sarcophagus of Vice-Admiral William Bligh is reached from a path inset with centuries-old gravestones. This path surrounds a square knot garden outlined in dwarf box, *Buxus sempervirens* 'Suffruticosa', enclosing two circles and four ellipses making an intricate pattern of flower beds of all sizes. At the centre an *Ilex aquifolium* 'Silver Queen' is clipped in the shape of a pyramid.

THIS sarcophagus carved with strange and exotic beasts, plants and buildings is where the two Tradescants, father and son, are buried. The tombs were blackened with soot and engulfed by long grass, the churchyard piled up with rubbish and the whole subject to a demolition order until in 1972 it was discovered and slowly restored.

THE TRADESCANT GARDEN: 'A CABINET OF CURIOSITIES'

A GARDEN FOR ENTERTAINING

In summer the white stucco front of this elegant early Victorian villa in Notting Hill Gate is the backdrop to a magnificent cascade of blowsy pink blooms, as the great buds of 'Mme Grégoire Staechelin' unfurl. Draping itself over the front door, the huge rose is simply smothered in richly fragrant semi-double flowers, astonishing both for their beauty and their sheer quantity. It is one of the earliest roses to come into bloom, and the glowing pink of its petals is a warm sight after all the yellows, mauves and blues of spring. A *Clematis armandii* twines through its branches, offering a more muted display of white flowers in spring and leathery deep green leaves throughout the year. A well-established winter-flowering jasmine clings hedge-like round a small bay window, and cheers the winter gloom with its sprays of clear yellow flowers, irresistible for flower arrangements when there is so little else in bloom.

Pale blue window frames complete the prettily countrified look of the street façade, and further interest is added by camellia bushes

A LARGE clump of the never-failing *Rosa* 'Iceberg' is planted in the border near one of the four crab apples. These are positioned so as to accentuate the main axis, and link the borders at the end of the garden with those near the house. Each rise from a square bed edged with box filled with Japanese anemones for late colour.

THE yew hedge that surrounds the rose garden also forms one side of a long grassy corridor which crosses the garden at this point, leading to semicircular niches at both ends. An antique urn stands at one end, *Bergenia cordifolia* covers the earth below the hedge, and white roses grow tall above a *Euphorbia characias wulfenii* heavy with flowers.

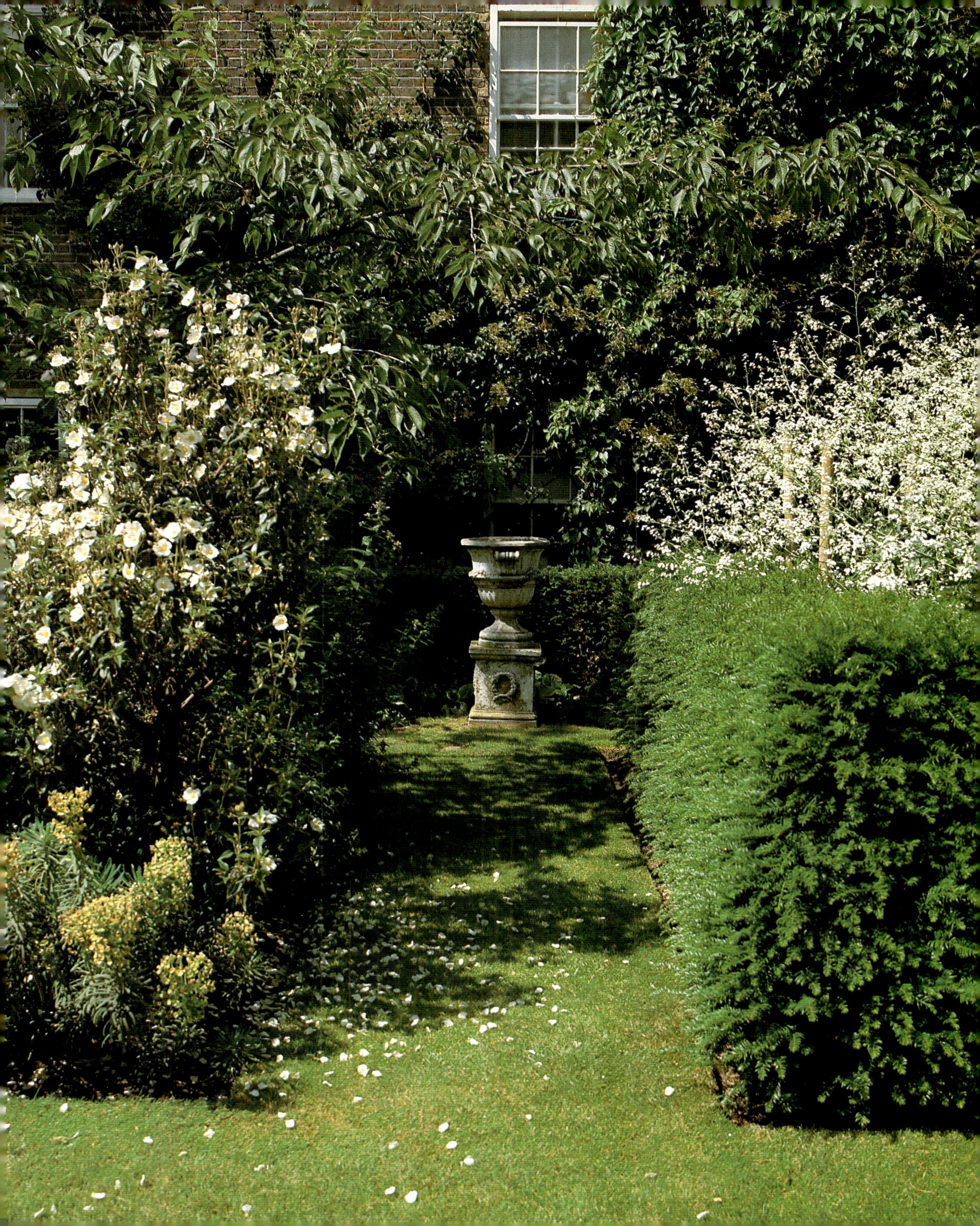

flanking the paved entrance area in Italian terracotta pots. Their sophisticated waxy flowers are of rare beauty in late spring, and their dark, glossy leaves are highly ornamental throughout the year. Their shape and colour are echoed by the larger leaves of a tremendous *Magnolia grandiflora* growing up beside the front door, its heavy branches shielding the entrance from the curious glances of passers-by and protecting the camellias against the strength of the summer sun.

Below the kitchen on this sunny side of the house is a small knot of dwarf box and silvery dwarf *Santolina chamaecyparissus nana*, with culinary herbs filling the gaps in the intricate pattern, and giving a clue to one of the owner's passions. For Pamela, Lady Harlech is not only a celebrated cook but also the author of several very good cookery books, and herbs play a prominent part in both her recipes and her garden.

This small front garden, intimate in parts and yet grand as you approach the house, seems full of sun and gaiety. Hidden behind the house is another garden, of considerable proportions and some splendour, a dramatic backdrop for the parties that Lady Harlech is fond of giving for friends and for the charities she supports. When Lord and Lady Harlech inherited the house from his parents the garden consisted of nothing but lawns and 'Queen Elizabeth' roses. The spacious house was redecorated with children and comfort in mind – huge sofas, roomy armchairs and fresh colour schemes give it the feel of a cosy house in the country – and then it was the garden's turn.

Ever aware of the need of room for parties, Lady Harlech was looking for a design which would lend interest to the rather unwieldy space. The greatest problem was that the shapes of the building and garden did not sit easily together: the building is an uneven U-shape, the original part being flanked by two later additions which protrude into the garden, the one to the right encroaching rather more than the one to the left. This created considerable difficulties as the owners and I tried to centre the design on the older main part of the house. Our solution was to create several separate gardens to complement the different sections of the building: a large one on an axis with the house, a small one outside the present drawing room in the left-hand addition, and a long thin one centred on the right-hand addition. There were also to be a white rose garden and, at the very bottom of the garden, a woodland walk.

THE way to the main garden lies through a wooden arch linking two borders and festooned with *Rosa* 'Albéric Barbier'. Two stone lions guard the way, one next to clumps of cranesbill and the other alongside the more ornate *Bergenia cordifolia*.

A GARDEN FOR ENTERTAINING

As you enter the house a large room opens off the hall with tall windows opening on to the back garden, which is screened on two sides by tall London planes. Their great canopies obscure the surrounding houses and provide privacy for the secluded 'drawing room' garden beside the house, and for the York stone terrace, laid to replace the original red tiles, under the large central windows. On the terrace, in the semi-shade of the house, are two large borders planted with lilacs, sweet-scented viburnums, the lovely lilac-blue *Hydrangea aspera villosa* and *Stachyurus praecox*, with its red-tinged branches hung in February and March with long racemes of tiny pale yellow flowers. A *Magnolia × soulangeana* 'Alba Superba' stands behind each border above a mass of iris, and a dark yew hedge serves as a backdrop while also marking the start of the next garden.

The way to the main garden lies through a wooden arch linking the two borders and festooned with the fragrant rambler rose 'Albéric Barbier'. The delicacy of the innumerable white blooms, tinged with the palest yellow, which smother the shoots of this rose belie its true character, for it is one of the toughest. It retains its leaves for most of the winter and – best of all – does not mind a little shade. Its sole failing is that it has only one flowering, but when it is in bloom it puts on such a spectacular show that this is easy to forgive.

Beyond are four crab apples, positioned so as to accentuate the main axis and link the borders at the end of the garden with those under the house. Each rises from a square bed edged with box and filled with Japanese anemones for late summer colour. In the sunny borders at the end are pink and white roses, blue delphiniums and soft mushroom-pink *Campanula lactiflora* 'Loddon Anna', hemmed in by *Euphorbia characias wulfenii* and woolly grey *Phlomis fruticosa*. 'New Dawn' roses are trained up tall wooden posts, and a variety of ground cover plants smother any weeds and complement the taller shrubs. Two *Prunus* 'Tai-haku', planted to either side of the outer edges of the borders,

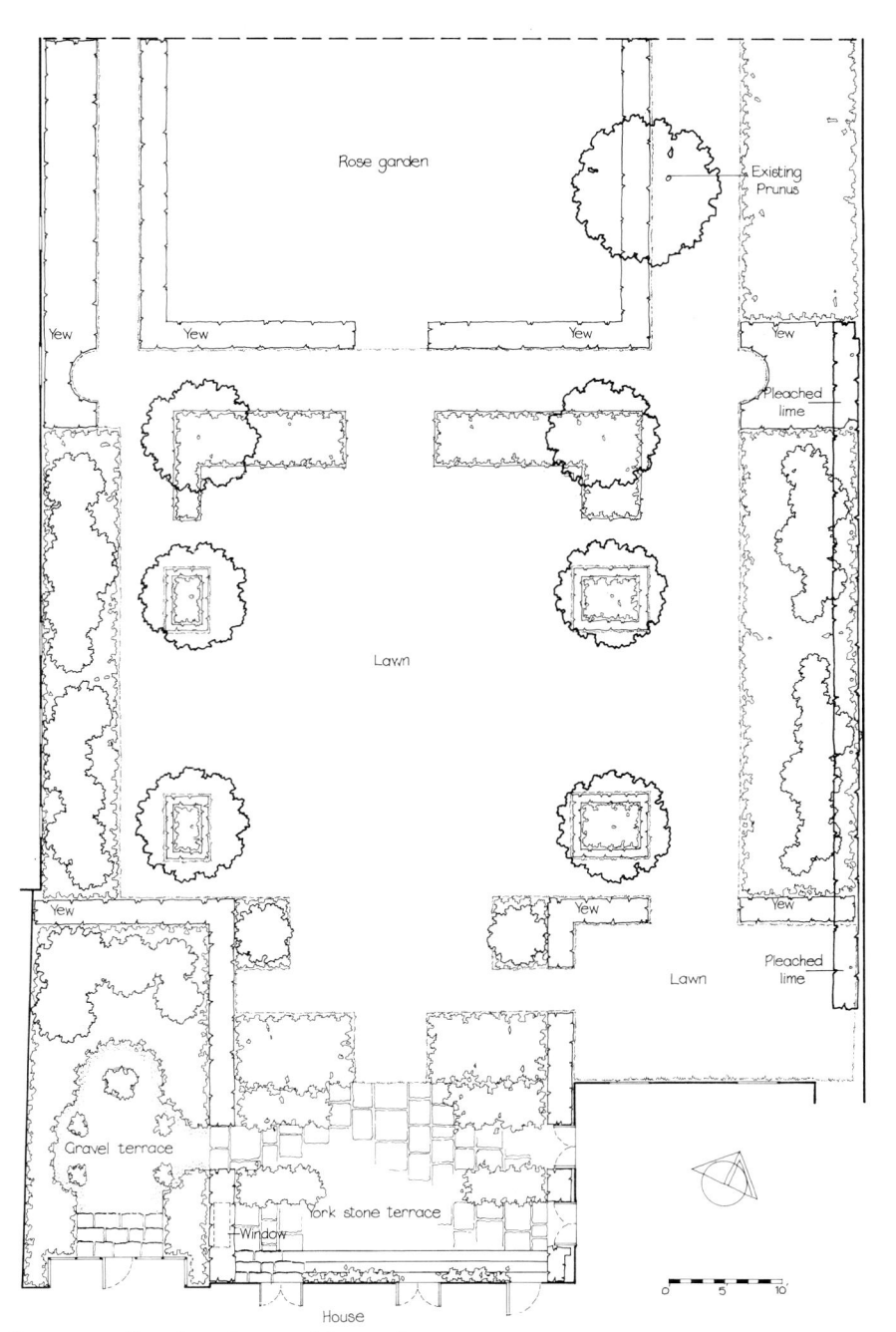

PLAN revealing the scheme of the garden as seen from the rear of the house. The rose garden gives way to a woodland garden, shaded by plane trees.

form clouds of dazzling white blossom against the coppery red young leaves in April. Behind is the yew hedge which surrounds the white rose garden. It also forms one side of a narrow grassy corridor which crosses the garden here, leading to a semicircular yew niche at each end.

FOUR crab apple trees accentuate the main axis of the garden. Each stands in a square bed edged with box, with box balls at the corners. In late summer the beds are filled with the tall, graceful stems and delicate flowers of Japanese anemones.

Before you enter the rose garden your eye is drawn to the niches to left and right; you glimpse an antique urn on one side, and, on the other, fragrant pink *Rosa* 'Sarah van Fleet' with geraniums at its foot.

A cherry tree already stood at this end of the garden, and now rises just outside the hedge, so that in spring its boughs decked with double white blossom overhang the dark yew enclosure. An ancient wisteria acts as a focal point at the far end, supporting itself on a wooden pavilion designed by the gardener, soon to be camouflaged by the wisteria's spiralling green tendrils.

Two evergreen *Rhamnus alaternus* 'Argenteovariegata' flank the entrance to this garden, where white is the prevailing colour. Tall wooden stakes support *Abutilon vitifolium* 'Album', with papery saucer-shaped white flowers from May to July, *Aralia elata* 'Variegata', bearing large panicles of white flowers in early autumn, and white pillar roses such as 'Mme Hardy', among the most exquisite of all the white roses, with perfectly shaped, green-eyed blooms. Beneath these tall shrubs are silvery artemisias, white geraniums and the late-flowering rose 'Yvonne Rabier', one of my favourites, with its fragrant clusters of delightful double white and perfectly shaped nearly evergreen leaves. The non-flowering *Stachys byzantina* 'Silver Carpet', pinks and lamiums are encouraged to spread underneath, as the tips of white delphiniums mingle with the other shrubs. At the centre of this garden is a small knot of box filled with the double white old-fashioned pink 'Mrs Sinkins', which is beautiful and highly scented when in flower, but sadly does not die gracefully and needs ruthless dead-heading.

The woodland garden beyond was never completed, but is nevertheless a delight in spring, when azaleas, camellias and bulbs all come into flower in the shade of the plane trees. It also hides the compost heap, essential in a

A GARDEN FOR ENTERTAINING

garden of this size for disposing of garden refuse, grass cuttings and vegetable matter from the house. Compost is the simplest and cheapest way of returning to the soil the nutrients consumed by the plants, and in London, where heavy clay lies immediately underneath the top layer of soil, it also helps to improve its structure.

Below a row of mature pleached limes which flanks the right-hand wall and screens the houses behind is a long border filled with shade-loving plants. These have been chosen for the shape and colour of their leaves, and in order to give colour at every season. Mahonias, philadelphus, deutzias and viburnums, together with variegated weigela and *Brachyglottis* 'Sunshine', are underplanted with *Geranium* 'Johnson's Blue' and pink *G. macrorrhizum*, lamiums, ajugas and ivies, while hostas and bergenias are used to emphasize the corners or to change the rhythm. This long border frames the view as you look out on the garden from the right-hand extension to the house.

On the opposite side, outside the drawing room, a small garden planted entirely with evergreens around a central gravelled area is wonderfully cool on summer evenings. The borders are filled with a dense planting of *Pachysandra terminalis* and the large-leaved ivy *Hedera helix* 'Hibernica', with not an inch of bare earth showing. From the middle of this sea of green rise rhododendrons and camellias, and terracotta pots with more camellias stand at the four corners of the gravel. Box balls underplanted with bergenias mark the corners of the beds, and the house wall is clothed with ivy and *Clematis montana*. The rich scent of a single philadelphus planted in a corner hangs heavy on the air in summer in this cool, quiet spot.

In a large area such as this there is great scope for seasonal planting, and in autumn as well as spring and summer the garden is full of colour: a small *Acer japonicum* tucked behind the summer borders turns to rich shades of gold, scarlet and ochre, an ampelopsis on a neighbouring house glows brilliant crimson, while the cherries and crab apples turn to gold and are hung with pretty yellow fruits.

Large open spaces are also made infinitely more interesting by being subdivided, so that there is always somewhere new to go and more to discover. This garden has its theatrical, gregarious side, which suits Lady Harlech's many public roles as trustee of the Victoria and Albert Museum, director of the South Bank Complex, chairman of the Women's Playhouse Trust, chairman of the English National Ballet, member of the *Evening Standard* Drama Awards panel, and many more. The yew hedges, dark and geometrical, strike a note of formality and of classical symmetry which is quite in keeping with this public world, but there is as well a more intimate, romantic aspect to the garden, expressed in its soft, flowing planting, its pastel shades and its secluded air; and each of these moods – public and private, architectural and romantic – is highlighted and intensified by the other. No longer just a large featureless space, this garden is now a group of smaller gardens each with its own distinct character – and proof of the maxim that the whole may be more than the sum of its parts.

ANOTHER long vista in this garden of many surprises. Below a row of mature pleached limes which flank the wall there is a border filled with shade-loving plants. *Rubus* Tridel with *Geranium endressii* at its feet together with mahonias, philadelphus and a variety of other shrubs have been chosen to give colour at every season.

AMONG MINARETS IN CHELSEA

'It all began', says Martin Summers with the air of relishing a favourite story, 'in 1978, on the night that Paddy the Irish cat-burglar broke in. I was lying in bed fast asleep. Rashly, perhaps, I launched myself at him, got my arm round his throat, dragged him downstairs and threw him into the littlest room in the house. There was no lock on the outside of the door, so I had to lean against it to stop Paddy escaping. Paddy was down but not out and embarked on a serious plea bargaining session through the door. If I would "go easy with him with the law" he would give me some good advice. "Your house is a pushover, guv'nor – you should put up the trellis. We all hate the trellis because it wobbles."'

The story has clearly been told before, but it bears the repetition. If Paddy were to see Martin Summers' garden now he would be impressed at how seriously his words were taken. Six-foot trellises were erected all round the roof by Keith Wilson of Teeways in Walton-on-Thames, and the effect was unexpected. The roof was transformed. No longer was it 'just a series of precarious parapets', but instead it had become an extension of the house, to be furnished and lived in. Bridges and balustrades, steps and a spiral staircase, statues and stained glass and yet more trellis followed. Then the planting started and terracotta pots appeared everywhere, starting with a single weeping willow (an ambitious enough start, one might think) and finally multiplying to the astonishing 900 or so plants which presently transform this Chelsea roof space into a bower of green.

There is considerably more variety here than is to be found in many earthbound gardens. Martin Summers puts this down to the fact that with pots you can change the soil to suit the plant, so that acid- and alkaline-loving plants will grow happily together. This is clearly only

TOP THIS courtyard is at ground level and marks the entrance to the house. Trellis is fixed to the walls and numerous pots are attached to it, planted with a variety of geraniums and other trailing plants. On the ground more pots, this time larger, are filled with hydrangeas and climbing plants.

A SMALL wooden statue of Buddha sits on a tree trunk, surrounded by a myriad of pots stacked one on top of the other and filled with azaleas, ivies of all kinds, bergenias and large-leaved hostas.

LITTLE bridges with white wooden balustrades lead you up and down, under pergolas covered in roses and past stained glass windows beyond which there is a view to a side garden where pots climb the wall.

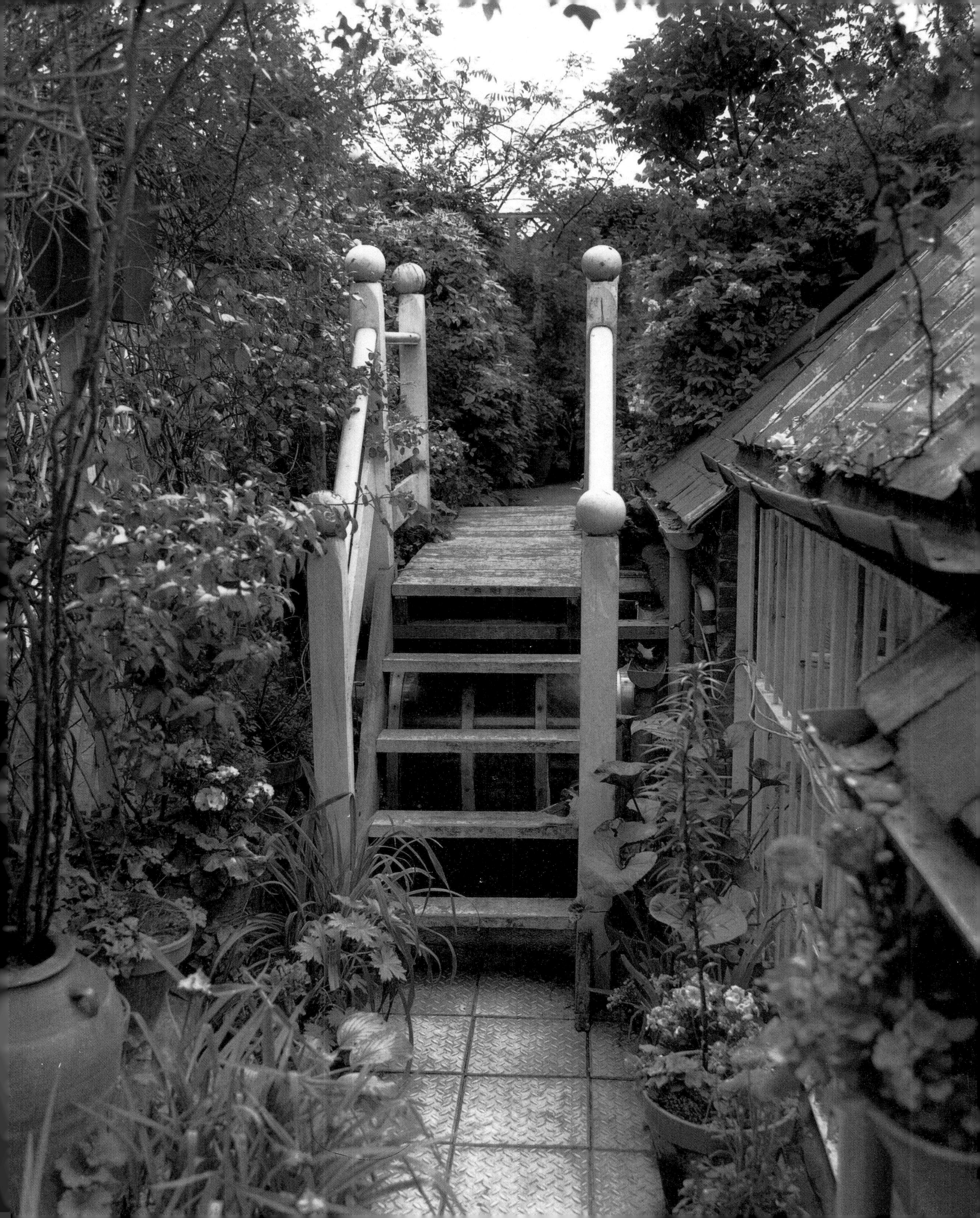

PRIVATE GARDENS OF LONDON

part of the answer, however: it takes a special flair and understanding to create combinations and associations of such consistent interest and vitality. He has a refreshingly workmanlike approach nevertheless: 'I had no real idea which plants went best with which, but I worked on the principle that if they flowered at roughly the same time they should get on well together in the same environment.' And on this cheerfully empirical basis he has managed to achieve some extremely successful groupings, such as a variegated weigela, *Philadelphus coronarius* 'Aureus', a purple maple and *Viburnum plicatum* 'Mariesii' with clusters of white blooms tinged with pink.

The choice of plants has been greatly influenced by colour, for this was to be a night-time garden as much as a daytime one, and Martin Summers felt that shades of red in flowers and leaves looked particularly well under floodlight. The list started with liquidambar and *Parrotia persica*, with their rich autumn tints of orange and amber, and grew to include *Amelanchier canadensis*, that unusually rewarding shrub which bears racemes of white star-shaped flowers in April, sweet-tasting black berries in June and soft red or yellow foliage in autumn, *Cotinus coggygria* 'Royal Purple' (the purple-leaved smoke tree), *Acer pseudoplatanus* 'Brilliantissimum', with its shrimp-pink young leaves, and a host of others.

Even the architecture of this garden seemed to grow more outlandish: interesting and complex initially, with different levels and four steep-sided studio roofs creating unusual interplays of light and dark, angles and planes, it was soon to become positively baroque. Martin Summers was offered four huge onion domes, fibreglass copies of ones that had originally graced the Royal Pavilion in Brighton. These they had replaced while they were taken down for restoration, and now that the restoration work was complete and the originals reinstated to their proper place the copies were no longer needed. Martin Summers accepted without hesitation, and there followed an operation planned with military efficiency. At half past seven one Saturday morning the domes arrived on the back of a lorry, followed half an hour later by the crane (with 180-foot jib) that was to lift them into position. Lunch was served to the patient and curious neighbours in the street, which was closed for the occasion, and by teatime the 'Hindoo'-Gothic domes were in

BELOW LEFT THERE is considerably more variety of planting on Martin Summers' roof than there is in many earthbound gardens. He has a cheerfully empirical approach, shifting pots around as they come into flower or begin to fade, and creating unusual associations of plants. The minarets hide tape recorders which play recordings of tropical birds or cicadas on summer evenings.

CONTRASTING leaf shape and colour is particularly sought after here. A pink rose climbs through a purple-leaved acer with *Weigela* 'Florida Variegata' near it. Plants with pink and red shades were chosen for they look well under floodlighting.

A LITTLE picket gate framed by trelliswork leads from one part of the garden to another, while nearby tables are set among bowers of hydrangeas or small orchards of fruit trees. As you wander round the garden, or simply sit and look, it is hard to believe that you are on a level with the surrounding chimneypots.

position, crowning the roofs above the streets of Chelsea.

Every perspective is now dominated by these exotic transplants. Furthermore Martin Summers has taken the opportunity of adding to the bravura of his garden by installing in them hidden tape recorders, which at the press of a button will play a selection of background noises: wild birdsong perhaps, or, on warm summer evenings when everyone is eating outside, cicadas.

Yet as you step out of Martin Summers' kitchen you might be forgiven for thinking that you were entering a more or less conventional back garden, though an exceptionally pretty one. In the small conservatory

PRIVATE GARDENS OF LONDON

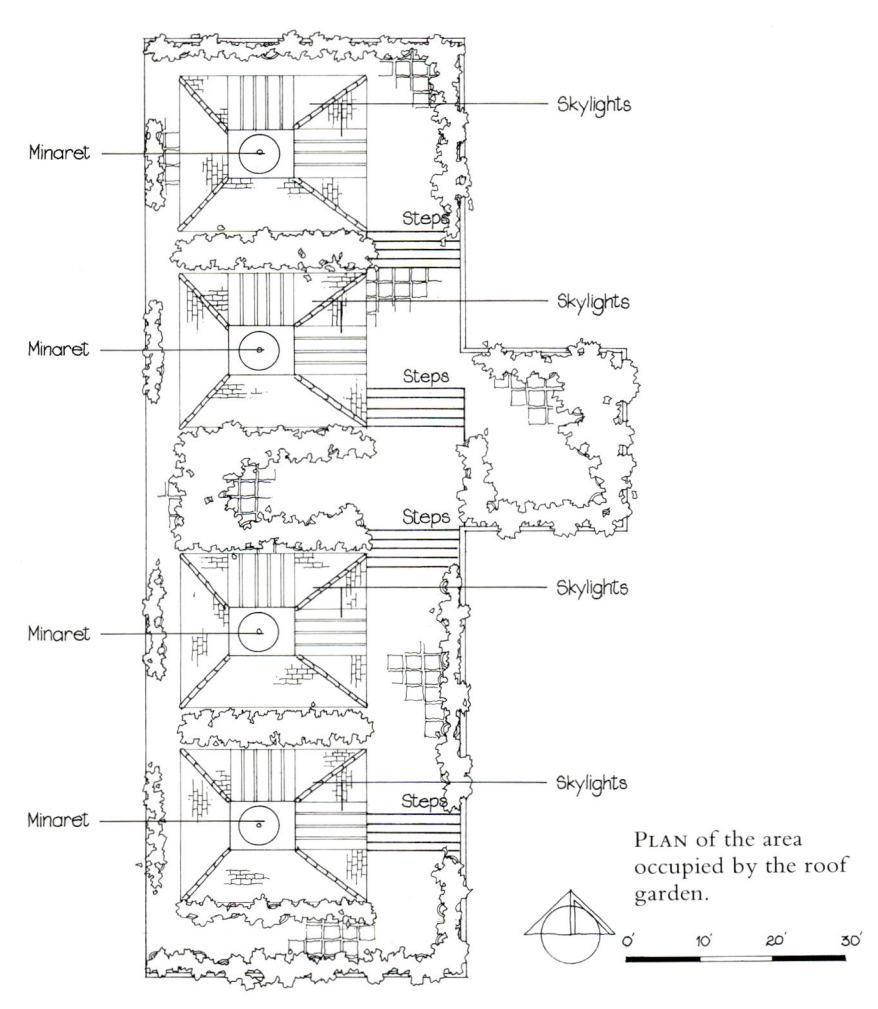

PLAN of the area occupied by the roof garden.

are the tell-tale signs of an unusually keen gardener: a small propagating frame is crammed with cuttings, and small pots of seedlings and bigger pots of herbs stand on the shelves, in a sea of *Soleirolia soleirolii*. It is only when you look harder that you realize that the profusion of greenery that surrounds, so natural and abundant, has its roots in nothing bigger than ten-inch pots. It is an achievement to be able to create imaginative combinations of flower and foliage colour, but in a roof garden it is a positive *tour de force*. Your eye leads you up a pretty wrought-iron spiral staircase wreathed with ivy, and your feet itch to follow to explore this extraordinary secret paradise. Once on the higher level you thread through a mass of foliage which towers above you on all sides. Here is a little table and seats in a bower of pink hydrangeas; there another, in the shade of a small orchard of fruit trees. Little bridges with white wooden balustrades lead you up and down, past some beautiful stained glass panels beyond which there is a view to a side garden (where dozens of pots hang from the walls), past a Buddha statue musing under the boughs of some azaleas, under trellises laden with clematis and roses ('Pink Perpetue' is a favourite, underplanted with lupins), and on and on. So abundant and many-layered is the growth here, and so frequent are the surprises and the twists and turns in the path, that a walk round the garden seems much longer than it really is.

The arrival of spring is unmistakable in Martin Summers' garden: all his neighbours are treated to a bird's-eye view of clematis, a weeping Korean cherry tree, jasmine, roses, viburnum, fuchsias, sweet peas and a host of other flowers, all bursting forth in an extravagant display which only becomes more luxuriant and immoderate as the summer wears on. Autumn in its turn brings a kaleidoscope of golds, ochres, scarlets and pinks.

IN a sea of greenery contained by high trellis, four huge onion domes, fibreglass copies of the ones on Brighton Pavilion, dominate the sky line. Large-leaved rhododendrons are amongst the myriad of plants grown in this roof garden.

46

This is not a garden that encourages reflections on the practical, mundane aspects of such an enterprise. Yet the potential problems are legion. Weight is an obvious one, as most roofs are not designed to carry heavy loads, but he positions the pots with care on load-bearing walls rather than give up his beloved terracotta pots for one of the many lightweight substitutes and uses lightweight paving on areas that will not take much weight. Watering has to be done daily (or nightly, as Martin Summers often does it in the small hours, when he believes plants do their growing), and an irrigation system with twelve short lengths of hose attached to taps has been installed for the purpose. Hygiene is more important in a roof garden, too, and there is constant sweeping and tidying and grooming of plants with the help of the invaluable George, and a patch of Astroturf is hoovered regularly.

Martin Summers is more impressed by the advantages than the disadvantages, however. He insists that pests and weeds are less of a problem than in ordinary gardens, and he never has to go through the agonies of other gardeners who can rectify their inevitable planting mistakes only by the risky business of transplanting. If Martin Summers is unhappy with a composition, be it a particular association of shrubs or the arrangement of a small grove of trees, he simply moves the pots around. If colours clash or proportions get out of hand, the answer is equally simple. And he is not faced with the problem of what to do with that glorious shrub in a prominent position when it has finished flowering: 'I like to wait until a pot is in full bloom and then lug it into the most obvious part of the garden. When it is over I move it to a less conspicuous place.'

It is not surprising that Martin Summers should make light of practical difficulties, for this is a garden of exotic dreams. Viewed by moonlight on a summer's evening, the onion domes silhouetted against the stars and the warm air heavy with scent of *Trachelospermum jasminoides* and pulsing with the whirring of cicadas, it is the sort of vision of orient splendour which might have risen before Coleridge's eyes in the opium trance that inspired *Kubla Khan*:

'*In Xanadu did Kubla Khan*
A stately pleasure dome decree;
Where Alph, the sacred river, ran
Through caverns measureless to man
Down to a sunless sea.

So twice five miles of fertile ground
With walls and towers was girdled round:
And there were gardens bright with sinuous rills,
Where blossomed many an incense-bearing tree;
And here were forests ancient as the hills,
Enfolding sunny spots of greenery.'

PLACING these large onion domes on the roof tops of the four studios was an operation planned with military skill. They arrived early in the morning and by tea time the Hindoo Gothic domes were in place crowning the roofs above the streets of Chelsea.

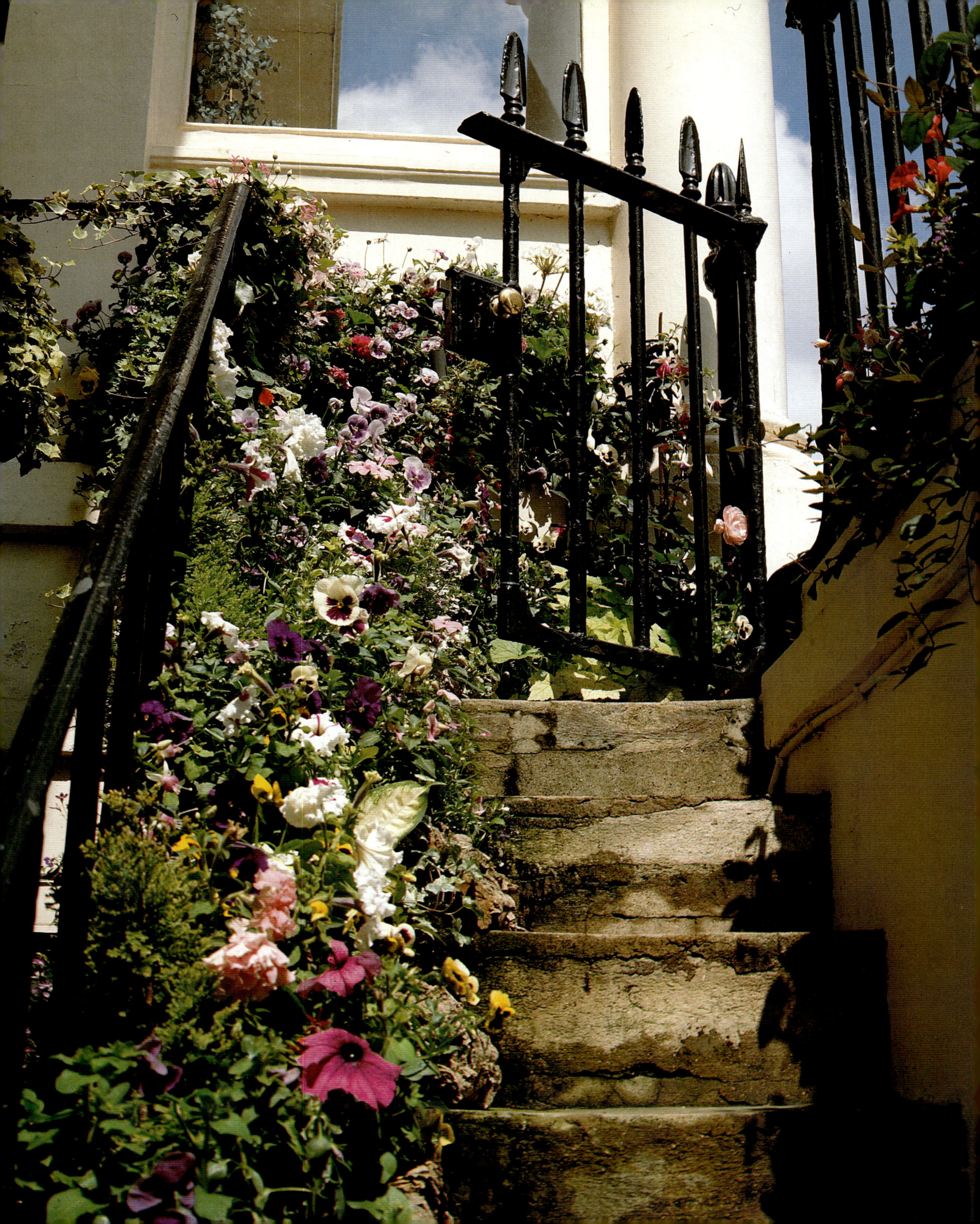

A BELGRAVIA BASEMENT

It would be hard to imagine a site more bleak or uninviting than this cramped, dark and narrow Belgravia 'area' a few years ago. Only the most dauntless of gardeners would even have attempted to do anything with it, and most of those would probably soon have given up the unequal struggle, abandoning the basement to its three red dustbins and air of genteel neglect. Not so Ann Bogod. Having discovered that some plants which she had put outside to hide some paint splashes were not only surviving but thriving, she decided to try something more ambitious. With splendid disregard for what the books say about which plants will tolerate shade, she set out to create a garden full of colour and perfume. Now pedestrians walking down this sober late Georgian street are greeted by the unexpected sight of a profusion of flowers and greenery wreathing the iron railings and spilling on to the pavement.

With an optimism bordering on the heroic, she concentrated on the site's good points. Although it receives only at most an hour and a half of direct sunlight each day, its open position on a west-facing corner and its white-painted walls meant that it was appreciably lighter than her former garden, a north-facing patio. Moreover it was extremely sheltered from the wind, as well as being protected from the worst of the frost, and it seemed also to be insulated by its sunken position. The result was a slightly warmer than average microclimate in which a surprisingly wide range of plants would flourish. Even limited space was turned into a virtue, for as the pots and containers multiplied so Mrs Bogod became convinced that plants thrive on close proximity, and do best when they are actually touching each other.

Pots are everywhere, marching down the steps, hanging from hooks and bars, clinging to narrow ledges and crowding together on the York stone paving. Most of them are tiny and filled with annuals, so that the planting scheme can be completely rethought every year. A winter 'skeleton' is provided by ivies and dwarf conifers, which Mrs Bogod combines with bark to form arches and other architectural shapes. Bark is one of her favourite materials for the 'woodland' feel it gives, and ivy creates a permanent skirt round the pots to hide them from view. The 'Goldheart' ivy which climbs through the railings in winter tends to clash with summer planting schemes, so it is camouflaged with two honeysuckles which grow through it, and strips of bark to plug the gaps. The conifers, too, are no longer a feature in summer, being disguised with flowers.

The entrance to the garden is through a pretty wrought-iron gate. To the left the honeysuckles twine rampantly through the railings, interspersed this year with pansies and busy lizzies; to the right a trough spills over with more pansies and busy lizzies, together with ivies, trailing pelargoniums, roses, carnations, clematis and fuchsias; and leading down the steps is a froth of pansies, busy lizzies and petunias in shades of mauve, pink, purple and white. Continuing this colour scheme below are a wall basket spilling frilly double mauve petunias and mauve, cerise and white trailing

ALTHOUGH the basement and steps of this Belgravia house receive only at most an hour-and-a-half of direct sunlight each day, its open position and the reflection of the light from the white painted walls mean that the microclimate is perfect for a wide range of plants to flourish. Pots are everywhere, down the steps, hanging from hooks and bars and crowding the York stone paving below.

A PIECE of cork provides a comfortable edge to this profusion of petunias and violas. Here is a further example of the ingenuity of the owner of this minute garden.

lobelia, and window boxes of pale pink busy lizzies, Virginia stocks and mauve violas set against a dark background of ivy.

Not an inch of space is wasted on this lower level, which at its narrowest measures only three feet across. Even the security bars on the windows are pressed into service as supports for the sweet peas. Here is the garden's only large tub, containing a standard camellia with a pink-flowering lavatera in front. One year regal and Pink Perfection lilies were spectacular here in combination with jasmine and a white lacecap hydrangea, but next year the scheme will be different again. Mrs Bogod never knows from one year to the next what theme she will choose for the garden. The two jasmines climb up a piece of trellising which forms an ingenious arbour, through which sweet peas are also threaded. Another clever feature is a mirror on the end wall, which reflects not only light but also space, so giving an illusion of greater depth.

An extraordinary number of plants thrive together in this limited space: there are no fewer than six roses, including David Austin's 'Mary Rose', 'Ballerina' and several ramblers. Another rose climbs up the wall, along with the hydrangea, summer jasmine, two honeysuckles (one deciduous, one evergreen) and three clematis. On summer evenings the scents of the honeysuckles, jasmine and roses combine to make a heady cocktail. Pots and troughs at floor level hold more annuals, together with shade-loving hostas, azaleas, fuchsias and a variegated castor oil plant, and above hangs a bird cage festooned with tiny ivies.

Mrs Bogod's passion for flowers embraces also the entrance porch, which is lined with suitably narrow troughs, and even the side wall of the house is hung with baskets of trailing pelargoniums. Inevitably she finds herself entrusted with other people's ailing specimens, and she never turns a plant away. She is equally careful, however, to remove dead or diseased plants or foliage, and admits to being fanatical about dead-heading. Her maintenance routine is strict and unrelenting: constant training (horizontal rather than vertical) is essential if this tiny jungle is not to run riot; and watering and feeding are equally essential to keep it growing. Most of the plants are in plastic pots, which are lighter and easier to manage than terracotta ones; they also dry out less quickly, but in summer watering is nevertheless a twice-daily chore. Mrs Bogod generally uses phostrogen as a feed, although she has also been known to make her own compost in plastic carrier bags.

Mrs Bogod's minute attention to detail in making a fully fledged garden in her basement is not only rewarded in full by the pure joy that the sight of it gives her and all passers-by but also proves beyond a doubt that no plot, however small, cherished and tended by a true gardener can fail to become a real garden.

A GARDEN AFLOAT

Alive with the shimmering reflections of stately mature trees, grand stucco terraces and barges painted in bright, primary-coloured trim, the towpaths of the Paddington Basin have an extraordinary un-metropolitan, and even un-English quality. It comes as no surprise that it was a poet who christened the area 'Little Venice' (possibly with a certain amount of poetic licence, for the pale northern light and the inspiration of the architecture are more Dutch than Venetian): Byron coined the name, and Browning, whose romantic idea it was to plant the island in the middle of the basin with weeping willows, followed suit.

This lowest part of the Regent's Canal, just above its confluence with the Grand Junction Canal, is among the finest stretches of waterway in London. The canal was opened in 1816 and, perhaps because the architect John Nash was the driving force behind it, its aesthetic properties were appreciated and exploited from the start (indeed Nash wanted the canal to flow right through the middle of his Regent's Park development, but the Crown Commissioners insisted that it be banished to the northern fringes, fearing that rough bargees would lower the tone of the area). Accordingly, noble tree-lined avenues of handsome,

BRIGHT colours are in the tradition of house boats, and these petunias, bright red geraniums, deep blue lobelias and white annual iberis contrast gaily with the blue of the hull.

stuccoed villas were constructed overlooking the canal; many still survive, as do the trees, whose great canopies cast a dappled shade on the water.

Some of the narrow boats that used to ply the canal, their original purpose lost, now line the towpaths as houseboats. Water-borne dwellings are rare, and gardens afloat are even rarer, but on the roof of his narrow boat, *Lady Venice*, Dennis Moore has made one of the most unusual gardens in London. *Lady Venice* is moored beside the beautiful wrought-iron Warwick Avenue bridge, just below the notorious Maida Hill tunnel where, as there were no towpaths, the bargees had to unharness their horses and, lying flat on their backs, propel the barges by pushing against the tunnel walls with their feet. In her livery of vivid blue and yellow *Lady Venice* adds a touch of brilliant colour to the canal at all times of year, but in summer her brilliance becomes truly dazzling. Then the array of pots, pails and troughs that cover the roof – over thirty of them, many painted in traditional bargees' floral designs – is filled to overflowing with flowers in sizzling shades of pink and scarlet.

Mr Moore, a former seaman, retired here with his Scottie dog (whose portrait is included in *Lady Venice*'s livery) for health reasons. He started gardening, which he had never done in his life before, as physiotherapy. Having cleared the towpath of rubble, within a year he had turned it into a true cottage garden: a higgledy-piggledy patchwork of colour, grown from cuttings, seedlings and other people's cast-offs. One of Mr Moore's most prized and showy dahlias was literally thrown through the railings one night. The dahlias, huge and crimson, stand at the back of the towpath, along with gladioli and tomato plants, which use the railings behind as supports. In front of them are everlasting flowers (helichrysum) in red, pink, yellow, white and orange, and zonal and regal pelargoniums with enormous salmon-pink, scarlet and white flower-heads. Bordered with clumps of orange and egg-yolk yellow marigolds, deep blue lobelia and white alyssum, this narrow bed is a kaleidoscopic display of pure colour in the unselfconscious tradition of the true cottage garden.

On the towpath stand flower-filled barrels and milk churns and overhead hang baskets brimming with petunias, pansies, busy lizzies, alyssum, lobelia and ivy, suspended from an old trivet now festooned with polygonum. But the *pièce de résistance* is undoubtedly on *Lady Venice*'s roof: a display of undiluted, exhilarating colour, set off by its bright blue background and reflected in the rippling water below. Here flame-red, salmon-pink, carmine and vermilion pelargoniums are paired with petunias in cerise, magenta, rose-pink and violet. Crimson and purple fuchsias mingle with plum-coloured pansies and busy lizzies in every shade from palest pink to blood-red. Only on closer inspection do you realize that among this kaleidoscope of colour there are dotted pots of herbs and of Chinese lettuce, the dog's favourite.

This is a garden full of exuberant, unstudied charm; it is also, judged by the cottage-garden criteria of colour, perfume and usefulness, extremely successful. The pure pigments of its colours dazzle the eye; its herbs and Chinese lettuce feed both Mr Moore and his dog; and, as *Lady Venice* moves gently on the swell, the sweet smell of alyssum fills the air.

IN this part of the Regent's Canal, which is just above the confluence with the Grand Junction Canal, amongst the narrow boats that line the towpath, is 'Lady Venice' with an unusual garden on her roof. In her livery of vivid blue and yellow she adds a touch of brilliance to the canal at all times of the year.

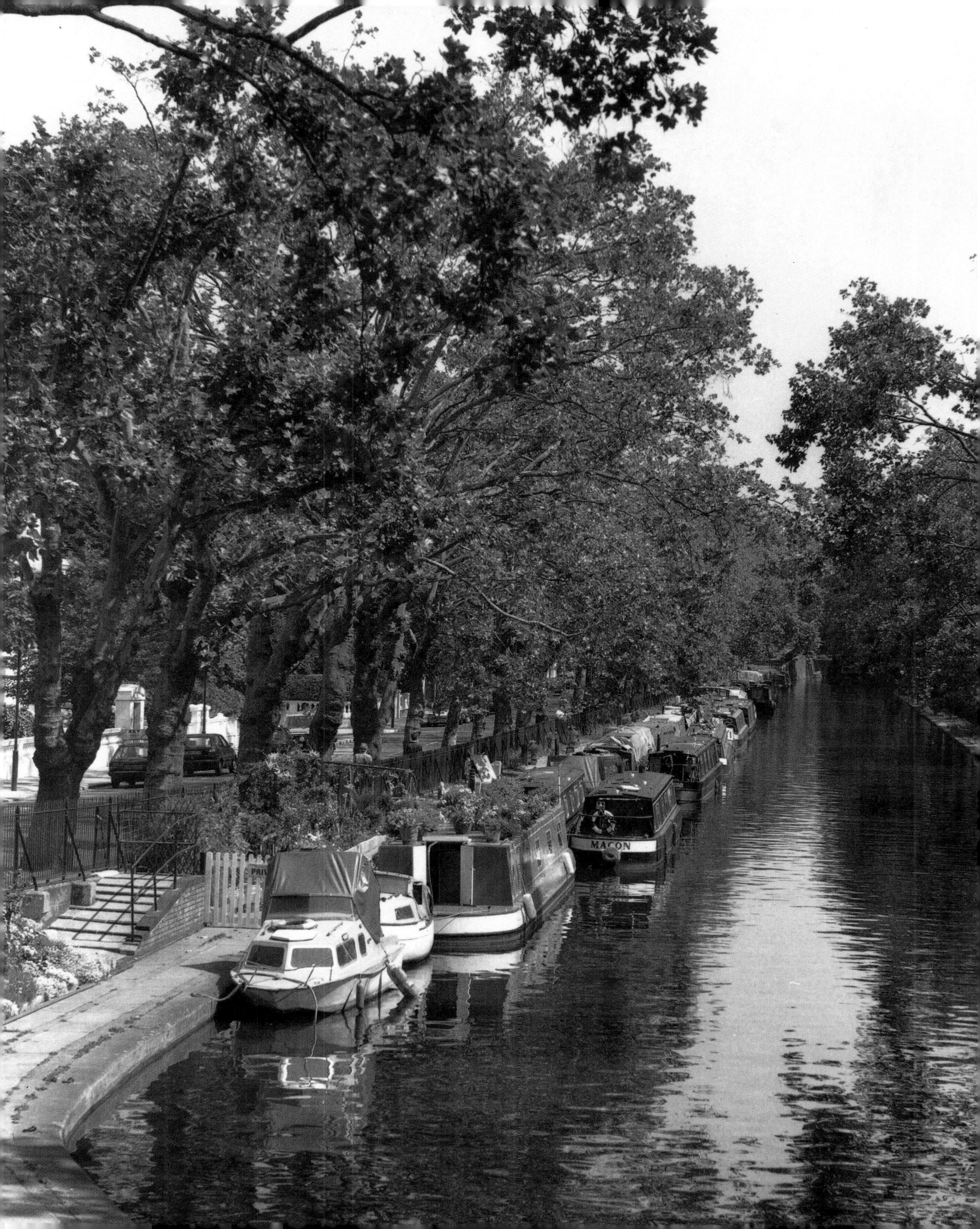
MACON

LUTYENS REVISITED

The elegant seventeenth-century façade of Lindsey House is a fitting prelude to the refined simplicity of the garden that lies behind, protected from the continuous hum of heavy traffic along the Embankment by its high brick walls. The only dwelling of its date to survive in Chelsea (it had just been built when the Royal Hospital was founded in 1681), the house is a reminder of the days when the only traffic noises to be heard were the clatter of hooves, the rattle of carriage wheels and – of course – the splashing of oars. When Sir Thomas More, ill-fated Chancellor to Henry VIII, chose to build his country manor here (within easy reach by river of the Palace of Westminster) in the sixteenth century, Chelsea was a tiny riverside fishing village, surrounded by open countryside which stretched to the east as far as the walls of the City of London. Ever since that time men and women of letters, scholars and artists seem to have been drawn to Cheyne Walk and the Chelsea Embankment as if by a magnet, attracted perhaps by its charm and the ever-changing light of the river.

WIRE and moss full-size monkeys are rapidly becoming clothed with ivy, a witty replacement for the statues that used to stand there. Yellow irises are planted at the foot of the red brick wall and ivy creeps along the ground at base of the big poplar.

THE west-facing border is planted with bold rectangular blocks of white variegated hostas, and box edged with blue flowering lavender. This rectilinear planting design makes a splendid foil for the roses that clamber up the brickwork and frame the two marble plaques.

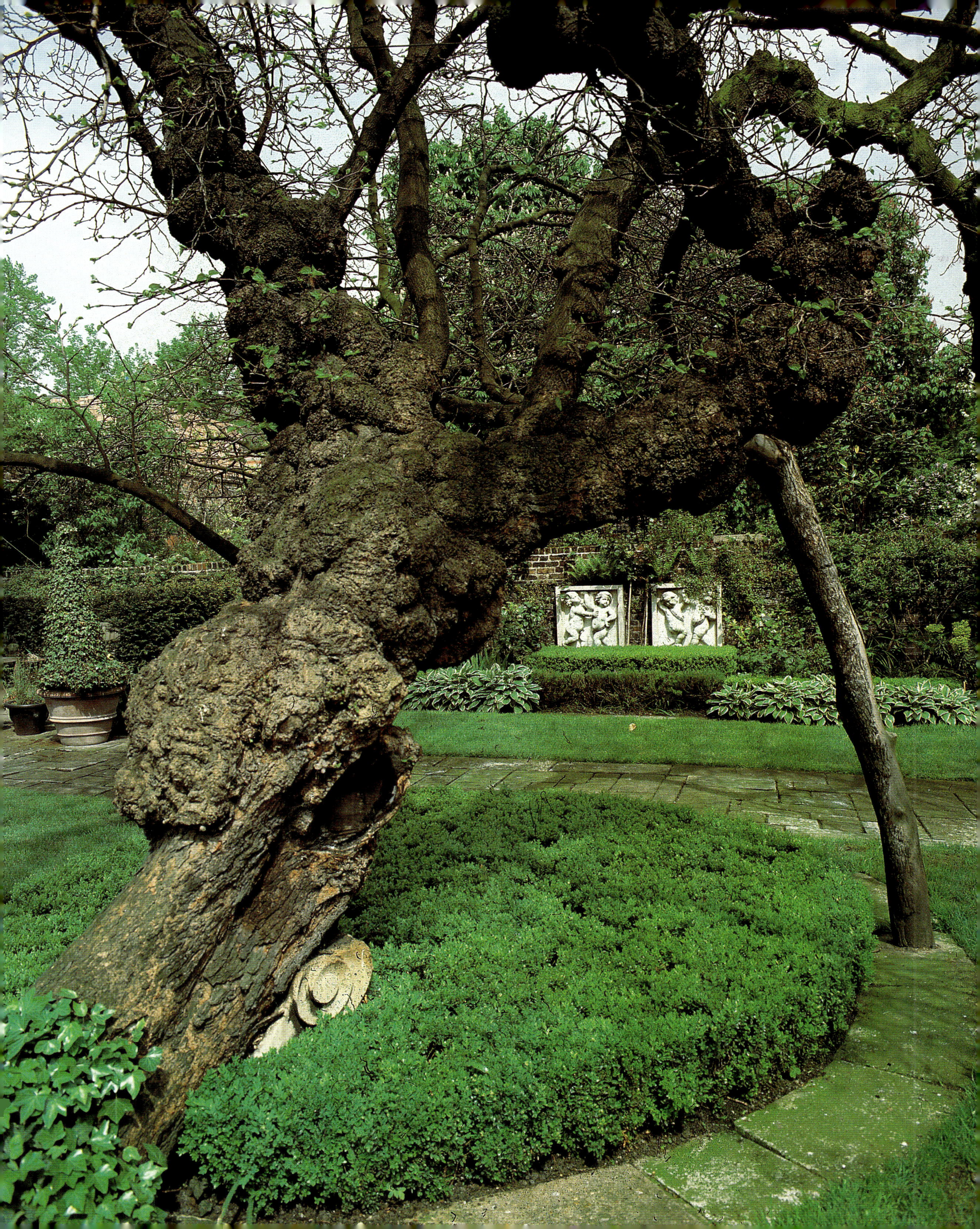

THE simple stone colonnade, designed to divide the courtyard from the rest of the garden, as it was when the garden was originally laid out.

The third Earl of Lindsey built Lindsey House in 1674, and in the succeeding centuries it has been home to a colourful array of people, including Isambard Kingdom Brunel, James Abbott McNeill Whistler and the Moravian Brethren. The garden too has undergone its vicissitudes. Its original formal layout must have suffered in the eighteenth century, not only because of changing tastes in garden design, but also because the house was then divided into five separate dwellings. These became three in the nineteenth century, and it was for one of the three gardens that Edwin Lutyens was asked to supply the design. This was a doubly fortunate choice, for Lutyens was predisposed, not only by his personal taste in garden design but also by his training as an architect, to respect and echo the simple formality of the house. Whether he intended it or not, his garden design must surely echo in spirit the garden through which the Earl and and his friends strolled over three centuries ago.

In this long, rectangular and (it must then have seemed) limited space, about fifty feet by thirty, Lutyens demonstrated a finely judged understanding of the possibilities and limitations of such a site. With commendable restraint he flew in the face of current fashion, choosing not to clutter the space with elaborate flower borders, nor to over-design it with the gamut of carefully contrived 'features' then in vogue. Instead he chose a linear composition of grass, water, trees and stone, modest in its elements and quietly restful in its effect. Two broad stone paths, echoed by two narrower, parallel paths at the far sides, ran the length of the garden, accentuating its rectangular shape. The inner paths flanked a central strip of grass, which was interrupted only by a circular lily pond under a venerable mulberry tree. A simple colonnade of stone marked the division between house and garden, and at the far end the boundary wall was enlivened by two pedimented niches, each holding a statue.

Fortunately the skeleton of this elegant composition was strong enough to survive many years of more or less abandonment and neglect. When John Stefanidis, the present owner, turned his attention to it some seven years ago, he found that the bare bones survived – and fortunately in him the garden had found someone who was prepared to devote a great deal of time and care to bringing it back to life. The mossy stone paths and green expanses of lawn were still in place, as were the pond and niches, though both were now empty, and the mulberry had grown even more gnarled and noble. With my help he set about completely reinstating the garden and adapting it to his own needs, approaching the project with his characteristic mixture of stylistic rigorousness and attention to detail, spiced with an instinct for experiment and sheer enjoyment. The ideas produced by this fruitful partnership were all carefully recorded in a garden book, together with notes of the work done.

The mulberry, it was decided, needed pruning – an extremely specialized task which is undertaken only rarely – and the fine stone of the paths needed cleaning. The empty pond was filled with soil and planted with box to create a raised circle of green, its slightly roughened surface forming a transition between the smooth green and grey of grass and stone and the wrinkled contortions of the mulberry suspended hectically above it. The extravagant asymmetry of the ancient tree strikes a note of jaunty insouciance, echoed in the witty replacements that have been created for the missing statues. Here the gravitas of the niches, with their stately classical pediments and flanking brick columns, is neatly undercut by cheeky wire and moss full-size monkeys, rapidly becoming clothed in ivy. Tails held high, they seem about to scamper up the walls and into the canopy of the surrounding trees.

The outer grass strips of the original design have been curtailed so as to create two small recesses at the end of the garden: surrounded by yew hedges and furnished with pretty wooden seats these now form very comfortable and secluded retreats. Pyramids of small-leaved ivy guard their entrances, and terracotta pots

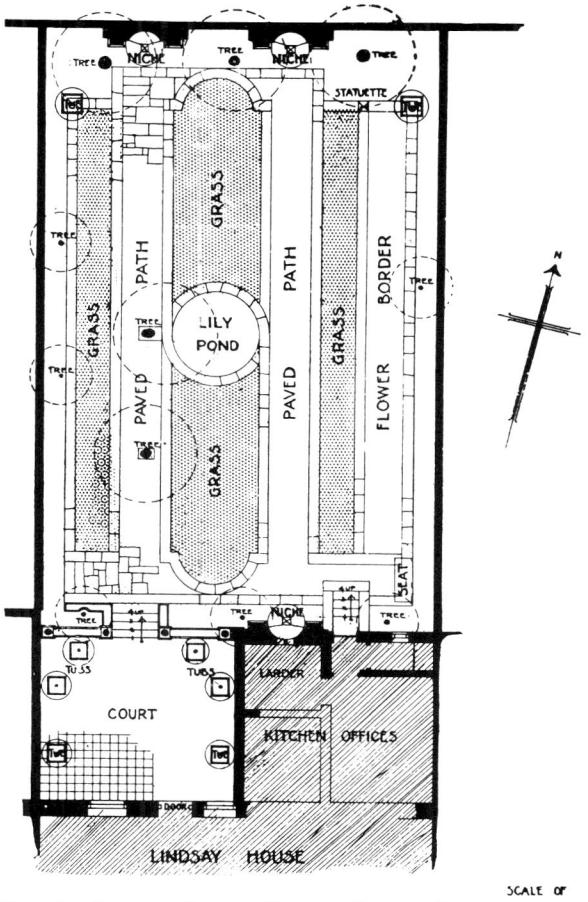

THE original design of 1911 by Sir Edwin Lutyens and Gertrude Jekyll for the garden at 100 Cheyne Walk, was described as 'a good example of what may be done in a limited space'. My revised plan retains the same essential form.

THE mulberry tree, described as already 'of noble growth' when the garden was laid out, originally overhung a lily pond. Statues occupied the niches where the monkeys now live.

PRIVATE GARDENS OF LONDON

WITH time, the roots of the mulberry tree encroached and the pond slowly dried up. Now box hedging fills the circle forming a raised mound of green.

overflowing with culinary herbs perfume the air. This heady concoction of Mediterranean scents is also contributed to by a *Wisteria floribunda* 'Multijuga', which bears extravagantly long white racemes, and a fig tree, with leaves which are not only ornamental but also aromatic, both of which are trained up the end wall. At the opposite end of the garden, overlooked by the house, is another sitting area, a terrace which forms a sort of antechamber to the garden. Here are giant terracotta pots filled with camellias, clipped bay and box balls.

The planting is discreet but imaginative. Under the far wall on one side is a geometrical pattern of dwarf box filled with a variety of plants chosen for their huge leaves. *Crambe cordifolia* and rodgersia, hostas and *Rheum palmatum* together create a feeling of lush vegetable growth, of almost tropical promiscuity, which contrasts admirably with the severity of the rest of the design.

Box, hostas and camellias fill the better part of the borders that flank the garden, with ivy used as ground cover. The camellias are trained as espaliers against the east-facing wall so as to allow light to reach the drifts of plain and variegated ivy with which they are underplanted. The west-facing border is planted with bold rectangular blocks of white variegated hostas and blue-flowering lavender, the fresh, variegated greens and broad, lanceolate form of the hostas' leaves and the lavender's silver-grey spikes making an especially successful combination. The uncompromisingly rectilinear design of the planting makes a splendid foil for the roses, including 'New Dawn', that clamber up the brickwork, taking full advantage of the sheltered position and framing two marble plaques.

Colour in this garden is fittingly subtle, relying largely on a seemingly almost infinite palette of greens. In summer the irises add a note of soft blue, the climbing roses give white highlights, and the old rose that spills romanti-

PALE pink camellias planted just outside the windows give a promise of spring early in the year, and the eye is drawn on past them and through the colonnade to the great mulberry, just coming into bud.

58

LUTYENS REVISITED

cally over the colonnade at the garden's entrance adds a dash of crimson; but still it is green, in all its subtle variations, that is the keynote. Even in spring, when the camellias flower in a profusion of pale pink and white, it is the contrast between the dark gloss of their leaves and the tender fresh green of the new shoots of box that draws the eye.

Sensitive management of each group of plants is necessary to maintain the delicate balance of design, planting and mood in this unusual garden. The opportunity to reinstate and adapt a Lutyens design is a rare one; the opportunity to do so while at the same time respecting the dictates of a house of architectural distinction and the needs of a discerning owner is not only rare but also extremely taxing. Minimalist in its conception yet with touches of romanticism; formal in design but at the same time idiosyncratic; faithful to historic precedent yet wittily original, this garden can happily be deemed a success on all counts.

AT the far end of the garden yew hedges screen two small recesses furnished with table and chairs. In front of the hedge, purple iris flourish while to one side a large terracotta pot is planted with small-leaved ivies, trained up four bamboo sticks to form a pyramid.

59

BEHIND THE STUCCO: THREE GARDENS ON THE LADBROKE ESTATE

'Ladbroke upholds the proper dignity of the English middle classes', it was observed in 1910; and indeed the stucco villas and terraces of the Ladbroke estate, picturesquely arranged on the undulating slopes of Notting Hill, exude an air of comfortable solidity. Laid out in the 1840s by J. W. Ladbroke, the estate was perhaps less aristocratic in its appeal than contemporary Belgravia, but its position on a breezy hill was considered to have other advantages over Belgravia's drained swampland. The avenues and crescents that fan out from Ladbroke Grove, the estate's central north-south axis, still have a quietly countrified feel to them. This is illusory now, of course (although there was a farm here as late as the 1880s) – and perhaps fortunately so, for in 1849 the nearby slum area known as the Potteries contained one hundred and thirty people and no fewer than three *thousand* pigs to the acre.

During the eighteenth and nineteenth centuries residential estates were built 'on spec' – that is, by speculative landowners and builders – to house London's ever-increasing population. Curiously, the Ladbroke estate owed its origins to the failure of a racecourse. Ladbroke's previous venture on the site had been the Hippodrome, a two-and-a-quarter-mile course encircling the area, which opened on 3 June 1837 to an enthusiastic reception, being described as 'a racing emporium more extensive and attractive than Ascot or Epsom, with ten times the accommodation'. Success was short-lived, however, for (as any gardener here will tell you) the soil is heavy clay which after rain turns to sticky, cloying mud. In bad weather the going became impossibly heavy, and within four years the Hippodrome was forced to close, its only legacy, apart from a couple of street names, being the Portobello Road market, which was started by gipsy horse-traders who came to do business there.

Evidently believing with John Claudius Loudon, founder of The Gardener's Magazine (first published in 1826), that 'the love of gardening is natural to man', Ladbroke provided each house on his estate with generous gardens, front and back. Between the elegant curves of Elgin Crescent and Lansdowne Road he even created a remarkable and extremely congenial communal garden, exclusive to the residents and reached through their own back gardens. In the dawn of Queen Victoria's reign gardening was to become a popular pastime as never before. With improvements in transport and the development of the Wardian case for importing specimens from overseas, new plant species were arriving at an unprecedented rate; and simultaneous developments in the fields of botany and engineering advanced the science of horticulture by leaps and bounds.

Popular interest was fuelled by periodicals such as Loudon's, and encouraged by a high-minded emphasis on the morally and intellectually improving qualities of gardening, which were deemed to be quite as important as any aesthetic considerations. Ladies were en-

THIS long rectangular garden is typical of the Ladbroke Estate and, indeed, of London itself. The shape makes it ideal for dividing into 'rooms', giving ample scope for imaginative design and planting.

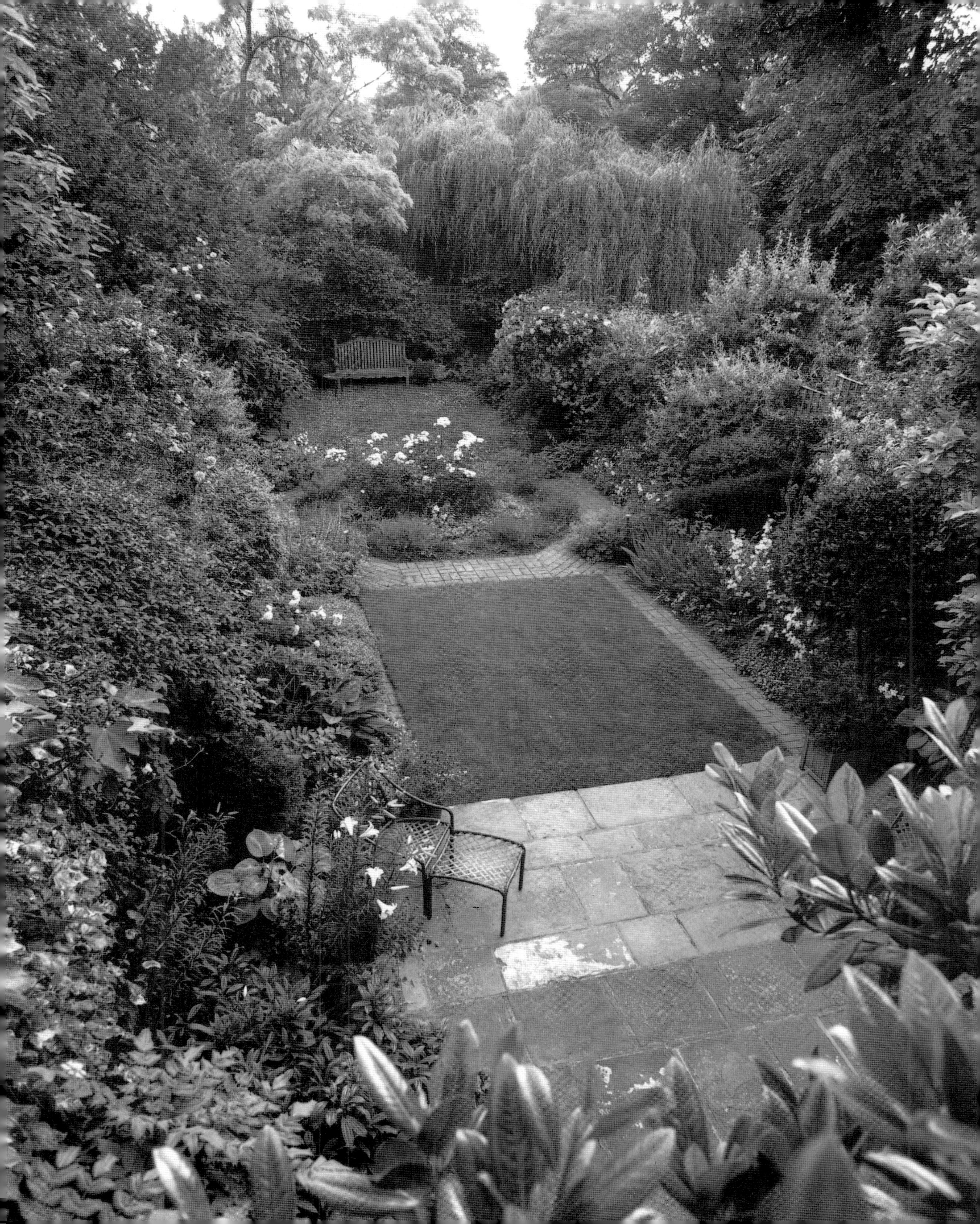

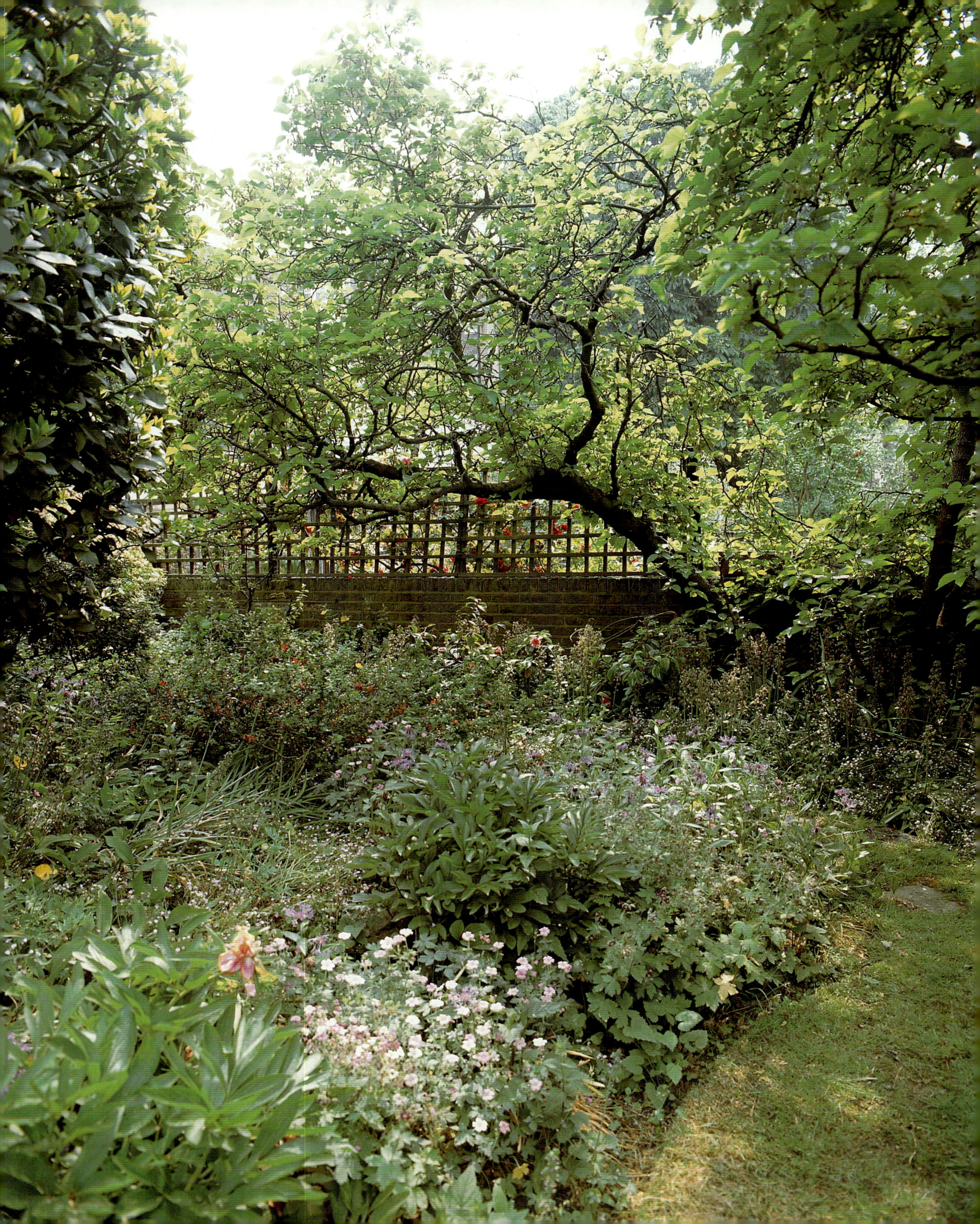

BEHIND THE STUCCO: THREE GARDENS ON THE LADBROKE ESTATE

couraged to indulge in it as a form of genteel and decorous exercise, and the labouring man was earnestly exhorted by the likes of the Reverend William Hambury to eschew visiting public houses and other reprehensible habits in its favour: 'Let him reflect upon Horses and Dogs, Wine and Women, Cards and Folly, and then upon Planting. Will not the last engross his Whole Mind, and appear worthy of employing *all* his Attention?' Edifying and humbling moral lessons were drawn from the cycles of growth and decay to be observed in the natural world, and the activity of gardening was deemed to be an excellent source of opportunities for the practice of patience, industry, perseverance and other Victorian virtues.

The gardens of the Ladbroke estate were duly and enthusiastically filled with laurels and lilacs, cabbage roses and acacias to create the leafy streets that we know today. In Lady Amabel Lindsay's garden on Lansdowne Road, particularly, you feel as if you might be in the country. All around are mature trees, greenery and birdsong; the garden is surrounded on all sides by other gardens, and the dividing walls are low – years ago, the owner recalls, the local children used to hop cheerfully from one to the next, considering the whole area to be their domain.

Simplicity and informality are the keynotes of this delightfully romantic garden. A typically long, rectangular shape, ninety feet by sixty, has been disguised with pretty curved beds and winding paths. A little way down the lawn is one of the garden's most cleverly evocative features, a tiny woodland 'dell', where in the shade of a gnarled mulberry tree a mass of bluebells flourishes, to be followed in summer by hazy drifts of delicate pale pink claytonia. In May, when the bluebells are out, a sea of blue seems to flood this part of the

AT the end of the garden there is a little woodland dell where masses of shade plants thrive. Cranesbill, peonies, violas and ivies smother the ground. In the summer the grass path is lush underfoot, and forget-me-nots and poppies dot the borders on either side.

A MAGNIFICENT Victorian wrought-iron garden seat of Moorish inspiration, painted brilliant peacock-blue, is positioned under the mulberry tree as an eye-catcher.

POTS planted with marguerites, the tightly packed pink petals of climbing rose 'Aloha' is trained round a stone plaque set in the house wall.

63

PRIVATE GARDENS OF LONDON

garden, as though a plot of ancient bluebell wood had miraculously been transposed to central London. The illusion is compounded by the front garden, where drifts of bluebells greet visitors with their scent, full of the promise of summer.

This note of welcome sets the tone here, for this is a garden designed for thoughtful hospitality. French windows open from the drawing room on to the stone-paved terrace, where a simple wooden table and chairs are surrounded by pots of pelargoniums, nicotiana and lilies. Everything is arranged with extreme simplicity and restraint and a great deal of thought. Against the house wall is a stone plaque showing a classical couple in profile and wreathed with marguerites and the heavy pink blooms of a rose trained up the wall; on the edge of the terrace is a tree stump clothed in *Clematis montana*; and positioned as an eye-catcher under the mulberry is the garden's one note of flamboyance, a magnificent Victorian wrought-iron seat of Moorish inspiration and painted brilliant peacock blue.

Following the garden's northern boundary wall is a wisteria tunnel, under which a flagged path bordered with delphiniums and peonies, tradescantias and geraniums leads to the little Gothic greenhouse. It would be hard to imagine a more charming evocation of the Victorian cottage garden. The path carries on past the greenhouse, where the owner raises plants for the house and the many lilies with which she fills the garden in summer, to the end of the garden, where it meanders round to bring you out beside the mulberry. Here it becomes a softly shaded woodland walk, where even in high summer the grass is lush and fragrant underfoot, and cornflowers, poppies and forget-me-nots brush your ankles to either side.

The gently curving herbaceous border, an informal tumble of old-fashioned flowers – aquilegias, peonies, delphiniums in carefree profusion – is backed by the wisteria pergola and a 'Kiftsgate' rose, its great trusses of single, fragrant white blooms making a shamelessly romantic display as it rambles through an old apple tree. For those susceptible to elegant restraint coupled with rustic charm (and who is not?) this garden must prove irresistible. Yet its simplicity should not lull us into forgetting the hours of back-breaking labour (which Loudon would have thoroughly approved) that go into the creation and maintenance of such gardens; for as Kipling noted in *The Glory of the Garden*:

'Our England is a garden, and such gardens are not made
By singing: "Oh how beautiful!" and sitting in the shade.'

A FLAGGED path bordered with delphiniums and peonies, tradescantias and geraniums is covered by a wisteria tunnel. In the distance is a small gothic greenhouse, where a good collection of plants for the house and lilies which fill the garden terrace in the summer are raised.

IN the shade of a gnarled mulberry a mass of bluebells flourish in the spring, to be followed by hazy drifts of the pale pink *Claytonia sibirica*

64

BEHIND THE STUCCO: THREE GARDENS ON THE LADBROKE ESTATE

Elgin Crescent and Lansdowne Road, echoing each other in a graceful curve, enclose a communal garden which is accessible only to the residents. Each house has its own private garden with a little gate leading to the communal garden where, on a broad sweep of lawn dotted with mature trees and a herbaceous border, the residents hold communal parties and their children play together. A walk round this garden has the added attraction of yielding tempting glimpses of the surrounding gardens.

Only five years ago one of the prettiest of these was merely a narrow strip of dereliction, over which the tall white stucco houses loomed rather ominously. When I was consulted on the design I concluded that within these narrow confines any satisfactory design was impossible. So the owner, spurred by her love of gardens and sustained by unflinching determination, persuaded her neighbours to allow her to remove the division between her garden and theirs, thus swiftly doubling its size.

As the garden would now be overlooked by the windows of the neighbouring house, our first concern was to ensure privacy from above. I therefore designed a tall wooden pergola to cover the entrance from the terrace behind the house, and to close in the gravel path leading down the side of the garden to the wooden gate. In spring this is festooned with *Clematis montana*, while in summer *Rosa* 'New Dawn', *Clematis* 'Perle d'Azur' and *C.* 'Marie Boisselot' transform it into a tunnel of white, blue and shell-pink blooms. The pergola below the steps from the terrace, meanwhile, is wreathed with scented honeysuckle and *Rosa* 'Zéphirine Drouhin', the carmine-pink blooms, carried throughout the summer and into the autumn, highlighted against the white stucco. At the entrance to the garden two cypress-like *Prunus*

A TALL wooden pergola made out of tanalised softwood encloses two parts of the garden thus providing some privacy and welcome shade.

PRIVATE GARDENS OF LONDON

'Amanogawa' stand sentinel, smothered in April and May with soft pink double flowers.

The pergola frames on one side a large octagon of grass and paving with triangular beds on its sides. The sunken octagon is bordered by a path of bricks laid in basket-weave pattern. This path, as well as being decorative, serves several purposes: it gives access to the triangular borders created on the corners as well as to the sitting area on the York stone terrace, and at the same time is a practical ruse for easier maintenance of the lawn. The sunnier borders are planted in pretty combinations of white, pink and silver: old-fashioned roses and peonies are bordered by santolinas, ruta, artemisia and hostas. More hostas cluster in the shady borders, together with astilbes, ferns (*Osmunda regalis*), hellebores and taller shrubs such as *Viburnum × carlesii* and *V. davidii*. Gathered together in one bed are acid-loving rhododendrons, camellias and heathers, all conforming to the pastel colour scheme. Clipped hedges of dwarf box line the paths and edge beds of *Rosa* 'The Fairy', and miniature box balls in pots mark the angles between the paths and the central octagon.

Clematis montana twines round the railings at the back of the garden, encircling with its shoots a brick pillar on which stands an urn planted with hostas and ivies, while above there rises a majestic mature horse chestnut, shading the seat on the York stone terrace beneath.

ON either side of the brick paving rise two standard *Viburnum carlesii*, the round clusters of white flowers are pale pink in bud and emit a deliciously sweet smell in late spring. The rounded heads can be clipped after flowering thus shaping them into formal features. An aged horse chestnut with a twisting trunk shades the table and chairs.

ANOTHER part of the pergola is a delight when sitting or working in the garden. In the spring it is festooned with *Clematis montana* and in the summer *Rosa* 'New Dawn', *Clematis* 'Perle d'Azur' and *C.* 'Marie Boisselot' transform it into a tunnel of flowers.

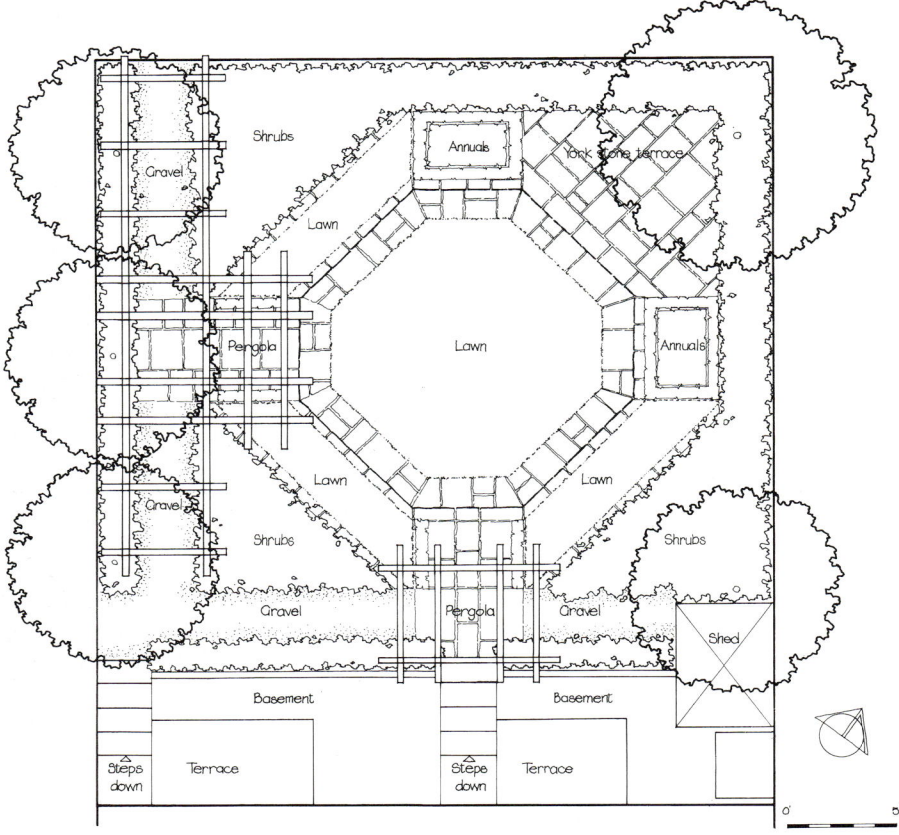

PLAN showing the main features of this delightful garden, which was doubled in size by combining the gardens of two houses.

BEHIND THE STUCCO: THREE GARDENS ON THE LADBROKE ESTATE

The owner's enthusiasm for gardening is not contained within the bounds of this garden, but spills over into the communal garden beyond, where she cultivates rhododendrons, philadelphus, *Viburnum plicatum* 'Mariesii' and other shrubs with a ground cover of ivy. Such communal gardens are a remarkable feature of this part of London, to which they lend a leafy, countrified air.

Parallel to Lansdowne Road is Ladbroke Grove, the central 'spine' of the estate. Here is another long, narrow garden, but with a crucial difference. Entered as it is from a first-floor balcony, this garden is first viewed from above; when I designed it I wished to take full advantage of this fact. The rectangular shape suggested a division into a series of carefully articulated 'rooms': a terraced sitting area, a lawn with herbaceous borders, a white garden and a woodland garden. There is a natural progression from one to the next, and together they create subtly emphasized perspectives from both first-floor and ground-floor levels.

Alterations started five years ago. To my delight and also that of the present owner, herself a plantswoman, the garden already contained some interesting and well-established plants, one of the finest being the superb *Magnolia grandiflora* which grows on the terrace. Its heady citrus scent hangs heavy in the air in late summer, when it bears its huge, bowl-shaped creamy white flowers; its great downy leaves, meanwhile, which brush your arms and forehead as you lean over the pretty wrought-iron balustrade of the balcony, frame and partly obscure the view, giving a rather tantalizing foretaste of the luxuriant growth to be found below.

On the York stone terrace outside the kitchen – which was lengthened so that it was big enough to take table and chairs – were placed pots of lilies, violas and an assortment of herbs for the kitchen, all framed by glaucous-leaved *Hosta fortunei* 'Marginata Alba' and the variegated ivy *Hedera canariensis* 'Gloire de Marengo'. An existing *Clematis armandii* was trained round the kitchen window, its leathery leaves providing a note of green throughout the winter and its flowers, delicately vanilla-scented, adding a welcome touch of white in April. Another existing plant, a fine *Lonicera japonica* 'Halliana', perfumes the terrace in summer and serves as a dense evergreen foil to the pretty rose growing through it.

Beyond the terrace lies a grassy rectangle set in a framework of brick paths and bordered by substantial shrub and flower borders. Here again the existing planting provided a useful framework; among other good plants were a Moroccan broom, *Cytisus battandieri*, which bears egg-yolk yellow pineapple-scented flowers in June and July, and a eucryphia, which in August becomes a mass of papery white blooms, each sporting a feathery tuft of stamens with prominent yellow anthers. Owners who, as here, inherit a quantity of mature and interesting trees and shrubs with their garden are extremely fortunate, for they already have an established framework within which to work, which will lend the whole garden an air of maturity.

As the eye travels further it is caught by a pretty wooden seat, a copy of an Edwardian design which I first saw at Holker Hall in

IN the summer *Clematis* 'Perle d'Azur' smothers shrubs and trellis with its pale blue flowers; below it white variegated hostas and a selection of shrubs provide interesting combinations of leaf colour and texture. The dazzling white flowers of *Rosa* 'Iceberg' in the foreground are astonishingly pretty when grown in its favourite conditions (sunny, warm borders and dry weather).

67

PRIVATE GARDENS OF LONDON

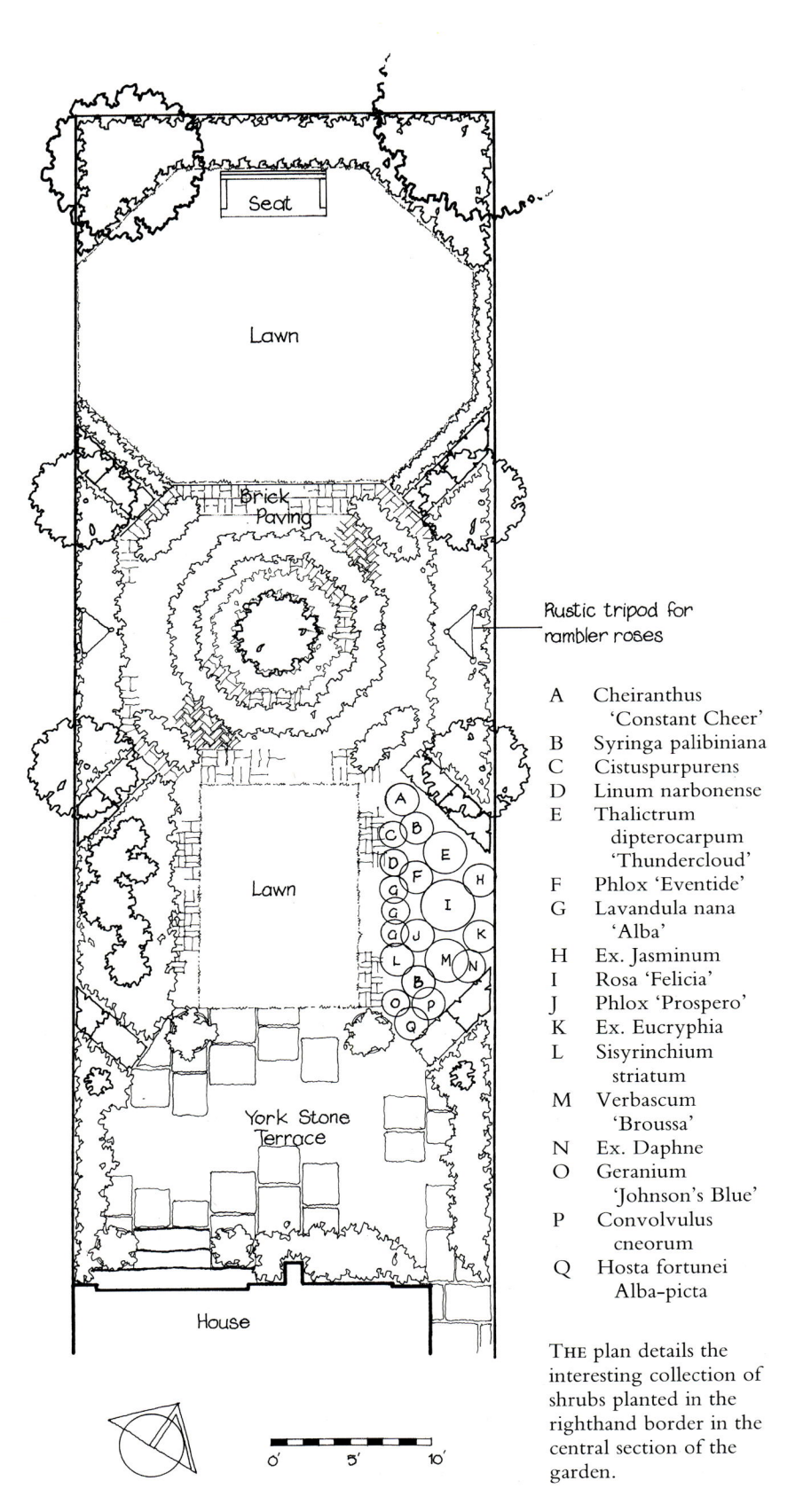

A   Cheiranthus 'Constant Cheer'
B   Syringa palibiniana
C   Cistus purpurens
D   Linum narbonense
E   Thalictrum dipterocarpum 'Thundercloud'
F   Phlox 'Eventide'
G   Lavandula nana 'Alba'
H   Ex. Jasminum
I   Rosa 'Felicia'
J   Phlox 'Prospero'
K   Ex. Eucryphia
L   Sisyrinchium striatum
M   Verbascum 'Broussa'
N   Ex. Daphne
O   Geranium 'Johnson's Blue'
P   Convolvulus cneorum
Q   Hosta fortunei Alba-picta

THE plan details the interesting collection of shrubs planted in the righthand border in the central section of the garden.

Cumbria, placed at the end of the woodland garden, at the vanishing point of the garden's lines of perspective. Above it there rises a fine old camellia, a magnificent sight in spring when it is laden with white blooms. Together with another camellia, a ceanothus and the useful shade-tolerant *Prunus laurocerasus* 'Otto Luyken' it forms a dark evergreen screen, suggesting the shady depths of a woodland glade. Breaking the skyline and framing the garden to either side are a cascading weeping willow and an airy *Robinia pseudoacacia*, its fresh apple-green foliage making a satisfying contrast with the camellias' glossy dark green and the willow's subdued grey-green tones. In the borders below ferns and *Azalea* 'Palestrina' flourish in the softly veiled light, while the carpet of lush grass in front of the seat is studded with wild flowers, like the flowery meadows of medieval tapestries. In summer Viticella clematis 'Royal Velours' smothers *Rosa* 'Kathleen Harrop' with its lovely hyacinth-blue flowers, which are particularly beautiful in combination with the silver-grey leaves of a weeping pear, *Pyrus salicifolia* 'Pendula'. In autumn the tall white racemes of *Cimicifuga racemosa* are silhouetted against the dark background as the robinia leaves drift silently down on to the long grass. Here, under the canopy of mature trees and with cool, sweet-smelling grass underfoot, you find yourself lulled into a mood of restful

The glorious pink-mauve flowers of this clematis are particularly successful in combination with variegated foliage.

contemplation, tinged with an irresistible sense of mystery.

As you step into the next 'room' the mood changes to one of elegant formality. Here a *Cornus alba* 'Elegantissima' and a *Weigela* 'Florida Variegata' provide an appropriately delicate backdrop to the white garden. Set at the corners are newly planted yew buttresses, gently emphasizing the stylized quality of this area while at the same time framing the prospect when seen from the house and lending it an illusion of greater depth. Their stark geometry and sombre green are highlighted by the white and silver tones of the rest of the planting. The central octagonal bed is filled with five 'Moonlight' roses, underplanted with *Salvia pratensis haematodes* and 'Hidcote' lavender, with ground cover of dianthus and helianthemums spilling out beneath. At the four corners rise clouds of *Alchemilla mollis*, and to the sides four *Pyrus salicifolia* 'Pendula', phlox 'White Admiral' and 'Iceberg' roses, hemmed in by santolinas and more alchemillas.

This garden's sense of luxuriant growth, flowing and romantic, is highlighted by a subtle colour scheme. A palette of soft mauves, blues, pinks, greys, silver, cream and white against a background of varying shades of green creates an extremely pretty effect and a soothing atmosphere, so that the garden is as delightful to look at as it is to be in. On summer evenings especially, when the white roses and the daisies seem to hold the light, glowing softly in the twilight, the effect is magical.

THE long rectangular garden was divided into three parts each with their own character and use. Midway, a central octagon breaks the vista with a clump of 'Iceberg' roses. Beyond is a lawn speckled with daisies, bounded with a seat and informal woodland planting.

A VIEW TO THE HEATH

The Grove, a fine row of seventeenth- and eighteenth-century houses overlooking a tree-shaded green on top of Highgate Hill, still looks and feels like the heart of a seventeenth-century village. As early as 1593 it was described as 'a most pleasant dwelling, yet not so much pleasant as healthful', and its 'grassy walks and shady avenues were the scenes of exercise and harmless merriment'. Two centuries later, when The Grove had become known as Quality Walk, the poet Coleridge lived at number 3, and would pace among the grove of stately elms, as Mr Thorne noted sardonically in his *Environs of London*, 'in meditative mood, discoursing in unmeaning monologue to some earnest listener like Wordsworth or Lamb'.

Numbers 1 to 6 The Grove have a stately appearance rather at odds with their quixotic and romantic origins. They were built in the grounds of Dorchester House in the 1680s by William Blake, a Covent Garden draper and an

SLIGHTLY off-centre in the brick terrace is a square pool, planted with an array of water-loving plants; self-seeded *Alchemilla mollis*, wild strawberries and marjoram grow in merry confusion. *Magnolia grandiflora* rises high against the houses to the right of the steps leading down to the garden.

AT the other end of the garden at a lower level, the eye is drawn to a laburnum tunnel, the yellow racemes drooping from the archway. The great retaining wall and its buttresses are shrouded with vitis, roses and lonicera.

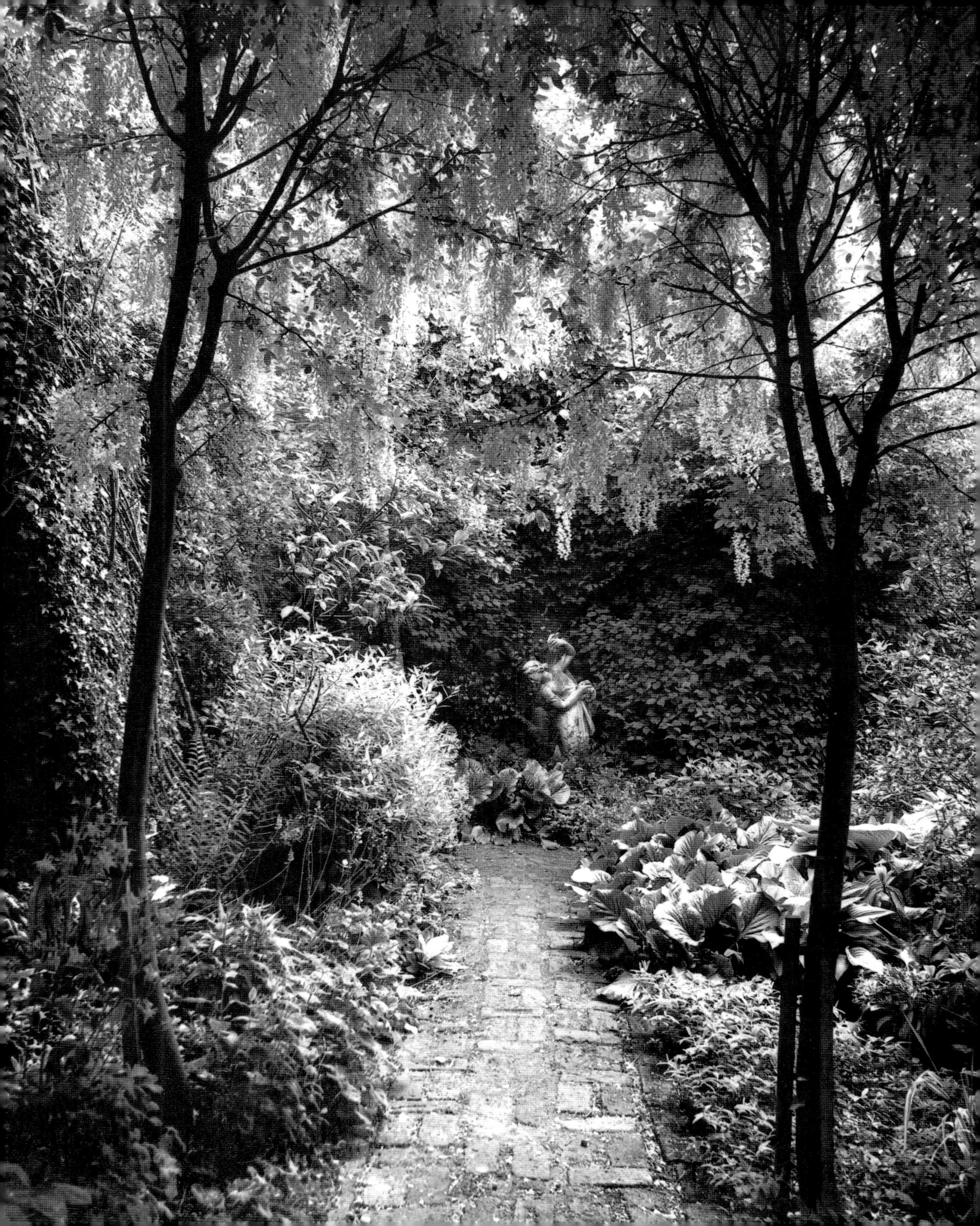

eccentric philanthropist. Blake bought the mansion for the not insubstantial sum of £5000 – his entire fortune – with the intention of establishing there a school or 'hospital' for forty poor or orphaned children. He sought to finance this venture by the twin means of publishing a curious book called *Silver Drops; or, Serious Things*, and building six houses, the rent from which would form the hospital's endowment. This was probably the first charity school, and it was not a success, which, as Edward Walford noted in *Old and New London*, was 'deeply to be lamented, as its only fault appears to have been that it was in advance of the selfish age which witnessed its birth'. The school was forced to close and the unfortunate Blake was incarcerated in the Fleet prison as a debtor; but he at least left a legacy of great architectural distinction.

Number 4 is perhaps the best preserved, as the front façade retains most of its original features, including the eaves and cornice, windows and front door. The door is elegant and of unusual height, and is shrouded with honeysuckle, *Parthenocissus tricuspidata* 'Veitchii' (the self-clinging Boston ivy) and *Clematis montana*. The shrubs below have all been chosen for their suitability to the north-east aspect: skimmias, magnolias, rhododendrons, *Garrya elliptica*, with its long grey catkins, and some hybrid musk roses, which do perfectly well here even though they would prefer full sun. The creeping evergreen *Gaultheria procumbens* is an extremely efficient ground cover, and *Campanula poscharskyana* 'Stella' and the ubiquitous wild strawberry seed themselves all around. *Rosa* 'Wedding Day' meanwhile wreathes its way through the railings and twines up and over the pretty wrought-iron lampholder above the gate.

The back of the house has a 'grand look-out Londonwards', as Mr Thorne observed: a sensational uninterrupted view westwards over Hampstead Heath, with hardly a house in sight. The ground falls away steeply, but had been terraced by the sixteenth century: the garden

THE dazzling blue of a ceanothus in flower is a real sight in the summer. Here it has been cleverly trained to form an archway leading to the steps that descend to the lower garden.

A FLIGHT of stone steps leads down from the drawing room to the terrace. *Clematis armandii* twines round the iron railings on one side, below *Cotoneaster horizontalis* forms a dense hummock and has seeded itself in every available crevice. A terracotta pot with a standard Portuguese laurel stands at the foot of the steps in front of a *Magnolia grandiflora*.

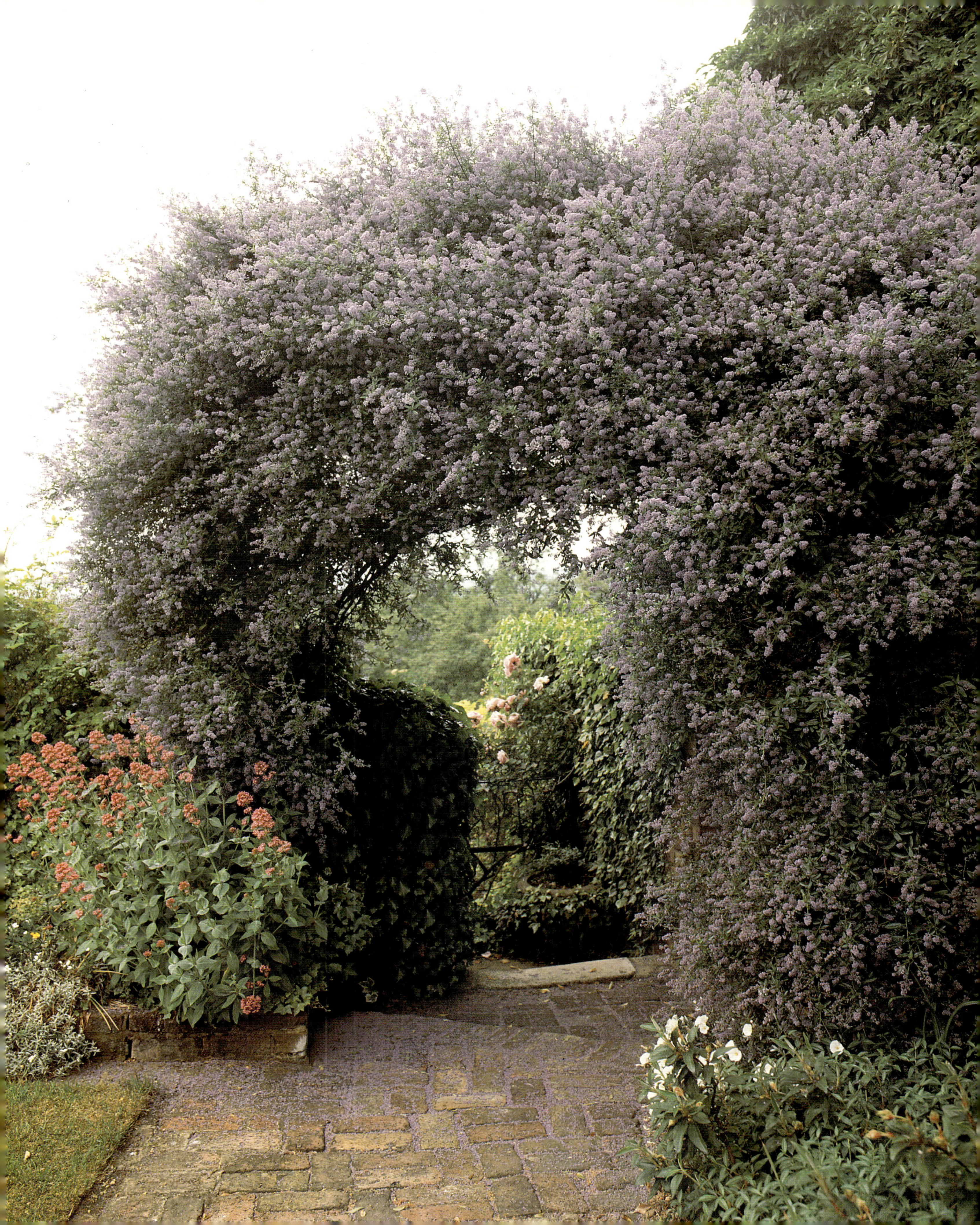

PRIVATE GARDENS OF LONDON

CLEMATIS *armandii* and ivy form a small alcove into which a statue is set next to the house.

ANOTHER statue stands pensively amongst the greenery of the ivy-clad walls. A bed set into the top of the low wall is also planted with a variety of rock plants such as iberis and helianthemums.

therefore has two parts, upper and lower, separated by an ancient brick buttress wall. With the help of Felicity Bryan and the landscape designer François Goffinet, Cob Stenham, the present owner, has laid out the flat upper part with a large terrace, lawns and mixed borders, while the lower part is wilder in character. Here the land slopes towards the Heath, and the rough grass is planted with shrubs and dwarf bulbs.

A flight of stone steps leads down from the drawing room to the terrace. *Clematis armandii* twines round the elegant iron railings on one side, its subtle perfume wafting into the house in early summer, and on the other a jasmine and a wisteria intertwine. A *Ceanothus thyrsiflorus* grows up the house and also reaches down to meet its prostrate cousin, *C.t.* 'Repens', their froth of intense blue flowers stealing the scene from a delicate *Cotoneaster horizontalis*, while the delicate, sun-loving *Rosa laevigata* 'Cooperi' thrives on the warm wall, its dark glossy leaves making a splendid foil for the large, scented white flowers. A *Magnolia grandiflora* comes into its own in August, when the huge waxy white flowers, sumptuous and fragrant, stud the brilliant dark green foliage.

The mossy brick terrace below is rectangular, and slightly off centre is a square pool planted with an array of water-loving plants: the giant leaves of *Gunnera manicata* shade lilies and agapanthus, *Iris ensata* and water lily species, while in early summer the exotic white blooms of *Zantedeschia aethiopica* seem to float above *Iris laevigata* and the enchanting *Myosotis scorpioides* 'Mermaid'. The surrounding wall is smothered with *Cotoneaster horizontalis* and masses of self-seeded *Alchemilla mollis*, with wild strawberries and marjoram in every crevice adding to the merry confusion.

Two Irish yews are an austere reminder that an element of formality is needed to strike a

GREEN ivies and *Clematis montana* smother the wall and form a dark backdrop to the white marble statue which throws its reflection into the dark water of the pool. *Iris laevigata* and *Gunnera manicata* are amongst the water-loving plants planted here.

proper balance, but the boundary walls to either side of them are engulfed by another riot of greenery. Ivies clothe them completely, with roses and clematis growing over and through them: an extremely successful way of enjoying the foliage throughout the year with the bonus of the flowers of other climbers to break the monotony in summer. It is not easy to achieve, however, as the rampant ivies must be kept in check and the roses carefully pruned each year if the less sturdy climbers are not to be swallowed up. Another wall-planting method is used on the low wall dividing the terrace from the upper garden: here a bed set into the top of the wall has been planted with a profusion of rock plants such as iberis and helianthemums.

Beyond this a large lawn seems to sweep away virtually into the ether, for at its end is the top of the buttress wall, and the eye is carried westwards, over the wooded heath to the blue horizon. Wide shrub and herbaceous borders edged with brick flank the lawn, and a brick path runs down the middle of the bed on the right. On the boundary wall side this is bordered by taller shrubs such as *Viburnum tinus*, the ever-useful *Choisya ternata*, *Prunus laurocerasus* 'Otto Luyken', one of the best of the laurels, and *Elaeagnus pungens* 'Maculata', whose spiny leaves have a central splash of gold. These and many others provide an evergreen and variegated backdrop to a mass of herbaceous plants, including phlox, cordateria and aruncus. To the other side of the path are mounds of lower-growing shrubs and herbaceous plants: santolinas, nepetas, *Alchemilla mollis*, *Geranium endressii*, rue and roses mingle with campanulas, echinops and *Sisyrinchium striatum* in loose and relaxed compositions of old-fashioned border plants. Rosemary and phlox growing into each other have their roots covered by *Lamium galeobdolon*, with silver-flushed evergreen leaves, while the fragrant faded pink blooms of *Rosa* 'Felicia' and translucent cistus flowers rise above an underplanting of vinca. Acid-loving plants such as azaleas, hydrangeas and cornus mingle happily, and in high summer the steel-blue flowers of *Echinops ritro* tower above day lilies and the slender bright blue flowers of ceratostigma. The shadier bed on the other side of the lawn, meanwhile, is planted with a more subdued collection of evergreen shrubs, including *Pyracantha* 'Orange Glow', more cotoneasters and the evergreen honeysuckle, *Lonicera japonica* 'Halliana', clinging to a weeping mulberry and quantities of hydrangeas. In the far corner is a bower of *Pyrus salicifolia* 'Pendula', a most original idea which creates an effect of airy softness around the inviting seat which looks out towards the view.

On the other side the brick path leads to another of the garden's highlights, a ceanothus arch which in summer is a dazzling cloud of sky-blue flowers. Beneath it time-worn steps lead steeply down to the lower level, burrowing their way through a tunnel of green: arches of *Vitis coignetiae* above and to the right; ivy to the left, clothing the ancient bricks of the retaining wall. As you reach the bottom some ten feet below, your eye is immediately drawn to another tunnel, this time of laburnum, tucked under the great brick buttresses and overhung by tall trees. When the laburnums are in flower and the tunnel drips with yellow racemes it is an arresting sight, and one can only admire the subtlety of its positioning. It is typical of this garden's talent for the unexpected that such a glorious prospect should be found in an unobtrusive corner, where its effect is doubly cheering.

The great buttresses of the retaining wall loom high above, and the old bricks in shades of red and ochre are shrouded with ferns and ivy, *Vitis coignetiae*, *Lonicera japonica* 'Aureoreticulata', *Rosa multiflora* and a very pretty single bright pink rose. Centranthus escaped from above has colonized every crevice, tumbling down the wall in cascades of minute pink flowers, which drop like tiny pebbles on the leaves of *Eucryphia glutinosa* in the deep shade of the border below. Cool and mossy beneath its ancient brick vaults and arches, this part of the garden has an intriguing aura of romance.

Fruit trees line a path that leads down the gentle slope from the bottom of the steps, past a thicket of *Cornus alba* and under an arch of yew and wild cherry to a shady corner where hostas and bergenias reign. The eye is drawn irresistibly to a bronze statue of a pair of elegant legs emerging from the shrubbery at the entrance to a secret garden encircled by yew. Here all is still, and a seat placed against the dark hedge encourages you to stop and rest among the muted colours and the silence. Tiers of

BEYOND the terrace, the sweeping lawn and the wide herbaceous borders is the garden's 'grand look-out Londonwards': a superb uninterrupted view westwards across Hampstead Heath from one of the highest houses in London. Beyond the end border the land falls steeply away to the lower garden.

green tones – fresh grass, gold-green euonymus and sombre yew; *Aucuba japonica*, mahonia and pachysandra – recall Andrew Marvell's lines from 'The Garden':

*'Meanwhile the mind from pleasures less,
Withdraws into its happiness . . .
Annihilating all that's made
To a green thought in a green shade.'*

Behind the yew hedge an old mulberry with a swing hanging from its branches encourages nostalgic thoughts of long Edwardian summer afternoons, and a winding grass path climbs back towards the high wall through a leafy passage of *Cornus alba* 'Elegantissima' and rhododendrons. This subtle combination provides interest at times of year when colour is hard to find, while at the same time giving a welcome foil to the rhododendrons, for when they are in full bloom their glowing colours might otherwise be almost overpowering. An old apple tree is completely smothered in the Victorian rambling rose 'The Garland', and in summer the sweet scent of its small semi-double blush-pink flowers wafts through the lower garden. Hostas and the dense leaves of *Bergenia cordifolia* line the path as you pass under the deep purple foliage of *Prunus cerasifera* 'Pissardii', and glimpses through the lilacs, laurels and eucryphias of the attractively designed greenhouse distract the keen gardener's eye from the focal point, an elegant stone statue clad only in heavily scented *Philadelphus coronarius*.

This is a garden of considerable scale and some grandeur, yet the judicious use of design and planting has contrived to give it an air of informality and seclusion. It is also a garden of contrasts: from the magnificent sweeping vista of the upper garden a series of arches, tunnels and twisting paths leads you ever onwards, with a constant sense of discovery. One focal point succeeds another, always tantalizingly half-obscured by a hedge or a group of shrubs; and the open formality of the top garden, tempered by soft cottage-garden planting, leads on to the lower garden's romantic wilderness of lush greenery and long grass.

A SMALL statue is placed in an opening in this secret garden encircled by yew. *Euonymus fortunei* 'Silver Queen' is planted all the way round at the foot of the hedge. Here all is tranquil among the muted colours of aucuba, mahonia and pachysandra.

THE great buttresses of the ancient retaining wall are shrouded with a romantic, tumbling profusion of ferns and ivies, centranthus and climbing roses. Below, in an unobtrusive corner, is a breathtaking tunnel of laburnum.

AN EMBROIDERER'S GARDEN

In the best tradition of city gardens, there is nothing at first to indicate that behind this elegant early Victorian house in south London lies a walled enclosure which, though quite modest in size, has the magical effect of making you feel you are in the middle of the country. Mrs Thomasina Beck used to have a large country garden in Dorset, and the knowledge she acquired there of plants and their preferences has enabled her to achieve what so many other London gardeners strive for with varying degrees of success – the re-creation of a rural atmosphere amid an urban landscape of bricks and concrete. Mrs Beck has another advantage, however, for as the author of *The Embroiderer's Garden* and a former lecturer at the Victoria and Albert Museum, she has been able to combine an artist's eye with a plantswoman's judgement to contrive a planting scheme full of original and carefully modulated associations of colour and texture.

As you walk through the French windows of the drawing room and on to a balcony with a delicate wrought-iron balustrade, an unusually welcoming atmosphere draws you down the steps and into the garden, among the well-furnished borders. Mrs Beck started the garden, now twelve years old, from scratch, and its perfectly balanced design is clearly the fruit of long and careful scrutiny from these windows, and perhaps even more from the windows of Mrs Beck's top-floor study.

The tall lime tree and horse chestnut in the adjoining garden provide a backdrop to the strong design which divides the well-proportioned rectangular space in two, and gives each part a clearly defined character. The first garden, an open, oval-shaped lawn framed by wide borders, has elements of formality in its statuary and topiary; the second is a softer, shady wild garden, romantic and overgrown.

At the bottom of the steps a small terrace set with a table and chairs marks the transition from the house to the garden. To one side of the steps is the sitting area, where Tuscan pots and dainty Victorian wirework *étagères* are filled with pink and white pelargoniums and fuchsias. To the other is a minute but generously planted garden, with wisteria and *Lonicera japonica* 'Halliana' overhead and a sea of *Campanula portenschlagiana* underfoot; erodium, geraniums, penstemons and *Clematis* 'Hagley Hybrid' make splashes of pink against variegated privet and the deep green leaves of a skimmia, and a topiary peacock and two stone putti disport themselves among the undergrowth. Already you are aware that each space is stamped with its own distinct character, an essential factor if such subdivisions are to be successful.

THE statuary in the garden is subtly placed: here a small child stands shyly among the leaves of the golden hop.

Two stone plinths supporting ornamental vases stand on either side of the elegant steps leading from the drawing room to the garden. In them are planted geraniums and trailing ivies. The wall beyond is thickly clad with wisteria and *Lonicera japonica* 'Halliana'.

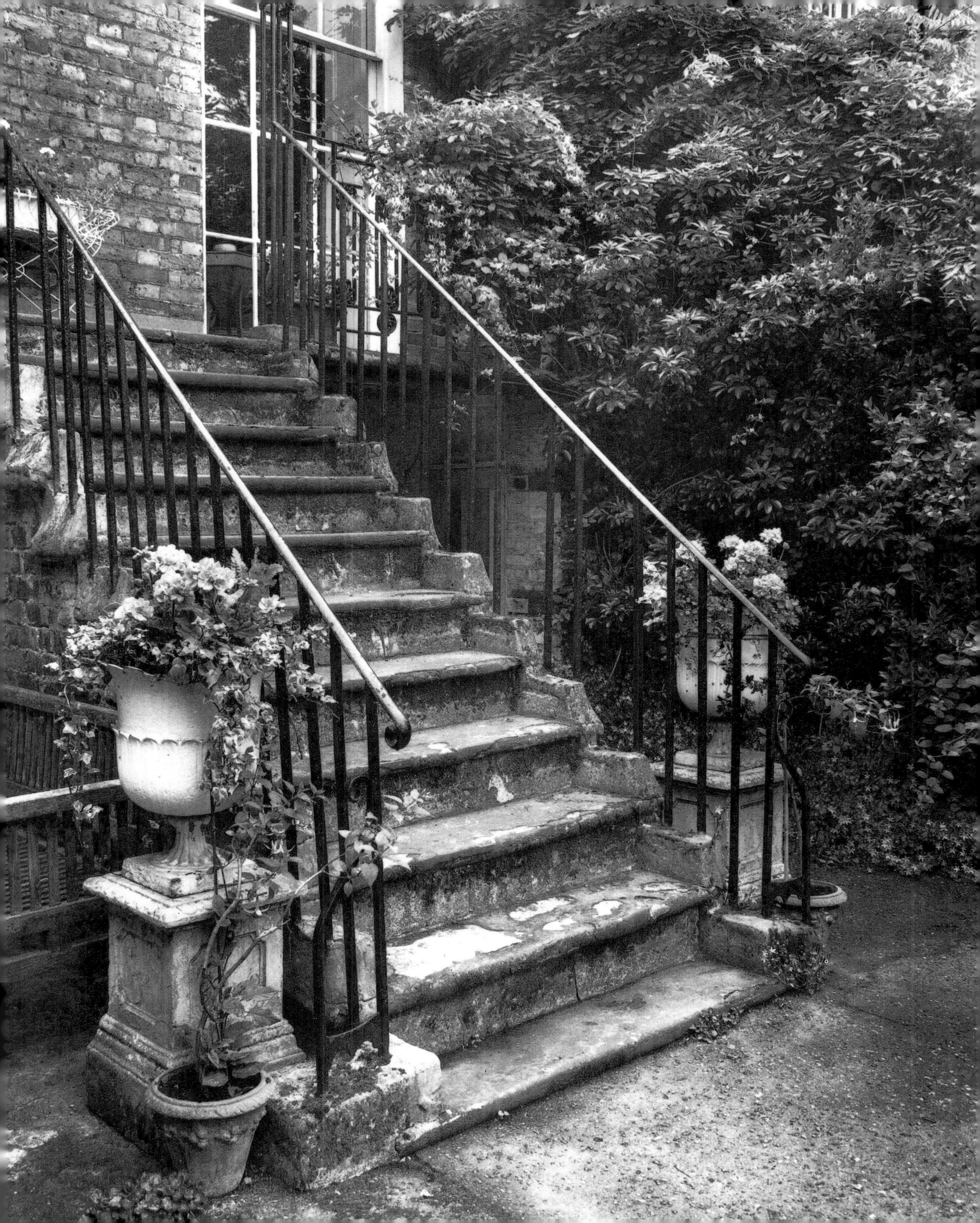

PRIVATE GARDENS OF LONDON

Moving towards the main garden you leave behind the open, practical terrace to be enclosed by high walls of green. Four conical clipped box brought all the way from Mrs Beck's previous garden are this enclave's formal skeleton; symmetrically placed in the right-hand border they provide an austere framework for the rest of the planting. It is here that Mrs Beck's enthusiasm for embroidery and fabrics becomes abundantly clear: tall shrubs and climbers chosen for the contrasting tones, textures and shapes of their foliage drape the walls like hangings, and beneath them mounds of low-growing shrubs like plump cushions and spreading mats of ground cover create yet more subtle associations and patterns.

Some groups are chosen for their mother-of-pearl colouring, others for their bronze-red tones. A golden hop runs through the metallic green leaves of a *Eucalyptus gunnii* above a rosemary bush, a pink tree peony and a silver-pink cistus, while their glaucous tones are picked up by the grey-purple leaves of *Rosa glauca* and the warmer pink shades by the beautiful cinnamon-coloured bark of *Luma apiculata*. Nearby is another myrtle, the enchanting *Myrtus communis tarentina*, which bears a mass of white flowers followed by white berries; its slender leaves, tiny and aromatic, are set off by a range of shrubs with variegated leaves, so useful for creating contrasts of foliage and here used to best advantage. *Ligustrum ovalifolium* 'Argenteum', with creamy-white margins to its leaves, *Pieris japonica* and a variegated fuchsia contribute to the tapestry effect, while yellow-leaved plants such as a golden berberis and *Filipendula ulmaria* 'Aurea' create intriguing plays of perspective against the dark foliage of the box topiary and camellias. Some plants are notable among these subtle permutations for the exceptional beauty of their foliage: the tender *Melianthus major*, which flourishes here, is outstanding among these, with its serrated, deeply lobed leaves washed with a grey-blue bloom.

Behind a large *Lavatera thuringiaca* 'Barnsley' an opening in a screen of espaliered apples, beautiful in spring for its blossom and in late summer and autumn for its scarlet fruit, leads the way to the wild garden. At the far end, acting as an eye-catcher from the house, are some unusual Puginesque Victorian wrought-iron seats, white-painted and grouped around a

PLANT associations in this garden tend to have a tapestry-like quality. Here a golden hop runs through a glaucous *Eucalyptus gunnei*, while the tender green leaves of the *Melianthus major* with their soft blue-grey bloom link the two extremes of the green spectrum.

ROSA 'Félicité Perpétue' smothers a tall *Forsythia suspensa* with its far-reaching shoots covered with pinky-white blooms. In the distance Victorian wrought-iron table and seats nestle in the dense greenery around and above.

table. Here you are tempted to linger and enjoy the cool of this leafy enclosure, with layer upon layer of soft greenery rising overhead. The high wall behind is clad with variegated ivy and an enormous philadelphus, which on summer evenings saturates the air with its intoxicating scent. Underneath there rises an *Abutilon vitifolium* 'Album', studded with saucer-shaped white flowers from May to July, and nearby is a tall *Forsythia suspensa*. Stunning in spring when it is a mass of pale yellow, in summer this is smothered with the creamy white fragrant blooms of *Rosa* 'Félicité Perpétue', its branches drooping to the ground under their weight. In its shade is a delightful bower, in whose veiled light you catch a glimpse of a mossy statue among pink foxgloves.

Framing the view on the other side is an old apple tree, perhaps a remnant of an ancient orchard, now wreathed with *Clematis montana* 'Elizabeth' and underplanted with the delicate violet-blue *Crocus tommasinianus* 'Whitewell Purple'. Behind, in the far corner, is an old summerhouse now used as a potting shed and shrouded in ivy and variegated jasmine. In the opposite corner, under a bank of ferns and ivies, is a white woodland bed, a mass of hostas and hellebores, *Lilium regale* and *Iris pallida* 'Variegata', *Cimicifuga racemosa* and white nicotiana, with little white violas tucked into any gaps.

Curiously, for something that is so enchantingly pretty, this is ultimately a utilitarian garden. Mrs Beck uses it as a source for her embroidery and chooses the plants with this purpose in mind. It is impossible to know which of her passions – her embroidery or her garden – influences the other more: each is so imbued with her fascination for colour and texture that the distinction between them seems almost to dissolve. In this symbiotic relationship her embroidery suggests her choice of plants, plant associations meanwhile inspire her needlework, and she judges each by the standards of the other. This lovely garden therefore also stands as a testimony as much to the beauty of her needlework as to her skill as a gardener.

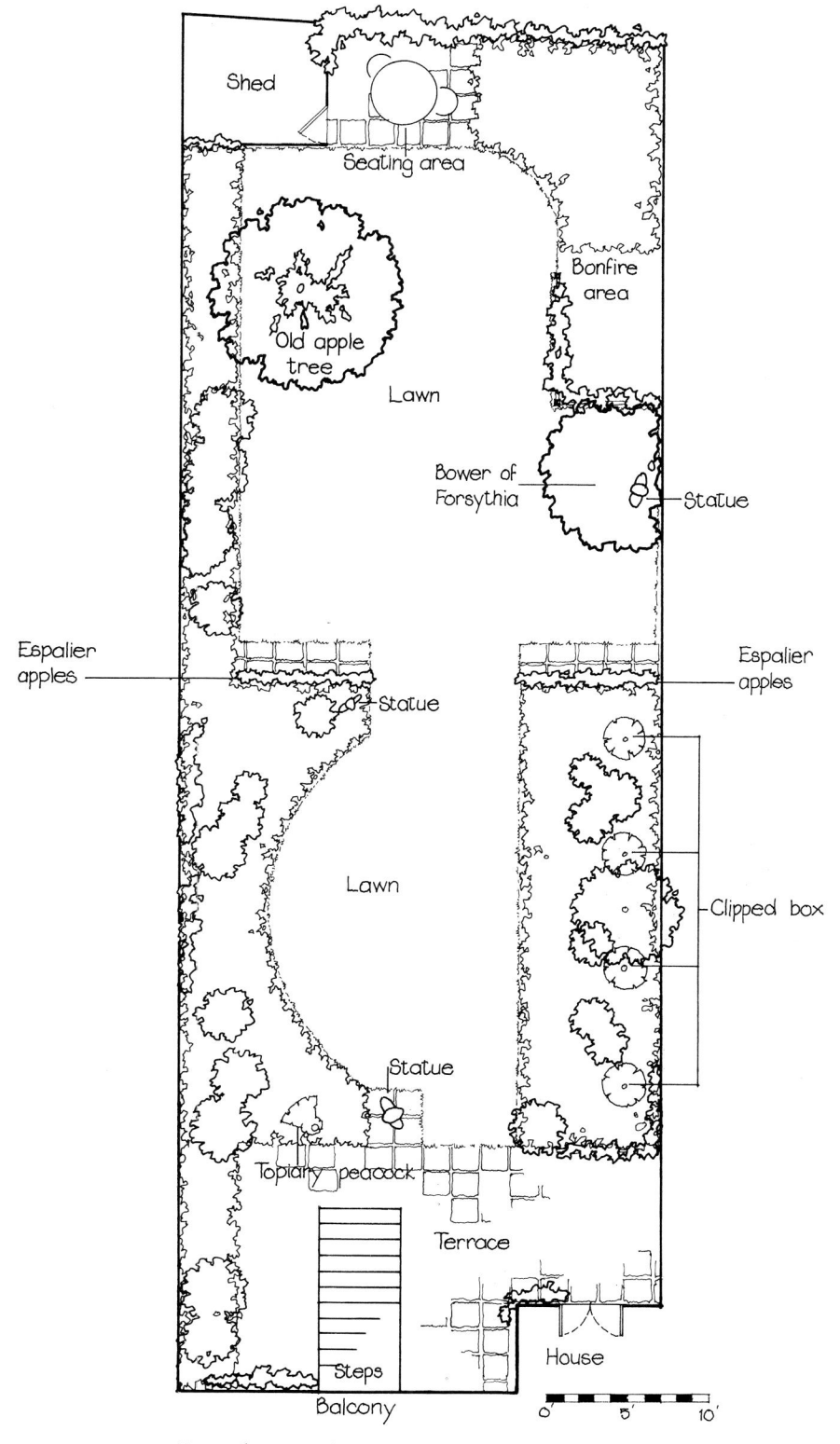

PLAN showing the overall layout of the garden. The lawn acts as a link between the two main areas which otherwise have their own identity.

A ZEN GARDEN IN FULHAM

With their tranquil beauty and their atmosphere of latent and mysterious symbolism, Japanese gardens hold a powerful fascination for Western minds. Alien and cryptic, they derive from a long and rich tradition that has evolved in complete isolation from Western ideas. The formal gardens that formed the Western tradition for many hundreds of years were descended ultimately from the Mediterranean gardens of Egypt and Persia, oases of fertility and shade amid a hostile, arid desert. Japanese gardens, by contrast, derived their naturalistic pattern of lakes, islands and peaks from Chinese models, inspired in their turn by the extraordinarily lush vegetation and flowery meadows of the rivers of the north China plain, and by the majesty of the mountains, gorges and waterfalls of southern China.

Hand in hand with this stupendous landscape

THE placing of rocks in a Zen garden is of paramount importance. A single rock might represent an island or cliff, waterfall or shoreline. The rocks in this garden were lowered from the back of a lorry by crane before being positioned using a block and tackle.

SURROUNDED by carefully placed rocks, small-leaved evergreen Kurume azaleas and other plants signifying a forest, chosen for their contrasting leaf shape, stands reflected in the water a *yuki-mi-doro*, or lantern for viewing snow, brought from Japan.

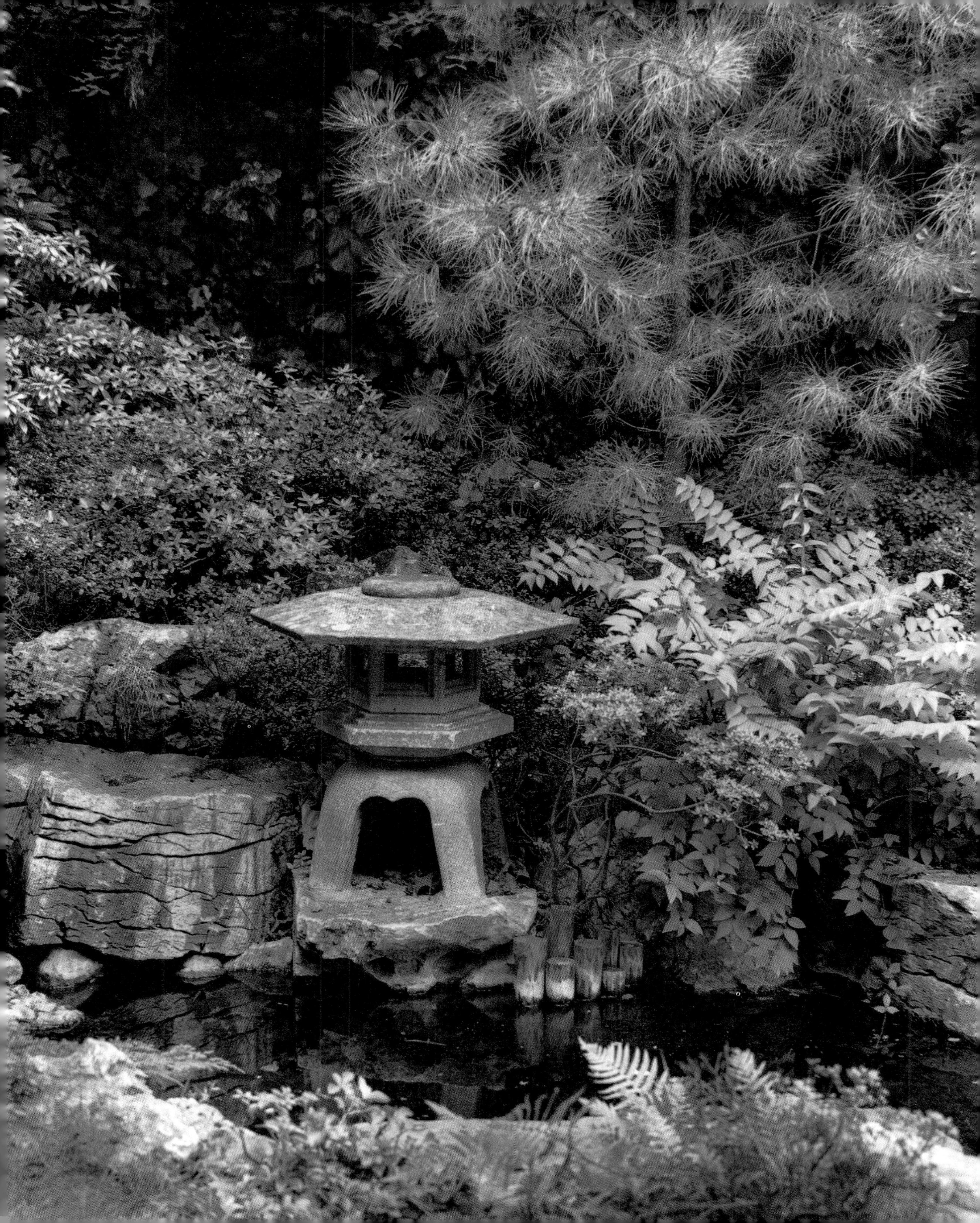

PRIVATE GARDENS OF LONDON

went a sensibility to nature which would not find its echo in the West until long after. Almost a thousand years before Petrarch became the first European to describe the beauties of landscape in 'modern' terms, Chinese painters, scholars, poets and courtiers were describing their response to nature in delighted detail, and with an awe and sense of mystery which seems to anticipate the romantics. Where Western gardens turned their back on their environment, creating artificial gardens of jewel-like beauty hedged in by high walls, Chinese gardens were a celebration of the natural world.

It was at the beginning of the seventh century that an embassy from the primitive kingdom of Japan arrived in China to learn what they could of the legendary Chinese civilization, of which hitherto they had only heard second-hand accounts. There the ambassador and his retinue would have observed, no doubt to their stupefaction, work in progress on an imperial park of unparalleled splendour, the most prodigious landscape gardens the world has ever seen. A contemporary chronicler estimates that no fewer than a million workers laboured to create the Emperor Sui Yang Ti's Western Park, sculpting, remodelling and planting an area some seventy-five miles in circumference. Rocks and earth were brought from which to fashion hills and valleys, which were then clothed with forests of mature trees and adorned with 'flowers, herbs, plants, trees, birds, beasts, fishes and frogs' requisitioned from every householder in the vicinity of the capital city. Four 'seas' and five lakes were excavated and connected by a network of canals plied by pleasure barges in the form of dragons and phoenixes. The largest lake, some thirteen miles in circumference, contained three island peaks, with pavilions and colonnades for the diversion of the emperor, at whose disposal there also lay sixteen pleasure palaces, each with its complement of twenty concubines.

TUCKED away in the corner opposite the pool is the tea house. The lantern is used to provide light for the tea ceremony which usually takes place at night. Autumn colour also plays a part in Japanese gardens. Here an acer has turned rusty red contrasting with the few remaining leaves of a magnolia in the background and the architectural leaves of a mahonia.

THE hollow bamboo which pivots over its support like a see-saw is called a *shira odoki* and is intended to scare away wild animals. One end rests on a stone, and the other end is a reservoir which fills with water. When the water reaches the required weight the reservoir end shoots down, and immediately springs back so that the other end hits the stone with a sharp crack. Rocks are positioned to suggest raging torrents while smaller stones and sand hint at quieter water with its eddies and ripples.

A ZEN GARDEN IN FULHAM

THE tea house is approached as is customary by a path of stepping-stones, the placing of which became an art in itself. Rocks are positioned to suggest raging torrents while smaller stones and sand hint at quieter water with its eddies and ripples.

Within a decade the influence of the Western Park was to be observed in Japan. The Japanese were surrounded by even more natural beauty, if anything, than the Chinese, and were equally susceptible to it. The gods of Shinto, the native religion, were nature spirits, and the trees, rocks and hills in which they were believed to live became the objects of veneration. To the Japanese mind the elements of nature were therefore not only familiar but also generally friendly; moreover they also held symbolic significance.

Lakes and islands, peaks and cliffs, rocks and waterfalls were the essential constituents of what was to become the Japanese garden. Mysterious, emblematic landscapes, at once elaborate and austere, began to spring up around royal palaces and temples. It was in the gardens of the temples, often quite small and dedicated to contemplation in the pursuit of enlightenment, that Zen scholars created the first Zen gardens as we know them today. Inspired by the paintings of Zen mystics, the gardens were full of symbolism representing man's spiritual journey, and their elements were viewed in a manner which perhaps has its nearest Western equivalent in Platonic ideal-ism: a rock, a tree, a waterfall was not merely itself but was also a paradigm representing the essence of all rocks, all trees or all waterfalls. The designs of such gardens were therefore conceived according to patterns of spiritual significance which were far more compelling than simple aesthetic concerns.

Such a garden is to be found in the heart of London, off the Fulham Road. A Zen garden cannot be created by imitation, so when Baron and Baroness Bentinck decided that this was the style of garden they wanted, they engaged a Zen gardener. In 1985, therefore, Toshiyuki Yoshimura, a gardener with a fourteen-year apprenticeship behind him, spent the summer arranging the rocks and water, earth and sculpture, trees and shrubs of the Bentincks' garden.

No element of a Zen garden is of more significance than its rocks: rocks which by their form suggested mountains were much prized and collected and displayed with care. A single rock might represent a craggy peak or island, several together a mountain range or cliff, cascade or shoreline, or even a sacred beast. Arrangements of rocks might also be valued purely for their rhythmic movement, or for their intrinsic beauty of texture, colour or form.

Here the rocks were dropped into the garden, which lies below street level, by crane from the back of a truck, and the larger ones were then manoeuvred – with meticulous precision and some difficulty – using a block and tackle. They have been used to create one of the garden's most intriguing and (to Western eyes at least) oblique features. The garden is rectangular, flanking the side of the house and protected from the street by a high retaining wall on two sides. From the corners of the longer side comes the sound of running water, and in one corner is a rocky pool fed by a waterfall. It seems to feed a stream that runs the length of the garden underneath the wall – until you look closer. For the meandering stream, edged by rocks and crossed by a little bridge, is composed entirely of small dry rocks. Dry cascades and streams suggesting water where there is none are an ancient feature of Japanese gardens. Rocks are artfully placed so as to suggest torrents of falling water, while smaller stones and sand suggest its eddies and ripples, interspersed with still pools of moss.

The rocks around and above the pool have been placed with equal care. Reflected in the water, surrounded by some of the acers, azaleas, pachysandras, peonies and ferns that make up the garden's planting, is a *yuki-mi-doro*, or lantern for viewing snow, brought from Japan. Other stone lanterns are placed elsewhere in the garden: a lantern of stones created by Toshiyuki Yoshimura stands under the wall, among the planting which signifies a forest, and another stands on a rise representing mountains. Along the valley in between, which in Zen symbolism would represent the cramped darkness of the material world, runs a path. In Zen paintings pilgrims are shown struggling up mountain paths to the soaring peaks of enlightenment.

The fourth lantern stands near a building which suggests a different gloss on this little path, however. Tucked away in the corner diagonally opposite the pool is a wooden building of the simple rustic design of the traditional tea house, and around it are the accoutrements of the tea garden. The Japanese tea ceremony is often seen as a secular expression of the spiritual simplicity of Zen, with the tea gardens having some of the same esoteric naturalism as Zen gardens.

Outside the building stands a magnolia underplanted with ferns and moss. To one side is a stone with a depression cut into it and filled with water, with a bamboo ladle laid on top of it. This is the place for washing hands before the tea ceremony, which must take place in surroundings of great simplicity and scrupulous cleanliness. Gravel would surround the washing place to prevent the ground from becoming muddy, and a lantern would be placed near by, as the tea ceremony frequently took place at night. In the earliest tea gardens tea masters were able to provide mossy, weathered lanterns from neglected temples, and ever since lanterns have been chosen with great care for their aesthetic effect.

OTHER stone lanterns are placed elsewhere in the garden. This one created by Toshiyuki Yoshimura stands under the wall among the planting which signifies a forest. Here Zen symbolism represents the cramped darkness of the material world.

THE rusty autumnal leaves of a plane tree fall gently over the green carpet of *Soleirolia soleirolii* as if deliberately arranged. Behind a bamboo screen is another stone lantern.

The essence of the tea ceremony was its ritual calm, its atmosphere of restful quiet away from the cares of the world. Decorous, measured conversation after the ritual sharing of tea was intended to restore tranquillity and equilibrium. The architecture, the furnishings and the surroundings of the tea house itself were therefore of considerable importance. A sylvan grove far from the city was the perfect setting, and if this was not possible it might nevertheless be suggested. The tea house was always approached by a path, known as the 'dewy path', covered with moss and set with stepping stones, the placing of which became an art in itself. Here they are suggested by grindstones set into the gravel, which also has patches of moss.

Mosses played an important part in traditional Japanese gardens, sometimes to the exclusion of all other plants. The garden of the Moss Temple on Kyoto contains up to forty different species and varieties, billowing and rippling in hummocks and seas of every texture and shade of green. Here the moss is supplemented by green carpets of *Soleirolia soleirolii* spreading under the ferns and azaleas.

The sound of running water nearby is punctuated at regular intervals by a loud thump: closer inspection reveals an ancient Japanese device known as a *shika odoshi*, intended to scare away deer and wild boar. A hollow bamboo pipe pivots over a support like a sea-saw; one end rests on a block of stone, and at the other end is a reservoir which slowly fills with water. When the weight of water reaches the critical point the reservoir end shoots down, spilling the water, and immediately springs back, so that the other end hits the stone with a sharp crack. Then the reservoir fills again.

Running along the house, parallel to the dry stream, is a sort of wisteria pergola called a *fujidana*. Bamboo poles are erected and tied with great artistry, and a single stem of wisteria is trained up each mainstay. At the top each stem is allowed to branch in three directions, straight ahead and to right and left, so that when the branches meet they form a right-angled grid. After ten to fifteen years of painstaking training and pruning the wisteria will support itself, and the bamboo framework will be removed.

This is a garden which cannot help but impress by its exhaustive authenticity. Even the existing native trees are pruned and thinned to take on an oriental aspect, in imitation of traditional methods of plucking leaves by hand to obtain the optimum level of sparseness. So fascinating is it that it is tempting to dissect and analyse it, element by element, and so become ensnared in a rather academic exercise. But by its very authenticity it rises above such scholarliness, for the *raison d'être* of a Zen garden is to encourage the mind to soar to an elevated spiritual plane, leaving far behind the practical, material concerns that dominate our earthbound lives. So, in the contemplation of this garden, if we tend to forget that it is the result of many hard hours of planning and building, digging and weeding, it is perhaps the ultimate tribute to the work of Toshiyuki Yoshimura.

A STREET IN PECKHAM

Rye Lane, just off Peckham Rye, has a deceptively bucolic ring to it: it is one of those nostalgic street names that reaches back over the centuries to more rural and (you are persuaded) gentler times. London is full of them, and they give fascinating clues to local history and topography. Sometimes, in the context of the urban blight that has sprawled over the pastures and villages of old London, they assume undertones of cruel irony, raising a wry smile from the nature-starved city dweller. Standing among the shops on present-day Rye Lane, breathing in the traffic fumes and temporarily deafened by the trains thundering past on the railway bridge that spans it, you need a robust imagination to picture the fields and market gardens which only one hundred and fifty years ago covered the land now swallowed up by the streets of Peckham, or the Kentish drovers who herded their cattle up the stony highway that is now the Old Kent Road.

Yet hidden behind Rye Lane, in the shadow of the railway arches, is a leafy lane which has earned the accolade of 'the prettiest street in London'. As you push open the wrought-iron gate you seem to enter a different world:

The tiny 'secret' garden at the end of the street is a haven for residents and cats alike. Reached through a gate festooned with honeysuckle and filled with old-fashioned plants and shrubs, it has a secluded, woodland feel which is especially welcome amid the streets of south London.

89

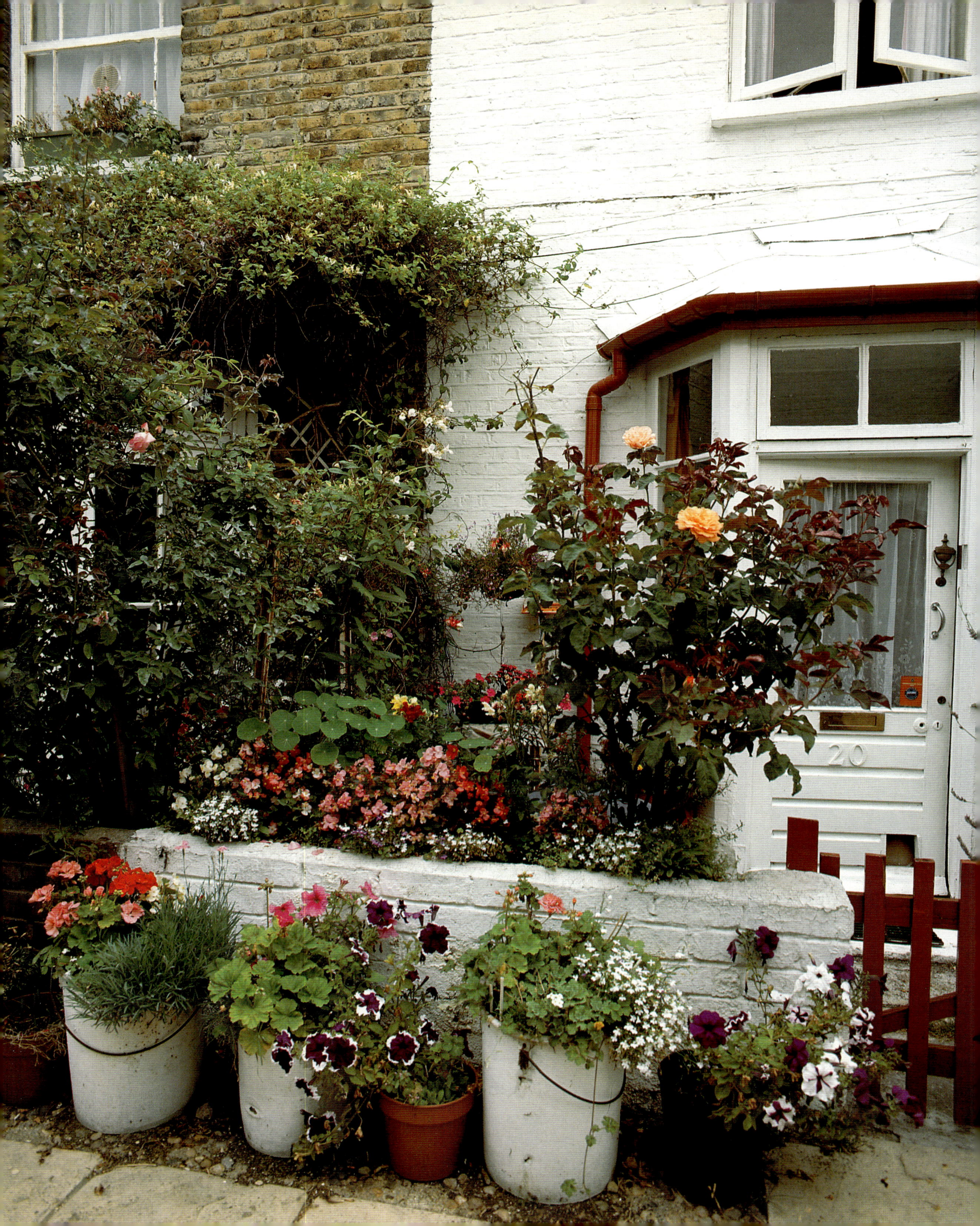
20

diminutive cottages line a long narrow path of weathered flagstones, and each Lilliputian front garden is a mass of flowers. Climbing plants and windowboxes decorate every housefront, honeysuckles and rambling roses festoon pillars and archways, and quantities of pots filled with a multitude of plants line the path and are tucked into every spare corner.

The railways came to Peckham in 1865, when the London, Brighton and South Coast Railway built the station and bridge at Rye Lane. From their architecture you might imagine these terraces were here before the railway, for the flat-fronted cottages seem early Victorian in style, with touches of picturesque Gothic, and their proportions even carry a hint of the Georgian. In fact they were simply old-fashioned when they were built by a speculative builder called Nunn in about 1880. Nunn bought the land from two sisters who lived in a mansion at one end of it, and who finding themselves in straitened circumstances sold off their drive. First one terrace was built on one side of the drive, then four years later the other side went up. Forty-six one-up-one-down cottages now lined the drive, with one communal wash house reached by a passage at the back. Landlords changed and rents fluctuated, and when half the street was sold off and rents went up in that end and not in the other passions among the residents boiled over. A pitched battle ensued, resulting in the erection halfway down the street of a second gate, now prettily wreathed with climbers, to keep the warring neighbours apart.

Now the only skirmishes are between the resident dogs and the innumerable cats that bask here in this feline paradise, shared out among the street on the same principle of relaxed cooperation that governs the upkeep of the gardens. No one here needs to worry about who will feed and water their pets and plants when they go away on holiday. One resident above all, however, deserves the credit for the luxuriant growth that now engulfs the street. Ten years ago, according to Mrs Ann Anderson, the soil was spent and full of soot, and very little grew on this awkward site, shaded by the house walls and the canopy of a large sycamore. Since then she has fed it and dug it, manured it and composted it tirelessly, and now plants need little encouragement to seed themselves everywhere. She also looks after a little 'secret' garden, reached through another gate at the end of the street, where residents can picnic or read, hold communal drinks parties in summer, or simply sit and look.

The profusion of climbers and shrubs, herbaceous plants and annuals that throngs the tiny front gardens seems to spill over irrepressibly into the pots and tubs that line the street in their hundreds. One garden has only species roses, including *Rosa glauca* with its purple stems and purple-grey leaves, and another has no fewer than six different varieties of clematis among a mass of other planting.

Among all the plant life in these tiny gardens the residents manage to pack in statues and ornaments and also tables and chairs, and on summer evenings everyone seems to live outside, undisturbed by traffic or passers-by. One garden contains the head of a statue of the

IT is hard to exaggerate the profusion of planting in these front gardens: every inch of space is covered with annuals, herbaceous plants and shrubs, and where there is no room to spread sideways plants are encouraged to grow upwards.

NOT content with troughs and trellises, windowboxes and hanging baskets, residents also line the street with all manner of pots and containers spilling over with flowers.

physician Linacre, which once adorned the old Royal College of Physicians building in Pall Mall East. After the war, when this became part of Canada House, all its statuary was sent to a breaker's yard, from where Linacre's head was rescued by one of his descendants, in whose garden it now reposes. Lack of space does not rule out dramatic associations either: the clustered blooms of the shrub rose 'Fountain' glow blood-red against the metallic grey leaves of a eucalyptus, and tall canna lilies strike a tropical note under the boughs of a crab apple.

The array of plants growing in pots is astonishing: camellias and mahonias, bay trees and conifers, ivies and cotoneasters, laurels and choisyas and a wealth of other evergreens provide a permanent green backdrop to an exuberant display of flowers virtually throughout the year. Because space is so limited all the plants have to work hard, and preference is given to those with pretty leaves as well as flowers, or which flower twice or recurrently. Those with scented leaves or flowers, or with ornamental or edible hips or berries are also deemed to earn their keep. Plants which spread or seed themselves freely serve the double purpose of filling any gaps and imposing a sense of unity on the planting – for it is easy to forget that this is not one long cottage garden but forty-six separate ones. Borage, poppies, the lovely *Impatiens balsamina* with pale pink orchid-like flowers, Jacob's ladder with its tiny mauve-blue pea flowers, foxgloves, hollyhocks, lemon balm, campanulas and a mass of others crop up everywhere, while lobelia and alyssum join the fringe of grass in the cracks between the paving stones.

Some of the houses are smothered in honeysuckle and clematis, others in roses and wisteria, hibiscus and abutilon. A large *Rosa* 'Buff Beauty' grows high against a soot-blackened wall, and the ethereal white blooms of *Zantedeschia aethiopica* float in a gloomy corner. Fuchsias, euphorbias and rhododendrons underplanted with violas, busy lizzies, ferns and periwinkles all flourish in the shade, while mallows and pelargoniums, geraniums and roses, nasturtiums and wallflowers fill the sunnier spots with splashes of hot reds, pinks and oranges.

Halfway down the path is a graceful *Robinia pseudoacacia* 'Tortuosa' which casts a deep shade over Mrs Anderson's garden and virtually

IN such limited space plants have to work doubly hard: evergreens are especially valuable, as are plants with attractive foliage as well as flowers, or with ornamental hips or scented leaves. Those which seed themselves freely are also useful, as they not only fill any gaps but also impose a sense of unity.

CLIMBING plants and window boxes decorate the front door of each house; honeysuckles and rambling roses festoon pillars and archways.

blocks the entrance to her neighbour's house – inconveniences which she happily puts up with for the sake of its tiers of pendulous, filmy foliage and its beautiful racemes of white pea flowers in spring. Another robinia, *R. pseudoacacia* 'Frisia' and a silver birch have been planted to replace two trees lost in the hurricane in 1987.

A gate under an arch of honeysuckle leads to the secret garden at the end, where in summer pots of pelargoniums and fuchsias sit in the middle of a patch of lawn with stepping stones set into it. The peripheral planting here is a romantic profusion of old-fashioned shrubs and herbaceous plants engulfed in a luxuriant tangle of climbers. A philadelphus is threaded with the slender stems of *Clematis tangutica*, valuable for its delicate, fern-like foliage, its nodding yellow flowers in August and September, and its silky seed heads. A herbaceous clematis which flowers at the same time grows up through its branches, and the feathery fronds of a huge asparagus fern arch overhead. Foxgloves, which have colonized every shady corner, lend this secluded spot a woodland feel, and tall double white hollyhocks, which have seeded themselves freely, are silhouetted against the dark walls and greenery.

Reduced to its essentials this is a difficult and most unpromising site: a long strip, much of it in shade, with a few pockets of poor soil, and a tiny patch of grass overlooked by high walls at the end. Yet by dint of a lot of hard work and good neighbourliness it has been turned into a quiet, leafy haven for the benefit of all the residents. As well as being a delightful spot to enjoy, it stands as its own eloquent testimony to determination and cooperative spirit.

As you go through the gate you enter a different world: small cottages line a long narrow path of weathered flagstones and each tiny front garden is a mass of flowers. Here the graceful *Robinia pseudoacacia* 'Tortuosa' casts a deep shade with its tiers of pendulous foliage and racemes of white pea flowers in spring.

WALPOLE HOUSE

Chiswick Mall – where coots and mallards paddle and preen under the willows of the riverbank, where boats large and small bob and swell on the incoming tide, and where the grey waters of the Thames lap against the narrow riverside gardens – is one of the most magical instances of *rus in urbe* in London. Only four or five miles downstream is the heart of London, but here the mood is gently pastoral and the call of wild geese haunts the air. The river adds a note of romance and a hint of sea breezes: finally flexing its muscles before its sullen, canalized journey through the city it spreads itself wide across its natural valley, capriciously flooding with every high tide the unembanked street and the gardens that line it. The architecture, too, seems of another time and place: as you walk past the substantial but

THE knotted and very aged trunk of a mulberry, leaning like the tower of Pisa, frames semicircular beds containing pink camellias, evergreen bright pink Kurume azaleas and a variegated ivy, 'Gloire de Marengo'.

ACER griseum, 'the Paper-bark maple', one of the most beautiful of small trees, rises, with its flaky cinnamon-coloured trunk, from a sea of *Helleborus orientalis*, covered with flowers of all shades of pink and white. In the far distance a neatly arranged pile of terracotta pots wait to be filled with precious seedlings.

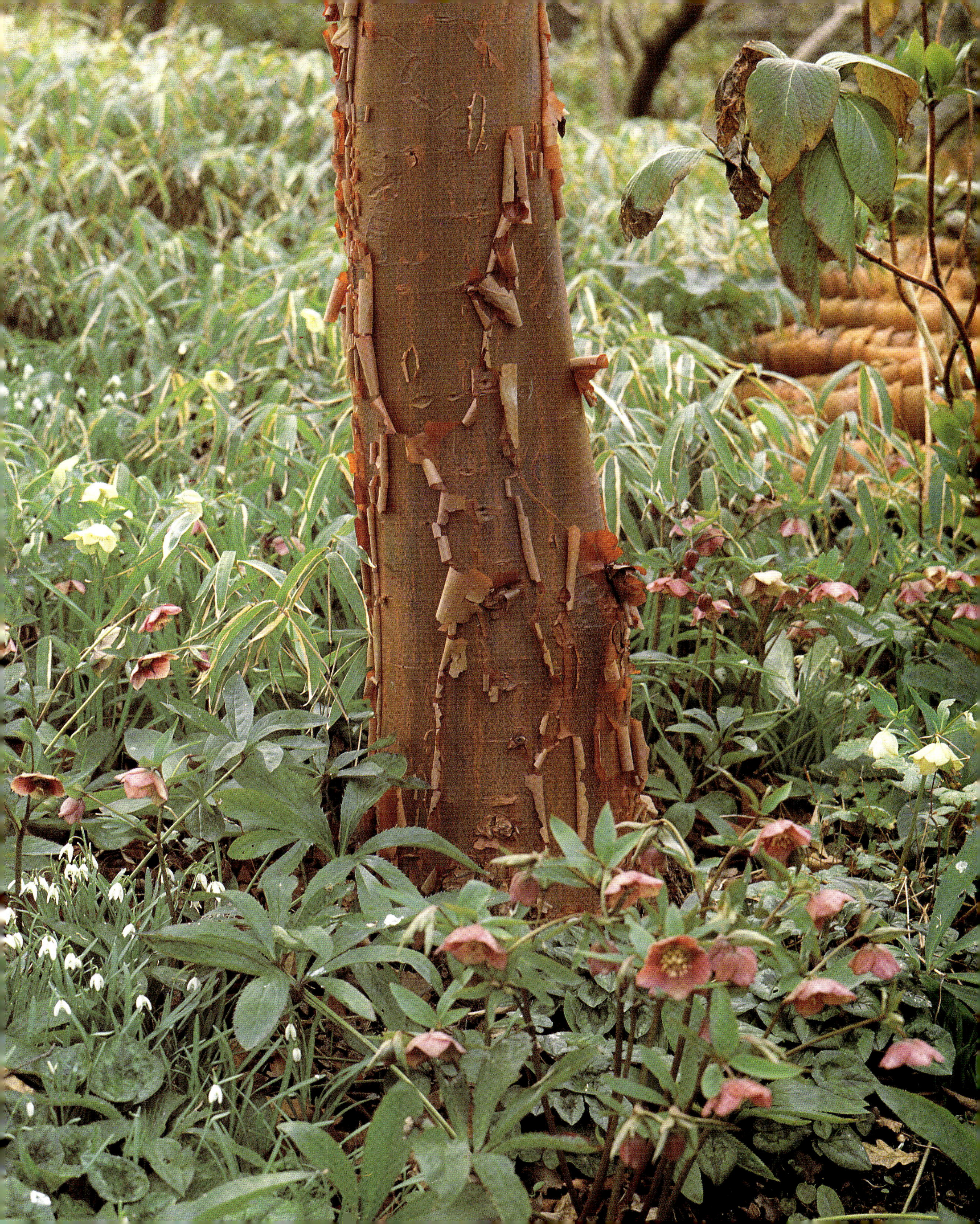

PRIVATE GARDENS OF LONDON

At the foot of the main lawn a yew hedge separates the lawn from the woodland garden. Here in this secret wild garden is a white painted metal seat surrounded by large borders crammed with drifts of cyclamen in the autumn, snowdrops and hellebores in the spring.

PRECIOUS seedlings are stored in neat rows in this frame. Here special treasures are cosseted and coaxed, some from seed collected both from the wild and from the garden. All are generously given away or sold on the opening days for the National Gardens Scheme.

elegant Georgian façades, with their graceful proportions and imposing porticoes, their simple ironwork and slender glazing bars, you could fancy yourself on the waterfront of a village in Georgian England.

About halfway down the Mall, on a low rise, stands Walpole House, one of the finest houses and probably the earliest. The lower part of the structure is Tudor, but the earliest records relating to the house date from the very beginning of the eighteenth century, when it was home to Barbara Villiers, Duchess of Cleveland and former mistress of Charles II. After her death it passed to the Hon. Thomas Walpole, nephew of Sir Robert Walpole (prime minister from 1721 to 1742), who gave the house its name. By about 1835 it had become a school or 'asylum' for young boys, among whose number was the young William Thackeray; it is thought that when he later came to write *Vanity Fair* he used Walpole House as his model for Miss Pinkerton's Academy. Later occupants included Sir Herbert Beerbohm Tree, the actor manager, and in 1926 it was sold to Mr and Mrs Robert Benson. Since 1947 it has been home to their grandson Jeremy Benson and his wife and children.

The river frontage of Walpole House gives no clue to the garden that lies behind. This comes as a revelation as you pass through the tall wrought-iron gates and between the Corinthian columns of the porch to the double front doors; for as you enter the house you find yourself on an axis that runs the length of the narrow hall to a glazed door and beyond, down a broad flagged path to the bottom of the spacious garden, where a white wrought-iron seat stops the eye. It is an unusually noble vista for a London garden: the path is flanked by sweeping lawns and lined with stone pedestals, and its perspective is heightened by a slight tapering of its width. As you enter the front door, therefore, all this lies before you, and the garden's light airy spaces beckon you through the shadowy hall to the garden door.

Camellias flank the door, which opens on to a York stone terrace which runs the length of the house and was part of the original design. The bones of this, laid out in 1926, were the work of Mrs Robert Benson, who planted most of the trees which have now reached maturity, built the low retaining walls around the lawns and laid the terrace. She also made a fine collection of hybrid irises for which the garden became celebrated, but which now seem not to 'do' quite so successfully, and many of the more elaborate and formal aspects of her design have also fared less well. During the war the garden inevitably suffered neglect, and in 1947 Mr and Mrs Jeremy Benson's first concern was to restore it. Practical necessity and changing tastes suggested simplification to the original design – and with it a general softening of the garden's outlines. Two symmetrical parterres, for instance, were replaced with beds where drifts of spring bulbs and wild flowers in shades of blue and yellow are followed in summer by roses underplanted with pinks and ground-covering lamium.

Shallow steps lead up to the first lawns, where raised semicircular beds to either side contain camellias, azaleas and a *Magnolia denudata* which casts its shade over a circular paved sitting area beneath. Fatsias and hostas grow happily in their shade, together with the first of the garden's impressive collection of tree peonies. The very double 'Souvenir de Maxime Cornu', with yellow petals shading at the edges to bronze, was one of which Mrs Robert Benson was particularly proud. As her grandson points out it is now much travelled, for at her death the plant was divided between her sons, Kew Gardens (where it still grows), and her butler-cum-gardener, Mr Ford. After an interval of many years Mr Ford returned to

SUN-LOVING plants colonize the cracks and spaces between the paving surrounding the pool. Pinks, violas, marjoram, flax and *Sisyrinchium striatum* thrive and seed themselves all around. At the centre of the pool is a clump of *Iris laevigata* 'Alba' which likes to have its feet in water, whilst on the sides two clumps of *Iris ensata* (*I. kaempferi*) thrive in the damp but not waterlogged beds.

PRIVATE GARDENS OF LONDON

Walpole House to help with the garden in his retirement, and before he emigrated to Canada in his seventies he returned the tree peony to its original spot, where it now thrives once more.

There is a sense of privacy and seclusion in this garden by the house, surrounded as it is by high walls on three sides, and overhung by the spreading canopies of a soaring *Ailanthus altissima* and a thirty-foot eucalyptus. Opposite these stands a knotted and very aged mulberry, its arthritic branches – given a severe pruning a few years back when it was discovered that the entire tree was developing a list like the leaning tower of Pisa – wound together with a mesh of wires.

From the relative intimacy of this area more steps lead up to the wide lawns which take full advantage of the garden's unusually generous proportions (it covers about two-thirds of an acre). The lawns are dotted with trees: an old pear tree, crowned in spring with white blossom which seems to float above the grass like a cloud, a tulip tree given to the Bensons by their children for their silver wedding anniversary, and two magnificent poplars planted by Mrs Jeremy Benson.

Beneath these lies another of her creations and one of the garden's dominant features, a large formal lily pond framed by York stone flags and surrounded by raised beds. The presence of five small children necessitated an encircling tall wire fence with secure gates, which Jeremy Benson planted with climbing roses and a pot of *Clematis alpina* 'Columbine' seedlings. These have now engulfed the fencing, making an effective and very pretty screen. The Bensons only misgivings surface at rose pruning time, an operation which has to be carried out with surgical precision if the fragile young clematis tendrils are not to be damaged.

Water lilies and *Iris pseudacorus* are reflected in the pool's still waters, and all around cheiranthus, ferns, rock roses and pinks have seeded themselves in the cracks between the paving stones, while terracotta pots placed around the pool contain innumerable varieties of sempervivum. *Sisyrinchium striatum*, pinks,

THE formal lily pond laid out by Mrs Robert Benson is especially lovely in summer, when its still waters reflect masses of iris and water-lilies. Against the informal cottage-garden planting that surrounds the pool, terracotta pots containing many different varieties of sempervivum strike a more architectural note.

WALPOLE HOUSE

PRIVATE GARDENS OF LONDON

THE pond laid out by his grandmother was a potential hazard to Mr and Mrs Jeremy Benson's five children. Their solution was to surround it with a tall wire fence: many years later, it is now smothered with climbing roses and *Clematis alpina* and is both functional and delightful to look at.

Campanula persicifolia and masses of self-seeded foxgloves and irises fill the beds under the clematis and rose screens, making a picture of cottage-garden appeal in summer. Tree and species peonies, including the coveted *P. cambessedesii* with beetroot-coloured stems and brilliant pink papery flowers in late spring, also flourish here in narrow beds against low walls; and in autumn, while other flowers fade quietly with the dying light, clumps of startling pink nerines make a courageous stand against the onset of winter.

At the foot of the main lawns a yew hedge, grown from seed, screens a secret wild garden, with a gap in the hedge permitting a glimpse of the pretty wrought-iron seat against its dark background of ivy. Here is an enchanting woodland planting of drifts of snowdrops and hellebores in spring, followed by a sheet of *Cyclamen hederifolium* in autumn. As you pass through the gap in the yew hedge, leaving behind the cool expanses of lawn, the change in mood from classical to romantic is marked and satisfying. Even the quality of the light changes, for here mature trees cast their shade, and the veiled light heightens this little garden's sense of mystery.

A path leads on along the ivy-clad wall that bounds the garden at the bottom, past deep borders filled with swathes of self-seeded *Helleborus orientalis* in every shade of dusty pink, cream and white. So happy are they here that Mr Benson is convinced that if the garden were left to run wild it would be completely overrun by hellebores, along with the equally wanton euphorbias and cyclamens. Under the boughs of a large eucalyptus, a large snake-bark acer and the beautiful *A. japonicum* 'Aconitifolium' with deeply lobed leaves which colour to rich ruby-crimson in autumn, are more shade-loving plants. *Geranium endressii*, *Euphorbia amygdaloides robbiae* and day lilies give way later in the year to foxgloves, ligularias and sedum, while delicate camellia blooms and Solomon's seal are followed closely by alchemilla, hypericum and smilacina, which raises its arching sprays of scented creamy-white flowers in May and June. Beyond, a graceful thicket of bamboo lines the path to the compost heap – the sign of a real garden.

A second gap in the yew hedge opens on to the lawn again, between informal beds where a *Magnolia × soulangeana* rises above more tree peonies, clumps of 'Iceberg' roses and the spring-flowering chaenomeles, its flowers silhouetted against the dark leaves of skimmias. Japanese anemones run between the shrubs, and in autumn the superb pink flowers of *Crinum × powellii* rise from rings of long strap-like leaves. Some fourteen varieties of tree peony flourish here, and Jeremy Benson's only regret is that they are so hard to establish, for over the years he must have planted at least forty. The pink moutan is the most free-flowering, but in Mr Benson's opinion the most splendid is a specimen of 'Superb', now nearly thirty years old and bearing as many huge cherry-red blooms every year.

Behind the bed to the right is hidden a little rock pool surrounded by lush ferns and rushes. A seat from which to enjoy this cool, shady spot is placed under the spreading branches of a huge *Paulownia tomentosa*, chosen for its immense leaves. This Mr Benson grew from seed: he is an enthusiastic propagator and a devoted collector of seed from all the plants in his garden, both rare and humble, and in the little raised greenhouse above the rock pool are row upon row of precious seedlings. Here special treasures are coaxed and cossetted: *Ferula communis*, for instance, brought back from Sicily as a seedling, which every few years throws up stems fourteen feet high smothered with innumerable golden flowers; *Euphorbia mellifera*, a present from Ireland; and a collection of species peonies, *P. mlokosewitshii*, *P. tenuifolia*, *P. mascula arietina* and, perhaps most treasured of all, *P. cambessedesii*. With the characteristic generosity of the true gardener Jeremy Benson shares these treasures freely with kindred spirits, and presses meticulously labelled packets of surplus seeds on visitors as they leave.

Mr and Mrs Benson are both architects, so it is not surprising that they should have enhanced their garden's strongly architectural design. Its changing levels, its long lines and its interlocking planes give them as much pleasure as the wealth of plants that grow here, from the simplest of woodland plants to the choicest rareties. All the modifications and changes they have introduced to a design which was originally extremely grand have been wrought with an eye to both their aesthetic and their practical benefits. There is not much time for planting out, for instance, so a permanent planting scheme has evolved, and with it a carefully worked out routine for chores and maintenance. Once rather formidable in its grandeur, this garden by the Thames now wears a gentler face, mellowed by softer planting and lent charm by its shady corners.

THIS superb Japanese cherry *Prunus* 'Tai-Haku' is at its best when planted in a lawn with nothing beside it to detract from its beauty. It has a profusion of dazzling white flowers which smother the wide spreading, drooping branches, often reaching the ground.

A GARDEN OF THE UNEXPECTED

Charles Caplin's Hampstead garden is a reminder that appearances can be deceptive. As you gaze over the broad sweep of flawless velvety lawn, flanked by beds well furnished with shrubs and herbaceous plants, your initial impression is one of ordered calm. This seems a placid garden, safely under control, where surprises will be few. Your first inkling that things are not perhaps quite as they seem comes as you venture down the path that leads down the side of the garden. Immediately you are engulfed in a jungle of teeming plant life of a variety, vitality and sheer quantity to take your breath away. And further exploration of the garden's periphery reveals an array of planting and features – a pond, a rockery, a fruit arbour, a miscellany of subtropical plants, topiary, bonsai and an encyclopedic collection of different genera and species – that is truly astonishing. A short walk round Mr Caplin's

IN this garden a single tree may shelter a density and variety of plants that is quite astonishing. Mr Caplin's enthusiasm for plants is irrepressible, and they all seem to thrive. Here a jungle of herbaceous plants and shrubs, conifers and annuals mingle happily under a standard wisteria.

AUTUMN colour is an added bonus when the flowering season is at an end and can be as varied as the riot of different colours in high summer. Here the spectacular *Vitis coignetiae* is in full autumnal glory with its large leaves turning from green to all shades of bright orange, red and yellow.

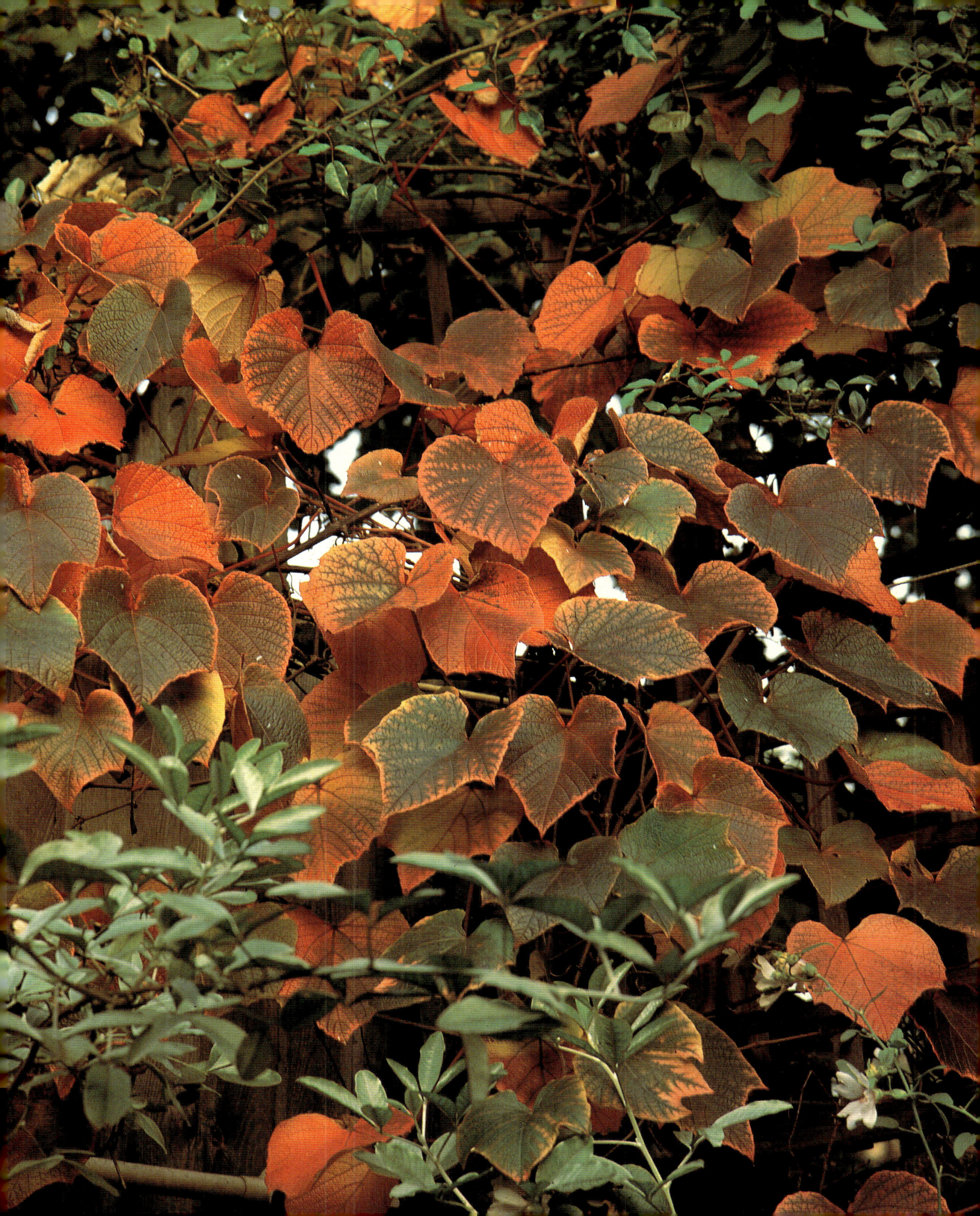

garden is sufficient to dispel your illusions of orthodoxy.

Although not set far back from the street, the detached red-brick house that fronts this garden is virtually concealed by greenery. Old sycamores rise above it, and in spring a screen of early prunus, rhododendrons, camellias, deciduous azaleas, a *Malus floribunda* and tree peonies is a study in pink and yellow, against the coppery new shoot of a pieris and the evergreen leaves of a huge yucca. In summer a mallow, fuchsias, clematis, a passion flower and climbing roses add deeper notes of pink and purple.

Charles Caplin's love of plants, already evident in the front garden, is not confined to outdoors. The back garden is reached through a large conservatory he has recently built in order to indulge his passion for tender and exotic plants. Here are lemons, gingers and bananas, toad lilies and lapageria and a host of other subtropical blooms. The boundary between house and garden is kept deliberately fluid: the garden surrounds the conservatory, and in summer the conservatory overflows into the garden.

The conservatory doors open on to the beautifully kept lawn, with York stone edging on to which spills the luxuriant planting of the flower borders. A few rocks in the middle

A PALM and a black bamboo make an exotic frame for the entrance to the path that runs down the side of the garden. Roses are planted on the wooden arches that span the path together with golden hops, clematis and *Actinidia deliciosa*. Chaenomeles, ribes and fig tree mingle together to make a tunnel of green.

distance suggest the outlines of a pond set into the York stone at the bottom of the garden. Graceful stands of cyperus (umbrella grass) rise like rushes from the water, and among them there stalks a metallic heron; in summer he is sometimes joined by his living counterparts, their great wings casting long shadows over the garden as they swoop down to snatch the goldfish. A waterfall bubbles from the rockery behind, which is planted with dwarf conifers, yuccas and a mass of other choice rockery plants, closely planted for best effect. The feathery foliage of *Phyllostachys nigra*, carried high on glossy black canes, shivers in the slightest breeze, above the sea-green shoots of *Leycesteria formosa*, which bears drooping panicles of white flowers on dark red bracts from June to September, and the beautiful red-tinged leaves of *Nandina domestica*, commonly known as the sacred bamboo. Contrasts of foliage colour and texture, of feathery and spear-shaped leaves, of the outlines of airy bamboos and compact conifers, create intricate plays of light and shade that are constantly reflected in the water.

To the right of the pond the stone edging fans out in three directions, and the intersection is marked by an extremely decorative *Eucryphia × nymansensis* 'Nymansay', smothered in white flowers in July and August, with a golden conifer beside it and astilbes covering the ground beneath. Behind is an *Acer negundo* 'Flamingo' surrounded by azaleas, which form the backdrop to a bed which cuts across the lawn, planted with another *A.n.* 'Flamingo' and a *Cornus alternifolia* 'Argentea'. Their pale and variegated leaves brighten this dark corner, while two clumps of evergreen azaleas, rhododendrons and tree peonies form a bank of colour in spring and early summer. They are overhung by the branches of a *Davidia involucrata*, the pocket handkerchief tree, draped in May (after twenty years or so) with its spectacular white flower bracts.

A small grove of trees stands closer to the house, including a cut-leaf alder, a mulberry, a quince, a *Paulownia tomentosa*, which if the buds escape a late frost will give a glorious display of violet-purple foxglove-shaped flowers in May, and – perhaps the most beautiful of all – an *Acer griseum*, with its flame-coloured autumn foliage and red bark peeling to reveal the cinnamon-coloured underbark.

A topiary spiral of bay stands at the corner of the conservatory against which climbs an old wisteria, and against the house on the other side are a tall *Magnolia grandiflora* and another wisteria, with beside them the corkscrew branches of a *Corylus avellana* 'Contorta'. Palms and a black bamboo make an exotic frame for the entrance to the path that runs down the side of the garden. Wooden arches span the path, planted with climbing roses, golden hops, hibiscus, clematis and kiwi fruit vines, their tendrils weaving together and through the branches of chaenomeles, ribes and

NOT an inch of space is left in this colourful border. A standard wisteria shows its gnarled trunk and branches above an array of different plants. Bamboos, *Lavatera thuringiaca* 'Barnsley' and *Juniperus scopulorum* 'Skyrocket' are planted close together, below them lavender, nasturtiums and other ground cover plants leave no part of the border uncovered.

a fig tree to make a tunnel of green. As you pass down this tunnel you become increasingly aware of the extreme intricacy and density of the planting in the beds to either side. Not an inch of space is left uncovered by a planting policy which, judged perhaps by more orthodox standards, seems designed more for dramatic effect than for the comfort of the plants – though they clearly thrive anyway.

The variety is almost overwhelming: in one small area under a large standard wisteria a *Mahonia × media* 'Charity', *Clematis × durandii*, a tree peony, an exquisite *Enkianthus campanulatus*, pampas-grass and three dwarf conifers jostle for space, with pelargoniums and nasturtiums coaxed into any tiny gaps. Elsewhere, above a sea of autumn cyclamen, a large rose 'Nevada' and a *Viburnum farreri* and *V. bodnantse*, which bear deliciously scented flowers throughout the winter, share a corner with a *Magnolia soulangeana*, a stewartia, a kerria and a black bamboo, all good-naturedly awaiting their turn to shine.

The enthusiastic Mr Caplin is moreover constantly introducing newcomers (and the temptation to succumb to new plants is ever present, for his youngest son runs nurseries at Alexandra Palace and Hounslow): a space can always be found for a few seedlings or pots of annuals, and when the spring bulbs and gentians in the raised bed along the boundary are over, the gaps they leave are soon filled. The choice is sometimes ingenious: the ornamental cerise and jade-green heads of purple kale and cabbage are often to be found peeping out between the crinums and the crocosmia. In front of the crinums is the lovely but tender rhododendron 'Lady Chamberlain', weighed

SOME vegetables can be extremely ornamental. Here the cerise and jade green heads of purple kale are often found peeping out of nasturtiums or crinums.

COLOUR combinations are not a concern in this garden. Pink *Lavatera thuringiaca* 'Rosea', pelargoniums and lythrums mingle unashamedly with bright red poppies and orange everlasting flowers, *Helichrysum bracteatum*, to great effect.

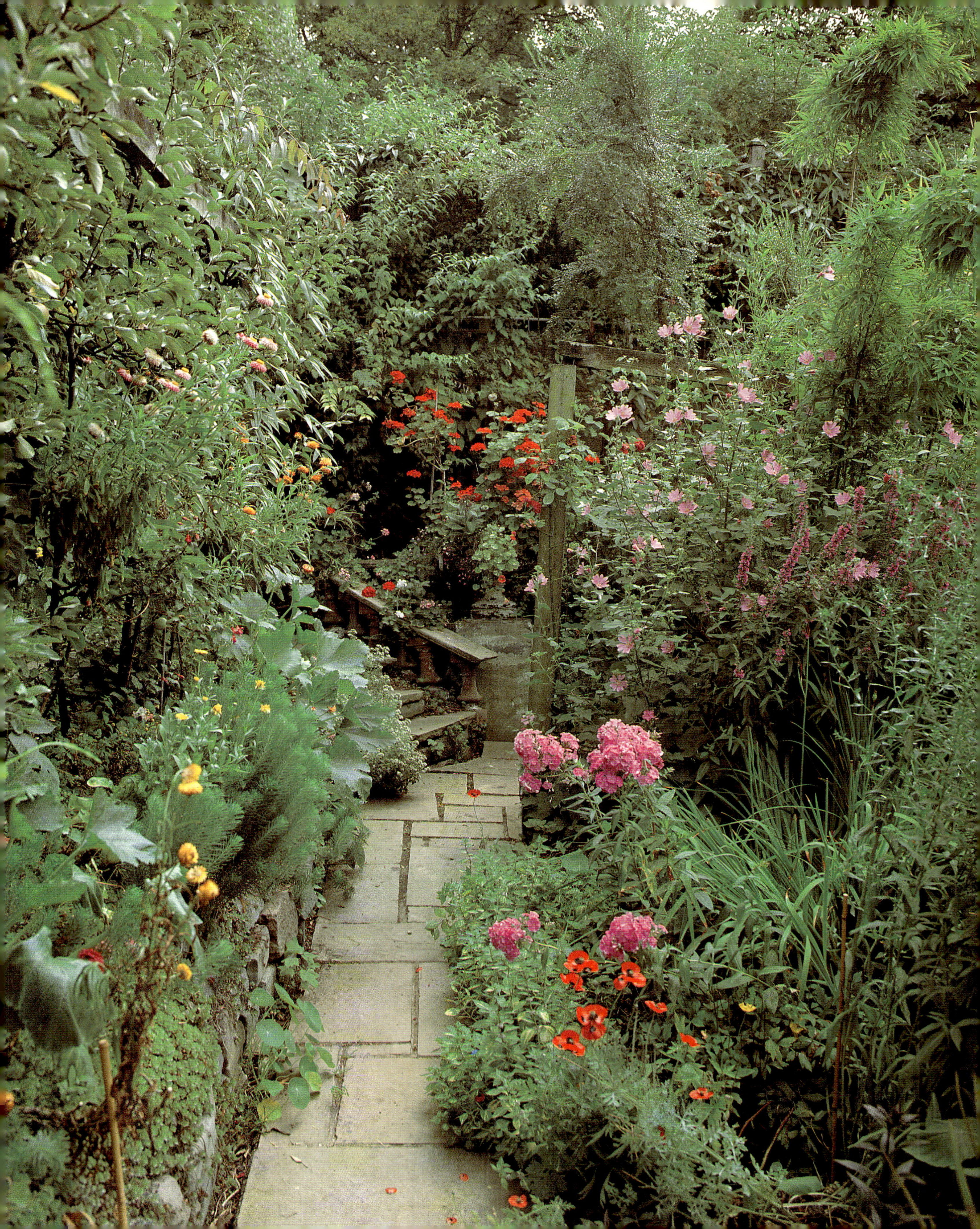

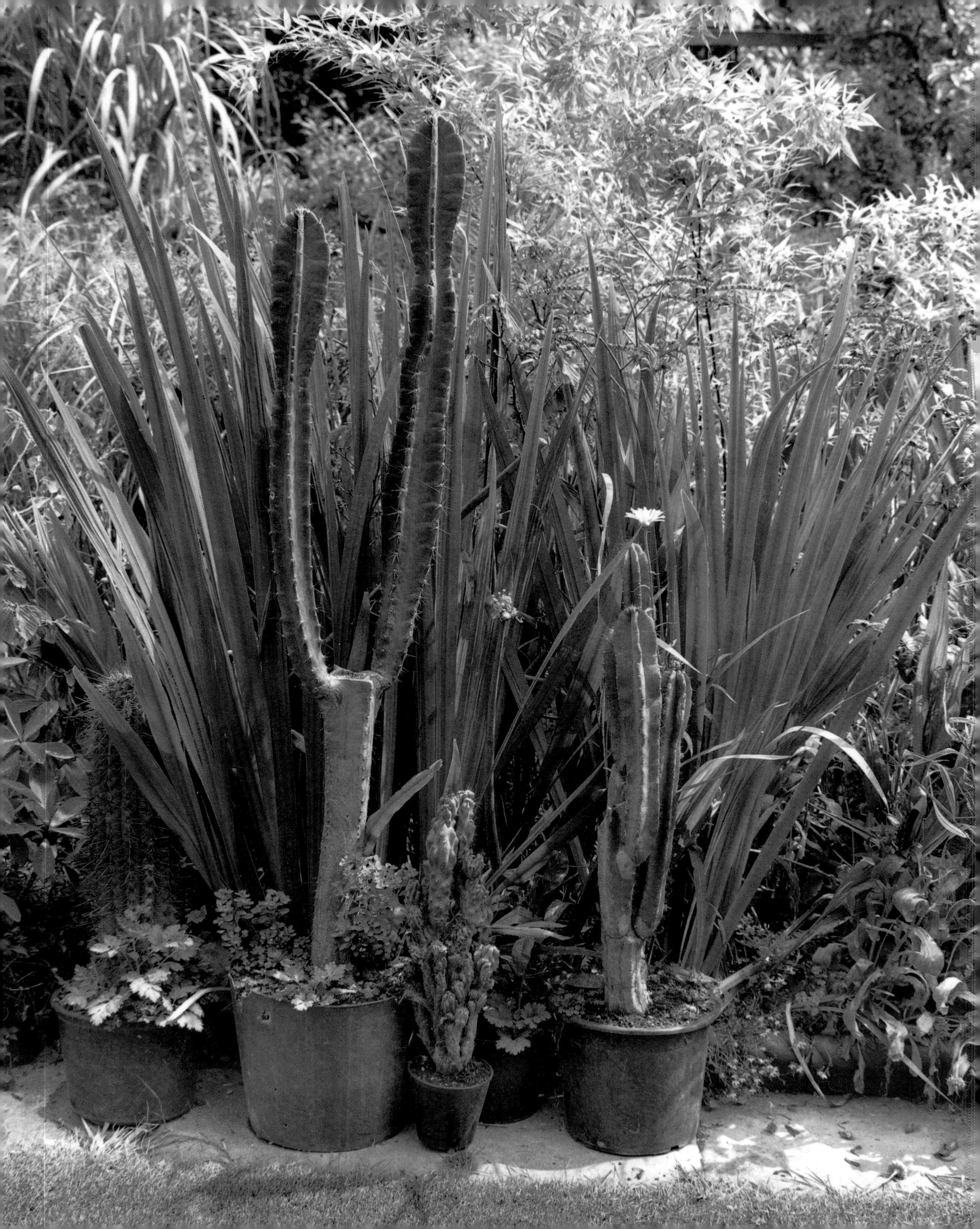

A GARDEN OF THE UNEXPECTED

down with cascades of bell-shaped mandarin-red flowers, and beyond this some steps lead up to a shady apple arbour wreathed with *Clematis armandii*. At the far end a *Lavatera thuringiaca* 'Barnsley' and the pineapple-scented *Cytisus battandieri* are overhung by a *Vitis coignetiae*, which turns red and gold in autumn.

The fruit tunnel overlooks a corner dotted with supports for soft fruit and climbing roses, where in summer quantities of flowers and fruits in shades of crimson, tawny red and purple are extremely pretty against the green foliage. One of Mr Caplin's most unusual and successful concepts is his use of fruit and vegetables for their decorative as well as their practical value. Apples and pears, raspberries, loganberries and alpine strawberries, as well as the purple kale and cabbage, are given equal status with the flowers and placed with just as much care for their aesthetic effect.

In high summer, when the greenhouse empties its store of tropical plants into the garden, jungle plants line the path and bromeliads hang from the arches. A cheerfully ad hoc note is struck by the assortment of materials – timber, stones, rocks and cobbles – used to retain the raised beds. There are no earnest attempts here to create special effects or colour combinations, but they seem to happen anyway; nor is the garden self-consciously 'designed', yet there is a fascinating contrast between the measured order of the open lawn and the exuberant vitality of the planting tucked away around its edges. And there is a tremendous variety of plants, acid-loving species mingling happily with others which prefer an alkaline soil, and Mediterranean and even subtropical plants jostling with hardy evergreens. It is above all the sheer versatility of London gardens – the quality that makes them the envy of gardeners around the world – that this garden demonstrates so well.

IN the summer when the greenhouse empties its store of tropical plants into the garden, jungle plants line the path. Here pots of cactus are tucked against yucca.

BROMELIADS hang from the arches and from the branches of this tree adding a touch of rain forest to the already eclectic planting.

PRIVATE GARDENS OF LONDON

A GARDEN OF THE UNEXPECTED

THE lovely but tender *Rhododendron* Lady Chamberlain weighed down with cascades of bell-shaped mandarin-red flowers thrives in this protected garden and clearly shows the versatility of London gardens with their different soils and microclimates.

A METALLIC heron stalks the goldfish in the pond amid graceful stands of cyperus. Sometimes his living counterparts swoop down to join him. A waterfall bubbles down the rockery behind, which is planted with dwarf conifers, yuccas and a mass of other rockery plants.

A MUSICIAN'S GARDEN

Towards the bottom of Lady Barbirolli's garden in north London is a specimen of one of the world's most remarkable trees, the plant world's equivalent to the coelacanth. Little over half a century ago the *Metasequoia glyptostroboides*, or dawn redwood, was known only from fossils, and was believed to have been extinct for millions of years. Then in 1941 Mr T. Kan found a single specimen in a village in central China, and three years later more were found in eastern Sichuan and western Hupei. In 1945, after careful analysis of specimens by startled botanists, the sensational news broke: a living survivor of a fossil genus had been found. Seeds from this remarkable relic were despatched around the world, reaching Britain in 1948; it proved to be vigorous and easy to propagate, and trees from the original seeds have now grown to over fifty feet – about half the height of the largest mature specimens in their native China.

Lady Barbirolli's metasequoia is a fine

ALTHOUGH well into the autumn, these hybrid tea roses surrounding the sun dial are still in flower. In the background the almost bare branches of *Metasequoia glyptostroboides* let the sunlight into an otherwise shady area.

A SCULPTURE of Don Quixote on his charger, surrounded by shrubs, faces the house at the back of the lawn. On the edge of the lawn pots and troughs are filled with ericaceous compost, one is planted with a pieris and another with *Rhododendron yakushimanum*.

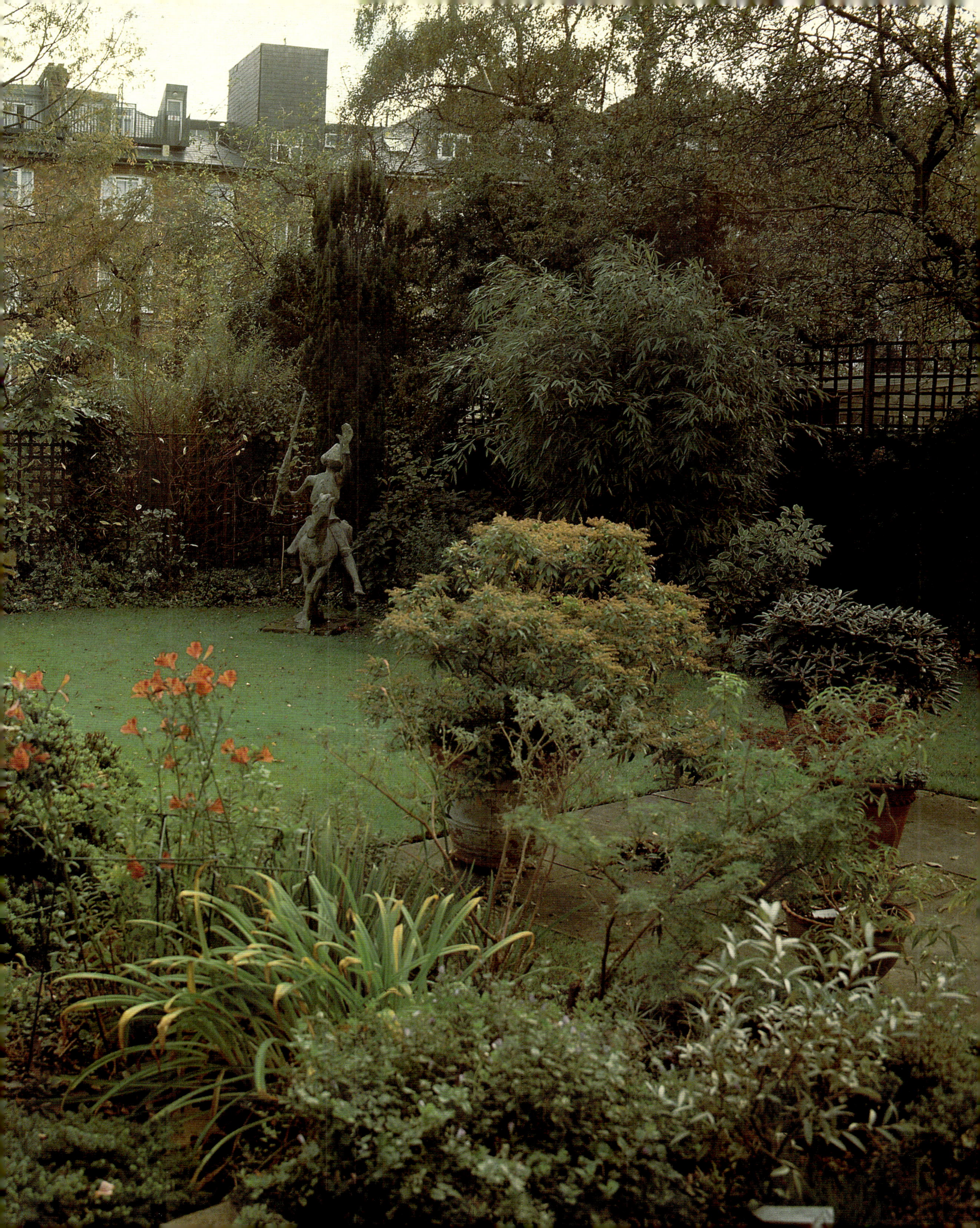

example, some forty feet tall and thirty years old. As well as having a remarkable pedigree, the tree is also valuable for its beauty, with feathery fronds rising in tiers to a conical crown, becoming more rounded with age. Through the branches, which reach down to the ground, its distinctive bark is visible, shaggy and cinnamon-coloured. The individual leaves are like flattened needles, and are borne opposite each other on softly drooping branchlets; these have an unusually light quality for a conifer, emphasized by the fresh green of the leaves' summer colouring. It is in autumn that the tree is at its loveliest, however, for then the deciduous foliage fades to subtle graduations of tones described by plantsmen, with unaccustomed poeticism, as 'tawny pink and old gold'.

Lady Barbirolli came to gardening late in life, after the death of her husband, Sir John. At the time she lived elsewhere in London, in a house that did not encourage an interest in gardening, for the only outside space was a basement courtyard, dark and bare. Nor did she have much time for it, for she was for ever dashing off to different parts of the world to give the oboe concerts and master classes for which in her own name – Evelyn Rothwell – she is famous, or to adjudicate at international music competitions. Eventually, though, it was her music which indirectly prompted her interest in plants; for it was her piano accompanist who, dismayed by the barren prospect outside Lady Barbirolli's windows, planted twenty-five pounds of daffodils in tubs. Lady Barbirolli was utterly smitten by the results, and has never looked back.

First the basement courtyard was transformed: brick troughs were built to raise the plants to the sunlight and filled with good soil; clematis in variety soon smothered the walls; and as Lady Barbirolli's ambitions and confidence grew so did her plants, culminating in a liriodendron destined in time to grow into a large tree. At the same time as increasing her practical skills she was avid for more theoretical knowledge, devouring books and attending as many lectures and seminars as she could.

Frustration inevitably followed, as she longed for more space and more encouraging conditions in which to put her new-found knowledge into practice. Then it was that an advertisement in the journal of the Royal Horticultural Society caught her eye. Mrs Mary Stein, who had spent the past thirty or so years making a garden on a third of an acre of land behind her London house, was moving, and was looking for a keen gardener to whom she could entrust her garden. After initial disappointment, when it seemed that she had been pipped at the post, Lady Barbirolli was thrilled to learn that the garden was to be hers.

The garden lies well hidden behind the stuccoed Italianate house, built in 1856. Mary Stein was an inspired designer, and had devised all sorts of ways of disguising the long, rectangular shape of the typical London garden: flower beds are gently curved, a trellis divides the space horizontally a little over halfway down, and the straight-lined symmetry of the plot is thrown off-balance by the skilful positioning of trees and shrubs. Mature sycamore and horse chestnut trees growing in neighbouring gardens screened the bottom, and against this backdrop stood the metasequoia, the main focal point from the house, in the bottom right-hand corner. Behind it is a tall, coppery purple *Prunus cerasifera* 'Pissardii', and to the side and in front of it are two of the garden's finest shrubs: hugging its trunk is a superb yellow jasmine, and nearby an exceptionally graceful *Cornus alternifolia* 'Argentea' rises in layers of white and pale green.

In the six years since Lady Barbirolli took over the garden she has altered the planting but not the design, which she felt would be hard to better. From the French windows that give access to the garden from the drawing room the view is framed by the cast-iron pilasters that support the first-floor balcony, wreathed in summer with *Clematis* 'Perle d'Azur' climbing up the perennial *Lathyrus latifolius* on one side, and on the other clouds of sweet-smelling jasmine against a background of variegated ivy. A spacious paved terrace runs the width of the house, sheltered by high boundary walls which curve up gracefully to meet the house. On the terrace is a raised, stepped brick bed filled with acid soil to accommodate the alpines for which Lady Barbirolli has a weakness, and which otherwise would not grow in her clay soil. Dainty *Salix serpyllifolia*, *Primula marginata* with fragrant lavender-blue flowers in April and May above dusty grey-green leaves edged in silver, gentians, anagallis and cushions of crassula are among the delicate plants filling the trough, with the clear blue flowers of *Convolvulus sabaticus* twining through them. Other lime-haters are accommodated in terracotta pots filled with acid compost. An azalea and a spreading, brown-leaved *Acer palmatum dissectum* fill one pair of pots; and on the edge of the lawn another pair contain a pieris which Lady Barbirolli doses with Epsom salts to encourage its red bracts, and a *Rhododendron yakushimanum*, whose neat, dome-shaped silhouette stands out against the smooth lawn. In May this delightful species is weighed down with trusses of bell-shaped flowers, delicate apple-blossom pink fading to white against the glossy dark green foliage and the silvery new growth.

Well-furnished beds curve round the corners of the lawn behind, with shrubs in variety banked against the trellis. On the left, by a clump of soft red alstroemerias, *Rosa* 'Aloha' is trained up a timber pillar, with the shell-pink flowers of *Clematis* 'Hagley Hybrid' twining among its fragrant pink blooms. This, together with the semi-herbaceous Texensis clematis 'Etoile Rose' which drapes its exquisite nodd-

Two long, straight borders run on either side of the path, packed with shrubs and herbaceous plants. On the right, the bed is punctuated by a wooden pillar with *Rosa* 'Aloha' growing up it, while mounds of low-growing plants edge the bed and spill over the path.

PRIVATE GARDENS OF LONDON

ing pink flowers over the branches and apricot-pink blooms of *Rosa* 'Compassion', is a clue to one of Lady Barbirolli's favourite plants. From the beginning of her gardening life she has been a devotee of clematis, and they sprinkle the garden in some number: *Clematis florida* 'Sieboldii' has white flowers with striking violet-purple stamens, rather like a passion flower, in June and July and is particularly beautiful; and the 'Hagley Hybrid' growing up *R.* 'Compassion' is one of no fewer than seven in the garden. The evergreen *Sollya heterophylla* has blue flowers in summer.

Roses are another feature of the garden. The trellis is clothed with crimson-purple 'Veilchenblau' and apricot 'Gloire de Dijon', and 'Schoolgirl', 'Magenta' and 'Buff Beauty' are among the many that bloom in the borders. 'Queen Elizabeth' stands next to a tall *Fatsia japonica* and a *Cornus controversa* 'Variegata'. A graceful bamboo arches over the lawn, echoed by another to the right, and between them, silhouetted against ferns, conifers and pyracantha, Don Quixote comes cantering out of the shrubbery. As well as being entertaining, this sculpture by Gerald Konstam plays an important role as a compositional device, drawing the eye off-centre and so increasing the garden's sense of depth.

Two long, straight borders edge the path that runs down the left-hand side of the garden, packed with shrubs and herbaceous plants and punctuated with roses on pillars, with mounds of low-growing plants edging the beds and spilling on to the path. Climbers are encouraged up the trellis-topped wall, which offers seclusion and protection from wind. A tall cotoneaster makes a buttress at the end of

AN interesting view of the cinnamon-brown trunk and delicate feathery lime-green foliage of *Metasequoia glyptostroboides*, or dawn redwood. One of the most attractive of conifers, it is deciduous and in autumn its foliage colours from gradations of brown to pinky yellow.

the first trellis, and a little further on a second, smaller trellis is marked by *Lavatera thuringiaca* 'Barnsley' and *Ceanothus* × *delileanus* 'Gloire de Versailles'. On the other side of the path is a round bed filled with Hybrid Tea roses surrounding a sundial.

A herb and vegetable patch fills the garden's bottom left-hand corner, dominated in summer by a magnificent lovage and the feathery plumes of bronze fennel, and from here a woodland path leads under the boundary wall. In this shady corner, under the canopy of the trees, clumps and drifts of violets, hellebores, ferns, snowdrops and other spring bulbs spread under an inviting rustic seat. A tunnel of green brings you back to the house down the other side of the garden, behind the metasequoia and Don Quixote, without breaking the quiet woodland mood. Complementing the rural feel is a bed filled with simple cottage-garden plants – campanulas, geraniums and roses – in shades of mauve and pink.

Lady Barbirolli describes herself as 'an awful tyro'; her garden, however, suggests otherwise. This garden has given her the opportunity to practise the skills and knowledge which she acquired so assiduously and in such a short time; and in return she has lavished on it all the time and care that a busy schedule allows. As she has gradually filled out the design that she was fortunate enough to inherit, she has been able to indulge her love for certain species and for colour and scent. In its choice of plants, its interesting compositions and its variety of moods, carefully encouraged and preserved, this garden is a living demonstration of the education of a late-flowering but dedicated gardener.

A COTONEASTER laden with red berries droops from the trellis over the silvery *Lotus hirsutus*, its silvery rounded leaves contrasting with a *Nandina domestica* and the evergreen *Choisya ternata*.

CHELSEA PHYSIC GARDEN

Chelsea Physic Garden, founded in 1676 and maintained in the succeeding centuries for the 'manifestation of the glory, power and wisdom of God, in the works of creation', is still a working garden, faithful to its strong tradition of medicinal teaching and research. It is also a botanical garden, engaged in the mutual exchange of plants and seeds with other botanical gardens all over the world since its foundation, and the first home in Britain for many of the plants brought back from overseas by the great plant collectors of the seventeenth, eighteenth and nineteenth centuries. Laid out in its original rows of narrow rectangular beds, with medicinal plants at the northern end and large areas of systematic order beds demonstrating the botanical relationships of plants, it is like a visual encyclopedia of the plant kingdom.

It was in 1621, in the same decade that saw John Tradescant the Elder starting his famous garden in Lambeth, that the first physic garden in Britain for the study of medicinal plants was founded at Oxford. Physicians and apothecaries depended almost entirely on plants for their medicines, and as the new science of botany developed and herbalism became more systematic, so physic gardens were established as centres of learning for practitioners of medicine, who were taught how to recognize and use the different plants.

Medieval habits of mind, which imbued everything in God's creation, down to the tiniest insect or flower, with a higher symbolic meaning and a specific purpose, tended to persist in the belief that if God had made all the plants then he must have done so for a reason, which only diligent study would reveal. But the spirit of enquiry that was to illuminate so many fields of knowledge during the Renaissance was no longer content to accept unquestioningly a body of knowledge derived from the herbalists of the ancient world, nor was it any longer convinced by later herbalists such as Paracelsus, whose remedies seemed to be based on a sort of eccentric anthropomorphism: hairy roots would cure baldness, for instance, and walnuts, being brain-shaped, were prescribed for headaches. The foundations of knowledge were shifting from mysticism to empiricism.

So it was that in 1673 the Worshipful Society of Apothecaries of London leased three and a half acres of land by the river at Chelsea in order to found a physic garden. The river was then the only means of access to what was then a fishing village, which already contained the gardens and orchards of great houses, including

To botanists this garden is a living encyclopedia of plant families, and their geographical location. Here can be seen large borders of South American plants with an *Araucaria araucana* the Chile pine or monkey puzzle, emerging through a variety of shrubs.

THE research and teaching areas of the garden contain collections of grasses, primulas, ericaceous plants, hypericums and native plants, together with collections of plants from California, Australasia and South America.

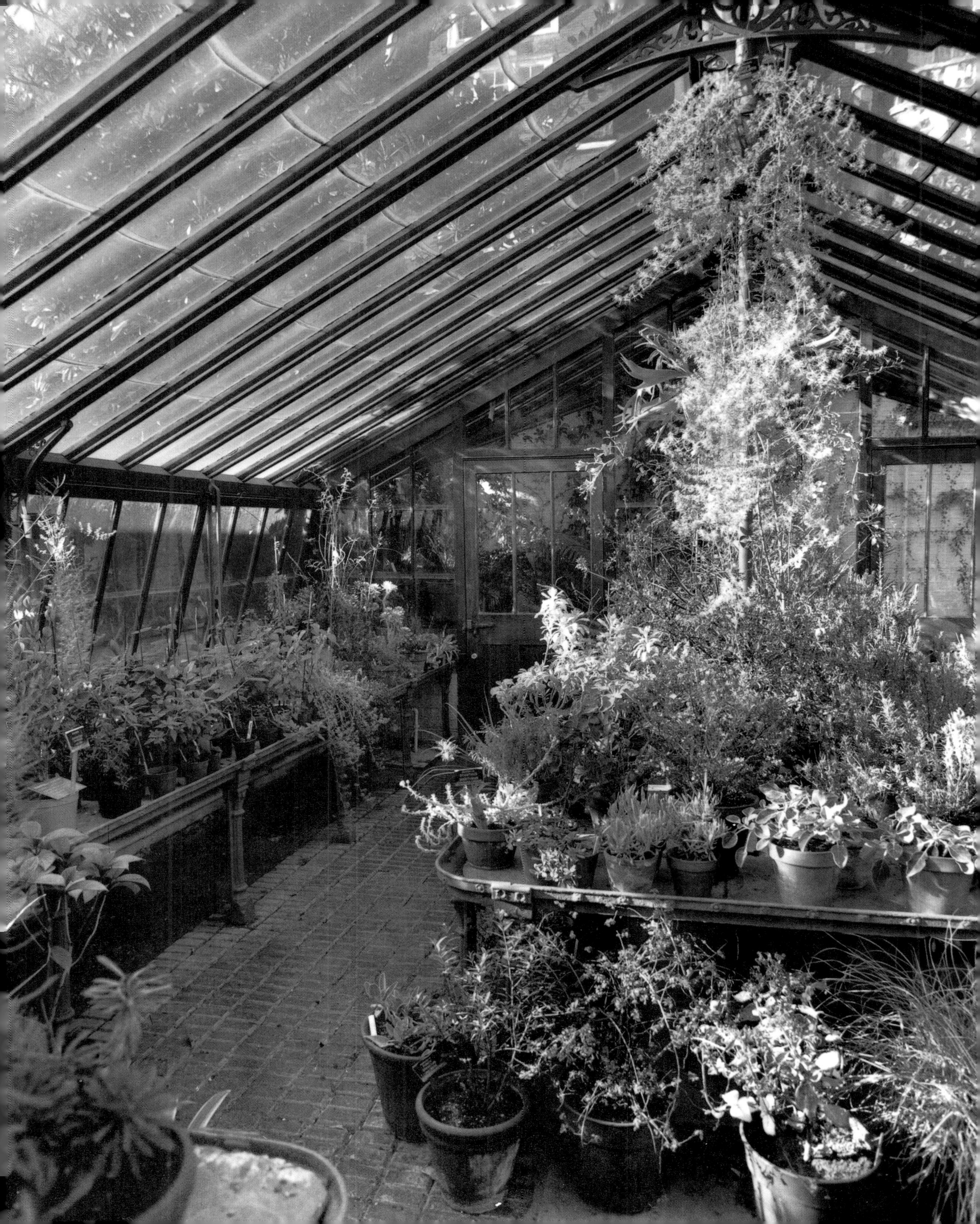

PRIVATE GARDENS OF LONDON

ONE of the most beautiful of all flowering climbers, *Lapageria rosea* has dark evergreen leathery leaves. The hanging bell-shaped flowers are pale pink, nearly white and truly spectacular. It will thrive on a very sheltered outside wall, but if in doubt it will make an excellent conservatory plant.

the mansion of Sir Thomas More. The south-facing, free-draining site was then surrounded by more or less open country; now it is a green oasis in a sea of bricks and mortar. Perhaps surprisingly, the surrounding buildings have proved of benefit to the gardens, for they insulate it from the worst of the cold and protect it from wind, thus providing a warm micro-climate in which some rare and tender plants are able to flourish.

The first plants were brought by barge from the Westminster gardens of the Apothecaries' Pastmaster William Gape, and for many years afterwards all the plants continued to arrive by river. Until the Thames was embanked in 1874 the garden stretched down to the water, where there was a natural basin for water-loving plants, and steps led down to a gate and landing stage. The Apothecaries' livery barge was kept in a boat house here, and flanking the river gate were four cedars of Lebanon planted by John Watts, the first Gardener, in 1683. These were among the earliest cedars to be planted in Britain and were the first to bear cones; the last one survived until 1904, when it was reputedly killed off by smog.

In 1684 John Evelyn visited the garden and was much struck by 'the subterraneous heate conveyed by a stove under the conservatory all vaulted with brick so as he [the Gardener] leaves the doores and windowes open in the hardest frosts, secluding only the snow'. Within fifty years, thanks to the energy and flair of Philip Miller, Gardener from 1722 to 1771, this had been supplemented by 'a Frame for sheltering such Exotic Plants as only require to be protected from hard Frost', and 'a large Bark Stove where the tender Exotic Plants of the hot Countries are kept plung'd into Beds of Tanner's Bark'. Such bark hot-beds were the latest thing, and had only recently been used to raise the gardener's equivalent of apothecaries' gold: the pineapple. The beds were made by laying quantities of tanner's bark over a layer of hot dung contained in a brick pit, and if laid in February were supposed to stay warm until October.

It was typical of Miller's progressive approach that he should have thought to introduce such a useful novelty. Miller it was who established the garden's reputation worldwide, engaging in correspondence with all the leading botanists of the day, many of whom sent him plants and seeds which had never before been cultivated in Britain, and writing works of importance, including a *Gardeners' Dictionary* which remained a standard work of reference for generations of gardeners.

The person responsible for Miller's appointment was Sir Hans Sloane, the great scholar and benefactor who had himself been a collector of plants in his youth, and who by virtue of marrying a rich wife was able to bestow on the physic garden its second great stroke of good fortune. In 1712 Sloane bought the manor of Chelsea from Lord Cheyne, and with it the freehold of the garden. Ten years later he presented the freehold to the Apothecaries' Company, on condition that they should give two thousand plant specimens to the Royal Society for the purposes of research, at the rate of fifty a year.

SOME fine trees punctuate the rectangular beds and straight avenues. A magnificent *Koelreuteria paniculata* brought from China bears large panicles of small yellow flowers in July and August.

A copy of the famous statue of Sloane by Rysbrack (the original is now in the British Museum) stands at the focal point of the garden, where the main avenues intersect. Beside it is the earliest rockery in Europe, built with some forty tons of stones from the old Tower of London and basaltic lava brought back from Iceland by Sir Joseph Banks in 1772. Now a listed building, it surrounds a pretty pond planted with aquatic plants. Some fine trees punctuate the rectangular beds and straight avenues: an olive (*Olea europaea*) is the largest growing outside in Britain and fruits almost every year, and a magnificent *Koelreuteria paniculata* brought from China bears large panicles of small yellow flowers in July and August. The research and teaching area contains beds of herbs, medicinal plants, culinary plants and dye plants, as well as the national cistus collection, part of the garden's work for national and international plant conservation schemes.

The present Curator, Duncan Donald, is the latest in a long line of distinguished gardeners and botanists associated with the physic garden: as well as Philip Miller and Sir Joseph Banks there have also been William Forsyth (of forsythia fame), William Curtis, William Hudson and Robert Fortune, who now have beds named in their honour and filled with plants associated with them. There is also a cool fernery, a woodland garden and a water garden, together with collections of grasses, primulas, hypericums, ericaceous plants, native plants, and plants from California, Australasia and South America. Along the Embankment is a wilder area of flowering shrubs and rare peonies. In this protected environment lichens, insects and birds that are rare in London have all been spotted, and recently a pair of long-tailed tits has successfully bred here.

Meanwhile the garden's education and research work, begun over three hundred years ago, continues unabated. It has its own research programmes – the taxonomy of early daffodils, frost tolerance, and the history of plant introductions into Great Britain – and it also serves colleges and schools. For King's College it grows feverfew, the subject of research into migraine treatments; for the British Museum (Natural History) it grows species of pelargonium for taxonomic research; and for Imperial College it grows crop grasses for research into fungal diseases.

This garden is many things to many people: to botanists it is a living encyclopedia of plant families; to academics and research institutions it is an irreplaceable resource; to schools it is a fascinating key to the world of the natural sciences. And as well as all this it is a place of beauty, a haven for wildlife and, once or twice a week in recent summers, a restful spot for Londoners to walk and sit, away from the noise and fumes of the city, under the spreading canopies of centuries-old trees.

PART of the garden is still laid out in its original rows of narrow rectangular beds, with medicinal plants at the northern end and a large area of systematic order beds demonstrating the botanical relationships of plants. In the foreground is a salvia, one of a large collection.

A PAINTER'S GARDEN

'Ancient' is the word Lady Dufferin uses to describe her Holland Park garden, although it is not especially old, and the house does not go back more than a century. Yet there does seem to be a patina of age to this garden, but not because of any element of pastiche or of spurious historicism; it seems rather to stem from a quality of timelessness. There is also a curious intensity here: colours are saturated, the air hangs still, and even the seasons change with unusual emphasis. Fanciful as it may seem, one of the most striking things about this garden is its atmosphere.

Lindy Dufferin designed the garden with a painter's understanding of colour and form, and it is simple and classical. Mature broad-leaved trees – planes, beeches and a wych elm – form a backdrop, and the view from the upper windows of the house is of Holland Park's great expanse of woodland. These woods are the remains of the 'wildernesse' which once formed part of the grounds of the Holland family's Jacobean mansion that stood here, and they are one of London's great wildlife havens. Garden and woodland birds abound, and birds that are rarely seen in London – flycatchers, blackcaps, nuthatches, long-tailed tits, gold-crests and tawny owls – can sometimes be spotted among the trees and undergrowth. The park also has a collection of exotic birds, including cranes and peacocks, and the cry of the peacocks carries into Lady Dufferin's garden, adding to the rural feel.

The garden is reached from the first floor of the house by a spacious verandah, which affords a good view of its attractive proportions, much squarer than the average long, thin London garden. The space is divided horizontally by a beech hedge which changes colour with the seasons: deepening shades of green in spring and summer, and rich amber throughout autumn and winter. The front part of the garden was designed as an outdoor drawing room, a space for entertaining and for summer parties, when tables and rugs are laid out on the lawn and the food is spread under an old pear tree to the right. The back part of the garden is the wilderness, wilder and more secluded, and shaded by tall plane trees and a thirty-foot brick wall and trellis clothed with ivy. Two herms, with rippling torsoes, mossy beards and Bacchic horns, bought by Lord and Lady Dufferin in Venice on their honeymoon in the sixties, flank the gap in the hedge that leads to the wilderness.

A wrought-iron spiral staircase leads down from the verandah to a York stone terrace dotted with mossy pots planted with single-

IN this corner of the terrace hidden behind a large philadelphus and a chamaecyparis is a small greenhouse. A luxury not to be foregone if at all possible, as it is agreeable to be able to grow plants for the house when there is little to pick in the garden and interesting to be able to grow ones own plants from cuttings or from seed collected in the wild or from friends.

THE beautiful self-clinging *Parthenocissus henryana* with its dark green leaves with silvery-white variegation smothers the handle of a lawn-mower placed at the foot of the house wall and also enlaces a pretty reeded vase in a niche in the wall.

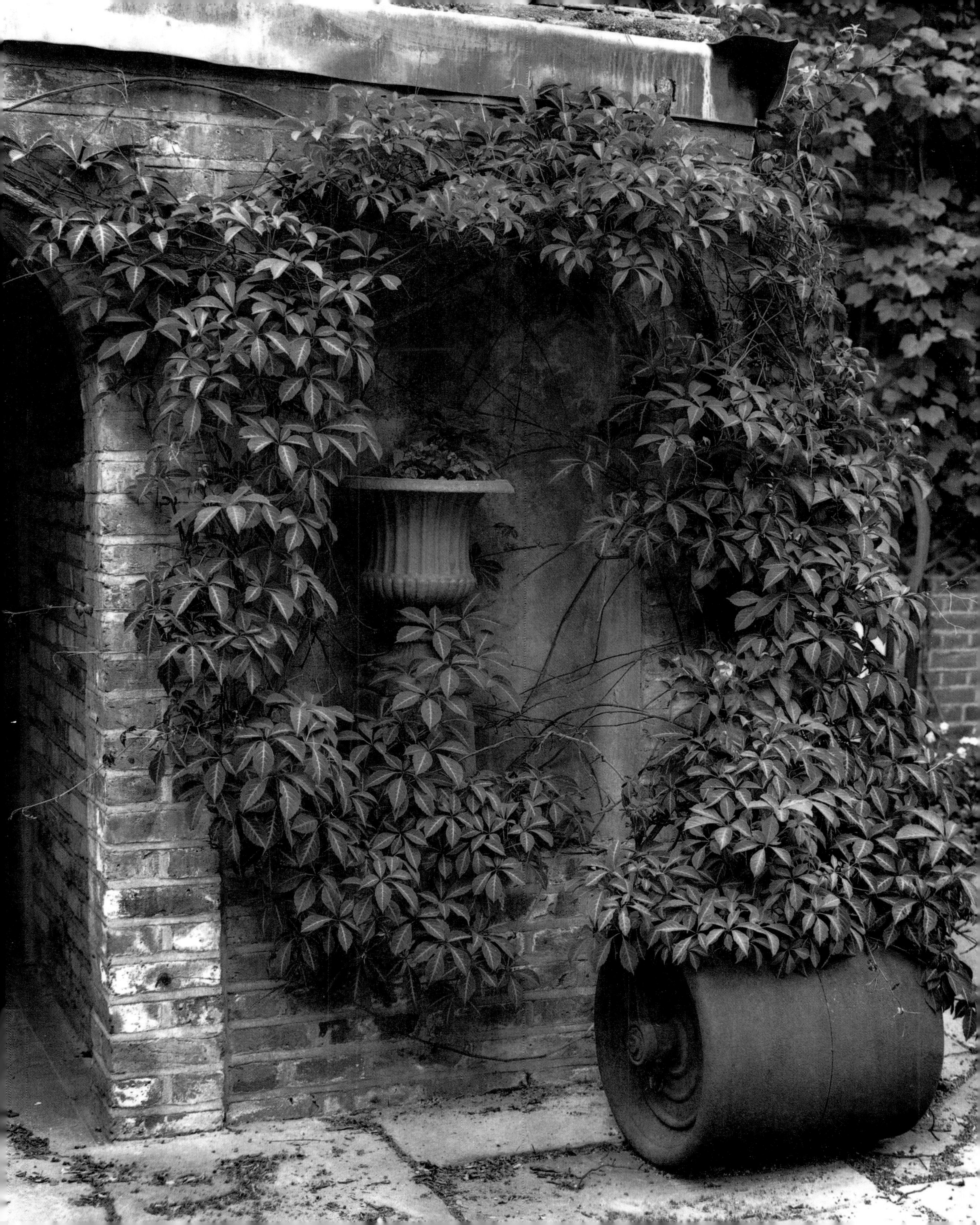

THE beech hedge cuts across the whole width of the garden, dividing the shady, secluded woodland garden at the back from the sunnier, more open flower garden at the front. Here, deep herbaceous borders are filled with a mixture of sophisticated and simple cottage-garden varieties.

flowering camellias, including clear pink *C. × williamsii* 'Mary Christian', white *C. japonica* 'Devonia' and *C.j.* 'Sylvia', carmine-red flecked with white, and some bulbs brought back in a suitcase from an Indian hill station. In one corner of the terrace is a simple greenhouse, soon to be superseded by a copy of an Edwardian conservatory attached to a neighbouring house and about to be demolished. Lindy Dufferin had hoped to be able to dismantle it and re-erect it, but this did not prove feasible; so instead she intends to build a replica in the wilderness. Up the house wall are trained a *Parthenocissus henryana*, rising three storeys, *Rosa* 'Apple Dawn', a pyracantha and a *Clematis alpina*.

An opening echoing the gap in the beech hedge gives access to the lawn, which is otherwise hemmed in by deep herbaceous borders. The planting is a mixture of sophisticated and simple cottage-garden varieties, many chosen for their scent as well as for their flowers. This is also where Lady Dufferin grows the iris and hellebores that have inspired many of her paintings.

Each of the flanking beds is backed by a high wall draped with green and variegated ivy. On the left-hand wall a *Clematis armandii* grows through the ivy, and the bed is backed by tall delphiniums, tree peonies, roses, foxgloves and *Campanula persicifolia*, among shrubs including choisyas, daphnes, dwarf philadelphus, *Viburnum davidii* and *Hydrangea paniculata* 'Grandiflora'. Towards the house in summer are the pink plumes of *Thalictrum aquilegiifolium*, rising above the silver-grey woolly leaves and white flowers of *Anaphalis triplinervis* and the creamy flower spikes of *Sisyrinchium striatum*. Galtonia and lilies, lavender and cistus and a mass of other old-fashioned plants fill the beds, with low-growing gentians, erysimum, phlomis, pulsatilla, saxifrage and geraniums edging the beds and acting as ground cover.

Towards the beech hedge *Achillea × taygetea*, *Helianthemum* 'Wisley Primrose' and santolina form a group of silvery-grey foliage tones, and beside them *Limonium latifolium* 'Violetta' flowers violet-blue from July to September, followed by lacy seed heads. Decorative seed heads are a particular feature of this garden in autumn and winter, and some of the prettiest belong to some *Stokesia laevis* near by. Above brilliant blue *Anchusa azurea* 'Royal Blue' and violet-blue *Geranium platypetalum* is a standard wisteria trained over French rose-holders so that its racemes cascade over them in early summer, and in some years when the leaves fall in autumn a birds' nest is revealed among the branches.

In the shady bed opposite, underneath the old pear tree, is a luxuriant mass of shade-tolerant plants. Around the base of the trunk is a collection of ferns and acanthus, and, on the wall behind, a marble plaque of classical drapery retreats behind the ivy. Astilbes, Japanese anemones, hemerocallis and herbaceous clematis grow among mahonias, golden philadelphus, *Buddleia davidii* 'Black Night', *Hydrangea aspera villosa* and the early-flowering pink-flushed white *Rhododendron* Cilpinense. At the sunnier end of the border, under the beech hedge, are the aromatic-leaved *Caryopteris × clandonensis*, with bright blue tubular flowers in August and September, *Acer palmatum* 'Osakazuki', which in autumn turns crimson against the amber of the beech hedge, and the dark magenta rose 'Cardinal Hume', underplanted with 'Mrs Sinkins' pinks, phlomis and twenty-year-old violets. Near by is a collection of single large buff-orange oriental poppies.

As you pass the Venetian herms you move into a secluded, shady woodland landscape. Soft green tiers of ivy rise at the back, and from them emerges an eighteenth-century south Indian statue of the elephant god Ganesh. Ivy also clothes the scorched lower trunk of a tall plane tree, around which the dried flower heads of a *Hydrangea petiolaris*, growing happily in very dry conditions, make a lacy petticoat in the autumn. A *Robinia pseudoacacia* 'Frisia' glows luminous pale green, and a glaucous conifer makes a sombre eye-catcher. Underneath the robinia is a fine *Viburnum plicatum* 'Lanarth', its statuesque horizontal branches covered with snow-like flowers in early summer. Among the tall grasses on the other side of the enclosure is a glade of camellias, the tender scented rhododendron 'Lady Alice Fitzwilliam' and the unusual *Sophora tetraptera*, with drooping clusters of yellow pea flowers in May. Underneath them spreads a carpet of *Saxifraga cortusifolia*, with feathery masses of white star-shaped flowers in October and November. Here Lindy Dufferin has planted two small *Quercus ilex* which, to her delight, will be the subject of preservation orders.

The garden is always changing with the seasons and with Lady Dufferin's new ideas – a *Stewartia sinensis*, valuable for its ornamental bark, fragrant flowers and rich autumn colour, is to replace a magnolia that has outgrown itself, and a blood-red *Rosa moyesii* is to supplant a fuchsia near the wisteria – but nothing seems to disturb its tranquillity. Perhaps it is the mixture of cottagey and sophisticated planting that gives this garden its atmosphere, or the counterpoint between the formality of its hedges and statuary and the informality of its borders, or the contrast between the garden visible from the house and the private wilderness, or the proximity of so many mature trees and the wildlife they support. Or perhaps it is all of them, or none; one of the most seductive things about this garden is that it is impossible to tell.

Two Venetian herms, with rippling torsos, mossy beards and bacchic horns, guard the entrance to the secluded shady woodland. The contrast between the soft formality of the beech hedge and the eighteenth-century statues is pleasing and adds to the charm of the garden.

THE ULTIMATE ROOF GARDEN

Anyone walking down Kensington High Street, feeling rather belittled by the large department stores and bewildered by the aggressive noise and weight of traffic, would be forgiven for dismissing as preposterous the notion of a modern Hanging Gardens of Babylon a hundred feet above their head. Yet there they are, six floors up, on the roof of the old Derry and Toms building: a Spanish garden, complete with Moorish pergolas, fountains and palm trees; an Elizabethan herb garden of rosemary, lavender and old-fashioned roses, its ancient stone arches wreathed with wisteria; a Tudor walk of warm old brick, reminiscent of the gardens at Hampton Court Palace; and a wooded grove of mature nut trees, their boughs overhanging a rippling stream where ducks fuss over their ducklings and – the final touch – pink flamingoes step fastidiously in and out of the

THE delicate arcading of the Moorish palace is garlanded romantically with vines and Virginia creeper. Both display their magnificent colours of yellows and all shades of red from late September through to winter time.

A COLONNADE of delicately twisted narrow columns runs along the two sides of the Spanish garden. Wrought-iron balconies follow the line of the arcade to form small viewing areas between each column. A vine is trained to frame the openings and cast dappled shade onto the balcony.

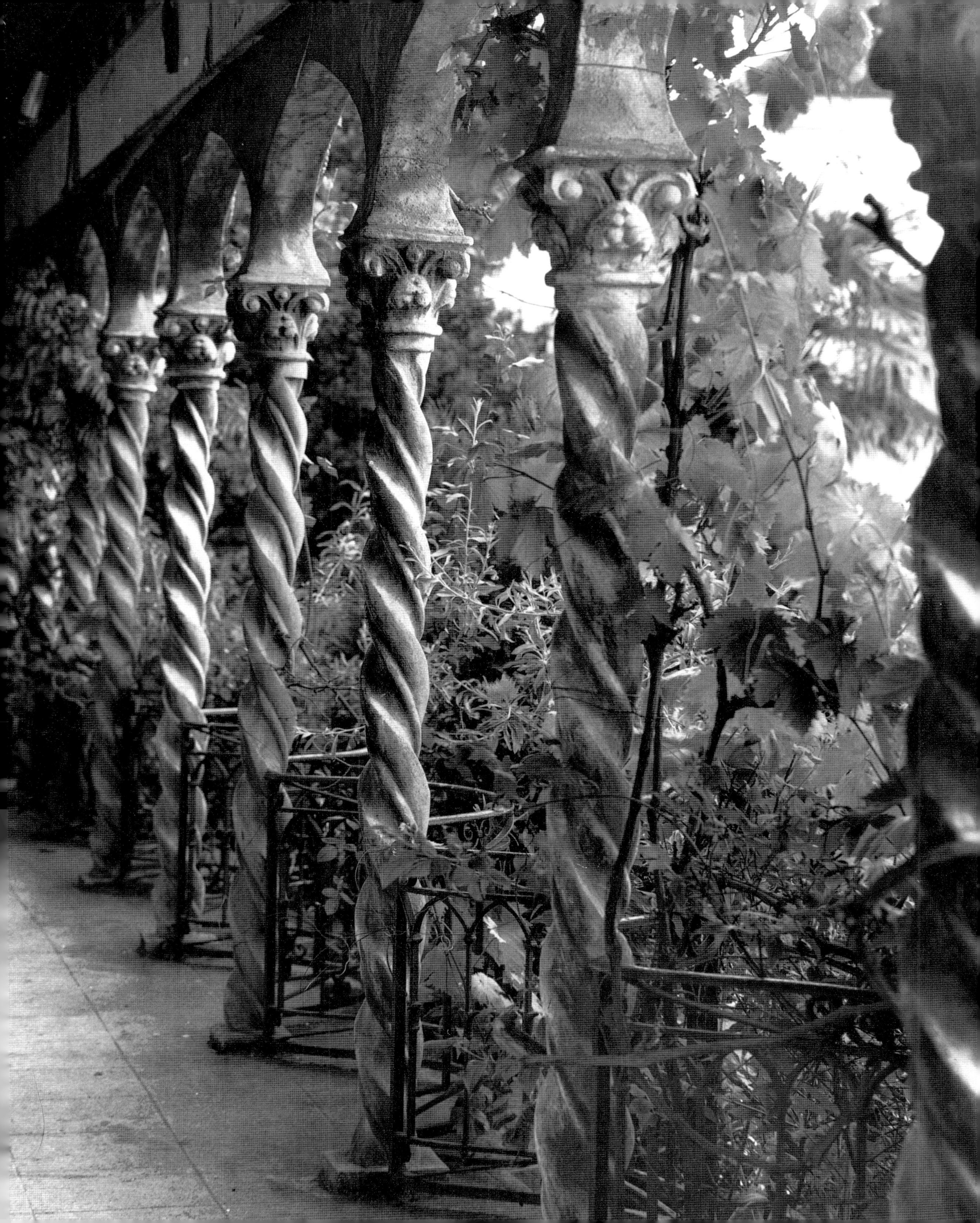

PRIVATE GARDENS OF LONDON

water. Even as you walk through these gardens, able to touch and smell the plants and with *terra firma* (apparently) beneath your feet, an air of unreality obstinately persists, and as you leave to return to the hubbub below it is hard to stifle the suspicion that when you turn your back on this *Alice in Wonderland* world it will simply disappear.

As you step out of the lift that whisks you up to this magical world your gaze is carried down an avenue of palm trees to the Moorish palace at the end of the Spanish garden. Moorish tiles and delicate arcading, garlanded with vines and Virginia creeper, add to the exotic air, while fountains play into the turquoise blue water channels sunk into the velvety lawns. The sound of running water lures you down the Tudor walk to the woodland garden, where a stream meanders peacefully past rocks and rushes under wooden bridges, and wild and exotic birds, mature broad-leaved trees and a tiny brick 'cottage' are reflected in a still pool. A narrow path tempts you towards the herb garden, and suddenly over the parapet you catch a glimpse of the Telecom Tower and the Royal Albert Hall. While traffic roars past below, the silence here is uncanny, broken only by birdsong and the splash of water. On through a brick arch, where the long racemes of wisteria and fronds of vines and roses frame the view, and you are in the herb garden, where a profusion of traditional cottage-garden herbs and flowers tumbles over low brick walls and hedges of dwarf box. Paths of soft red brick laid in a herringbone pattern lead to a central fountain, where you are tempted to pause to absorb the silence and the restful calm, and to ponder on the many remarkable aspects of this extraordinary fantasy.

It was the brainchild of Trevor Bowen, one-time chairman of Barker's, the parent company of Derry and Toms. And curiously it was the rather prosaic combination of fire regulations and the London County Council which was to prove the catalyst. It was in the early 1930s that a new building was erected in Kensington High Street in order to rehouse Derry and Toms next to Barker's. The building, designed by the architect Bernard George, was planned to have seven floors, but the top floor was vetoed by the LCC because the ladders then in use by the London fire brigade would be too short to reach it in the event of a fire. The seventh floor was therefore simply left off, and a roof was laid above the sixth floor, finished with mastic asphalt and laid to falls for drainage.

The structural potential existed for another floor, nevertheless, and Trevor Bowen was reluctant to waste it. Here was an area of two

THE stream that runs through the English woodland garden opens out at one end into a pool, its waters overhung by graceful grasses and a mature weeping willow. Over thirty species of tree flourish in this extraordinary roof garden.

A WOODEN bridge of Chinese design crosses over a brook in the English woodland garden. Here there is a grove of mature nut trees, their boughs overhanging the rippling stream where ducks and flamingoes live.

THE ULTIMATE ROOF GARDEN

acres, in a fine exposed position, on a site which would bear a weight equivalent to another storey of bricks and mortar and a roof. A roof garden was the answer. Having taken three years to build, the gardens opened to an astonished public in 1938.

The landscape architect responsible for designing and building the gardens was Ralph Hancock. Initially the planting included over 500 shrubs and trees, and despite the fact that there are fewer today the impression is still of a well-furnished, fully fledged grand country garden, with different compartments to delight and impress visitors. The practical difficulties of such a garden were obvious – even, it might be thought, overwhelming. But it seems that the whole structure was effected with maximum simplicity and minimum fuss.

The construction of the roof – hollow pots covered with a layer of screed and topped with three-quarters of an inch of mastic asphalt – was not modified, and a garden drainage layer was simply laid on top of it. A layer of house bricks was laid flat with one-inch spaces between the bricks, which were covered with a layer of coarse clinker and blinded with breeze to a total depth of nine inches. A layer of turf two inches thick followed, and finally the topsoil. This silt loam varied in depth from twenty-four to forty inches, and was enriched with generous quantities of peat and farmyard manure. The overall weight adds up to some 184 pounds per square foot, which is sometimes as much as doubled in the deeper areas.

The fall of the roof (about 1:100) was sufficient for good drainage, with the water being channelled through holes in the perimeter walls and into the building's main drainage system. Amazingly the original system still functions perfectly, apart from a few spots of waterlogging where the drainage material has compacted, and has never caused any problems more serious than the need to clear the drains of leaves periodically.

Watering is not too much of a problem either, for unlimited amounts of water (except at times of drought, when voluntary restrictions are observed) are available from Barker's own private borehole beneath the store, an essential factor in this garden where the only other water comes from the skies. A water main runs round the outside of the garden, and watering has always been done by hand, with hosepipes. These are sometimes left for hours on the roots of large trees, and the grass is watered on a daily basis. This is naturally very time-consuming, but because there is a slight risk of water penetration behind the water tanks, where the height of the walls had been raised without added protection, great care is taken over the watering, and the luxury of a sprinkler system has always been resisted.

Considering the exposed nature of the site the planting is remarkably varied, and includes some rare trees and shrubs. The heat that rises from the building seems to warm the soil, so encouraging root growth. The arrangement seems to be of mutual benefit to both building and garden, for the soil also acts as an extra layer of insulation. Because of the unusual warmth palms and vines flourish, and every year the garden experiences an early spring, for up here plants come into leaf and flower some three weeks before their earthbound equivalents. The woodland garden then becomes a breathtaking mass of almond, apple, cherry, crab apple and plum blossom, among the fresh green leaves of the willows and birches planted on the margins of the stream.

Over thirty species of tree flourish here, growing to a height of thirty-three feet and more. Beautiful lime trees border the herb garden; palms, catalpas and figs lend the Spanish garden its exotic air; horse chestnuts and laburnums line the Tudor walk; and as well as its orchard of fruit trees the woodland garden has leafy arbours of poplar, walnut, birch, ash, oak, maple and the full panoply of English deciduous trees. It also has some choice rarities, including several trees of heaven, a ginkgo, a mulberry and even a koelreuteria. The trees seem to enjoy a starred life, for even in the hurricane of October 1987, when London's parks and streets were devastated, not one of them was lost.

The gardens' most difficult period came after

A FORMAL water feature of Moorish design runs the length of this garden, which is complete with Moorish pergolas, fountains and palm trees. A narrow border on the edge of the long pool is planted with annuals according to the season.

the liquidation of Derry and Toms in 1973, when for five years the building was unoccupied and the gardens virtually untended. Now they are in the care of the Virgin group of companies, which uses them not only for company parties but also hires them out for private functions, and which once more employs a full-time gardener for their upkeep. One of the oldest and largest roof gardens in Britain, these gardens have many practical and useful lessons to teach. It is not for their usefulness that we prize them, however, for who would not agree with Abraham Cowley?

'Who, that has reason, and his smell,
Would not 'mong roses and jasmine dwell,
Rather than all his spirits choke,
With exhalations of dirt and smoke,
And all th' uncleanness which does drown
In pestilential clouds a pop'lous town?'

A SMALL GARDEN IN BATTERSEA

Moving house is always traumatic, and it is especially so when it involves leaving a much-loved garden, the fruit of a good deal of hard thought and even more hard labour. Will the new owners look after it? Will they do even the bare minimum necessary to maintain it, let alone cherish it? Will they understand the fragile balance of the garden's structure, the careful thought that has gone into the placing of trees and shrubs? Will they keep in check the stronger plants year after year in order to prevent them from overpowering the subtler, more delicate ones on which you have lavished so much care?

Christopher Masson, formerly assistant to Lanning Roper and trusted with the upkeep of the great designer's London gardens, need have had no such worries when he entrusted his Battersea garden to its new owner, though as a professional garden designer himself he had probably devoted more energy to its creation than do most of us. The terraced Victorian

THE rectangular garden rises towards the back in a series of gentle terraces, with a pool and fountain at the bottom near the house. Densley planted borders flank the path but, largely owing to the confident sense of scale used in both its design and its planting, there is no sense of overcrowding or clutter.

POTS of lilium cluster on the terrace and fill the air with their delicious smell. Their pale yellow and white colours brighten the shady terrace which is covered with a vitis, a solanum and a beautiful burgundy-red clematis.

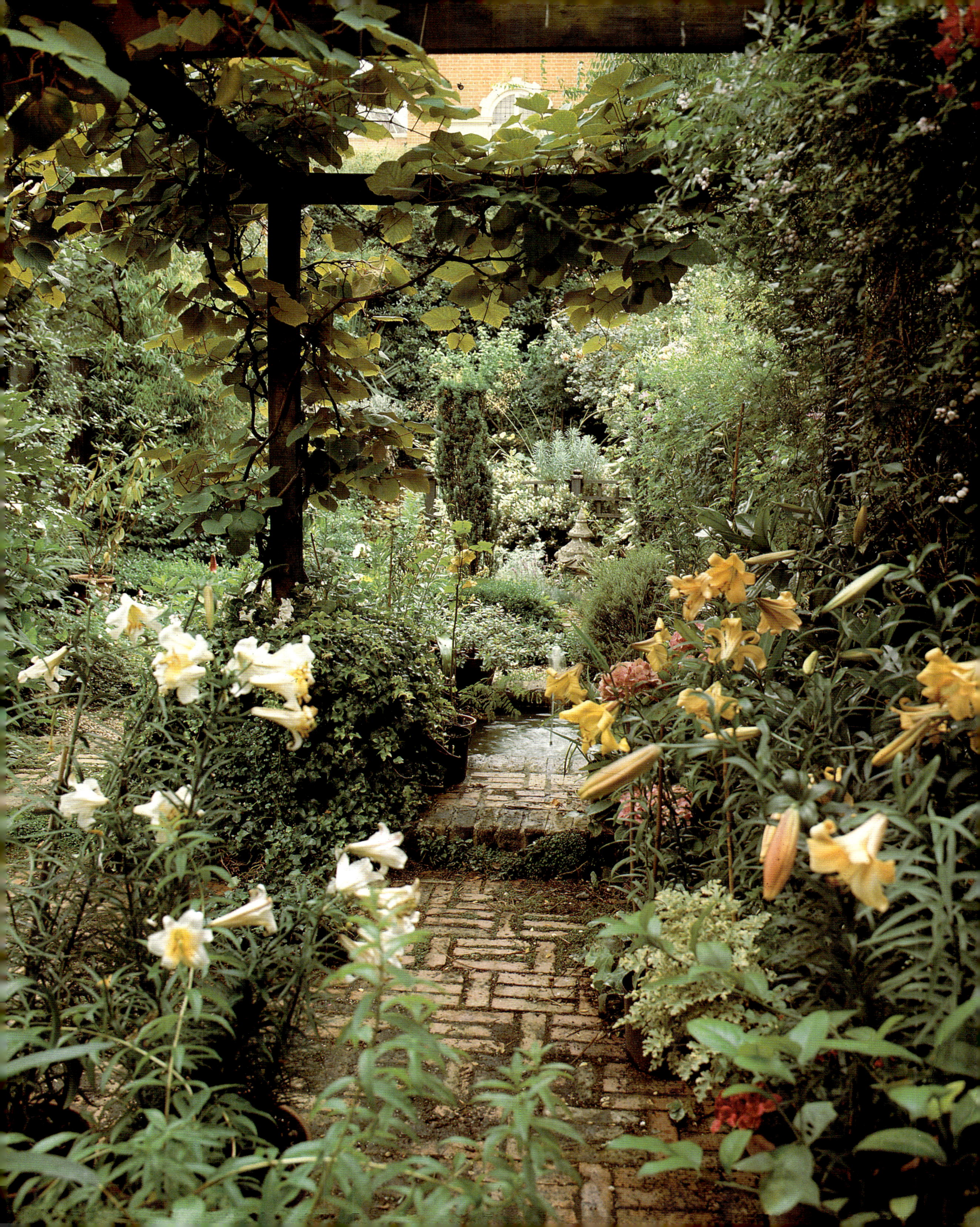

PRIVATE GARDENS OF LONDON

house stands on the edge of the Shaftesbury Park estate, a philanthropic venture by the Artisans, Labourers and General Dwellings Company to provide decent housing for local workers. The houses were built in the 1870s on the site of the market gardens (famous for their watercress) which used to cover most of the area, and each was provided with its own garden, varying in size from small to tiny.

Already a passionate gardener, the new owner of this delightful little garden has also gradually become an extremely knowledgeable one. While carefully guarding its spirit, she has also introduced many new additions (including a greenhouse) which make it even more of a pleasure to look at and walk in. At the same time she carefully weeded out and replaced its few failures, including an aloe which, unhappy in the wet English climate, 'had become a large patch of misery with its rotten leaves, and the smell from them was so bad that it had to be removed'. Rectangular in shape, the garden slopes up towards the back, and also away to one side (the gardens below always benefit from any watering done here). Within this small space Mr Masson created a design of some intricacy, based on a series of gentle terraces, with a pool and fountain at the bottom near the house. Although a great deal has been fitted into a modest area, there is no sense of clutter or fussiness, thanks largely to an unerring sense of scale.

The doctrine of the survival of the fittest has no place here. Every shrub, however small or apparently insignificant, is carefully nurtured for the part that it plays in the glory of the whole. Moreover at every time of year there is something special to admire. In the winter months the small conservatory built against the south side of the house fills with colour and scent. On the floor stand big terracotta pots which can be brought into the house, one of which holds a *Rhododendron lindleyi* with huge, scented white flowers, while *Pandorea jasminoides* clambers up the wall. On the shelves masses of pots are filled with exotic plants waiting their turn to be noticed. One of the most remarkable things about this unusual and beautiful collection of plants is that nearly all of them have been grown – with great enthusiasm and success – from seed. The rampant *Passiflora antioquiensis*, with bright pink helicopter-

AT the far end of the garden is a high, informal hedge of ceanothus, escallonia, laurel and pyracantha. At its foot, and acting as an eye-catcher from the house, is a tall yucca, which flowered for the first time in 1989. Ivy covers the ground beneath it, curling up around some weathered decorative stonework.

shaped flowers, smothers the glass roof, while underneath cymbidiums, *Osbeckia stellata* with its four-petalled mauve flowers and eucalyptus jostle for position. A furry-leaved *Asarina erubescens*, which if grown in a greenhouse and treated with care will bear its trumpet-shaped pink flowers almost continuously, also stands here. But it is when the tuberoses (*Polianthes tuberosa*) bear their spikes of pure white flowers that the house and greenhouse are filled with the most intoxicating of scents.

The kitchen, filled with pots from the greenhouse and terrace in winter, seems like an extension of the garden, which it overlooks from a huge window taking up the whole of one wall. The mossy brick terrace is shaded by a wooden pergola, up which twine a *Solanum jasminoides* and a *Vitis coignetiae*. The large, heart-shaped leaves of the vine, which turn glorious rich shades of gold, crimson and bronze in autumn, contrast beautifully with the small and glossy evergreen leaves of the solanum. They both frame the garden and, because of their unusually large scale, lend it added depth when viewed from the house.

On the terrace beneath stand innumerable pots which fill every available corner. In June and July their numbers are swelled yet further by rank upon rank of magnificent lilies – including *L. regale*, Pink Perfection, the late *L. speciosum* and the beautiful deep yellow African Queen – over which you must climb to reach the garden. Together they make a prospect of breathtaking opulence, while filling the air with their deliciously overpowering perfume. Other pots hold plumbago, scented geraniums, abutilons with masses of pure yellow bell-shaped flowers and the architectural, pineapple-flowered *Eucomis bicolor*.

To the right of the pergola is a *Robinia pseudoacacia*, and to the left a *Fatsia japonica* and

THE view out from the kitchen is framed by the large leaves of a *Vitis coignetiae* trained up a pergola. The effect of these large leaves in the foreground is to heighten the garden's perspective and to lend it added length. They also turn wonderful colours in autumn.

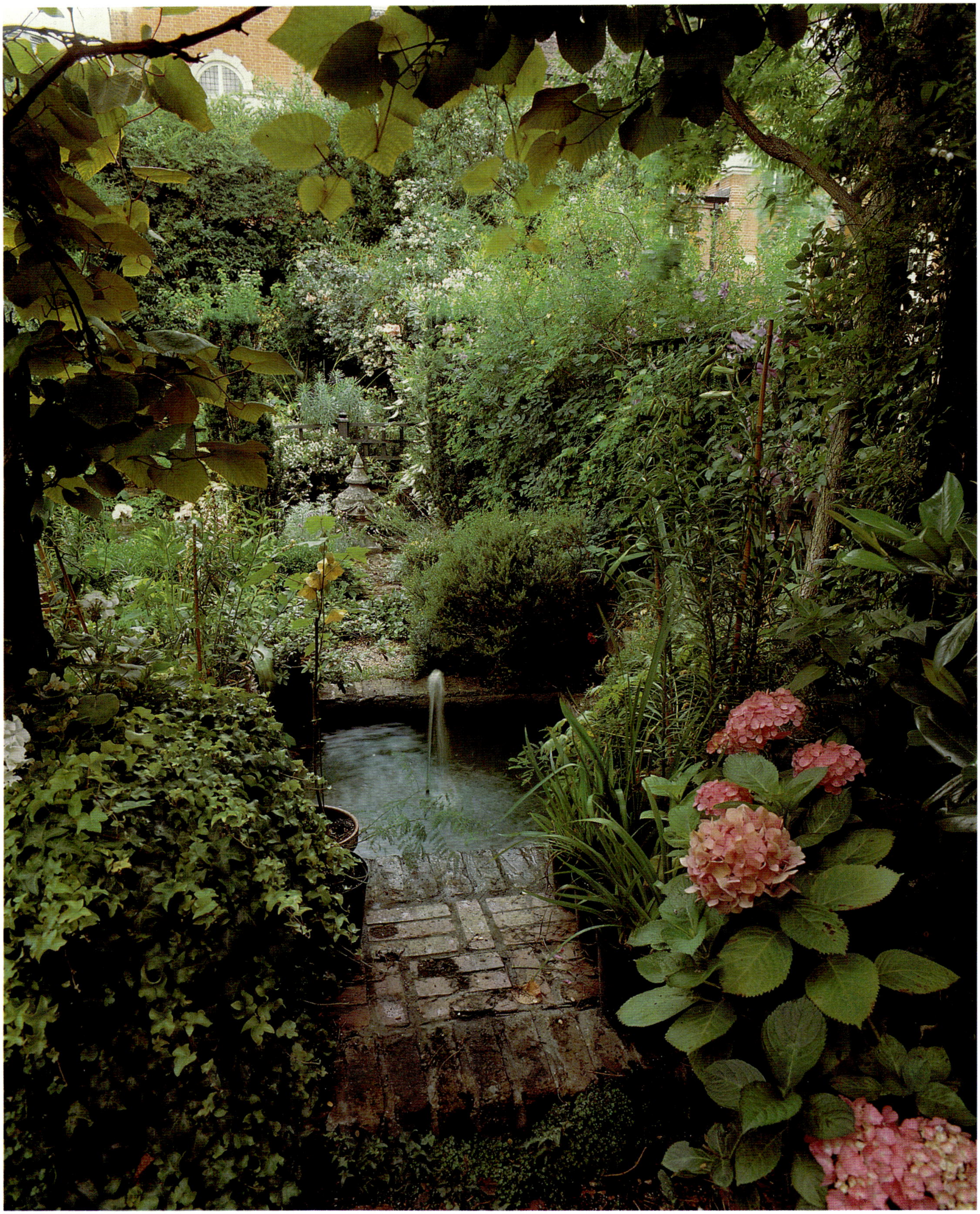

the compact, dome-shaped mound of a *Rhododendron* 'Grumpy', a hybrid of *R. yakushimanum* which in the wild is only found on the inhospitable mountain peaks of the Japanese island of Yakushima. Beyond the terrace a narrow, stepped brick path rises up the gentle slope to the end of the garden, with shrubs and densely planted raised borders to either side.

At the far end there rises a high, informal hedge of *Ceanothus arboreus* 'Trewithen Blue', a small-leaved variety with vivid indigo blue flowers, escallonia, pyracantha and *Laurus nobilis*. Framing the garden to either side are large pink- and white-flowering camellias and roses, including 'Ballerina', delicate as apple blossom, and the pale pink cabbage rose 'De Meaux'. Rambling through the other shrubs are *R.* 'Compassion', which bears large double salmon-pink blooms throughout the summer, and the beautiful Bourbon 'Mme Isaac Pereire', whose deep pink blooms are perhaps the most fragrant of all roses. Philadelphus and euphorbias spill over the path, underplanted with clumps of candytuft (*Iberis sempervirens*), lavenders, the tender *Erigeron karvinskianus*, *Anthemis cupaniana* with grey, aromatic leaves, and many different ivies. In spring miniature daffodils such as Hawera and Thalia, crocus and fritillaries poke through the ivy ground cover. Throughout spring and summer the clematis that scramble through the shrubs in the garden, including 'Kermesina', 'Perle d'Azur', 'Comtesse de Bouchaud' flower in shades of red, blue, and pink. In late summer the beautiful papery blooms of *Hibiscus syriacus* add a more restrained note of pure white, acting as an eye-catcher from the kitchen window. And at the far end of the garden towers a yucca, flowering for the first time in 1989.

The designer has managed to introduce so many ideas into a small space that you can walk through it, admiring plants to left and right, as though it were a much larger garden. Steps and shrubs divide it horizontally into a series of small compartments, each crammed with plants, while the different levels create an illusion of greater depth and space. With some ingenuity the present owner has added further interest by prolonging the flowering season and bringing the garden into the house. She has planted a *Lippia citriodora* and *Grevillea rosmarinifolia*, both of which are slightly half-hardy shrubs and bear out her belief that in London you can grow virtually anything, for the soil is generally suitable and in certain sheltered gardens the microclimate is such that very tender plants can be grown with great success. This little garden must be especially fortunate, not only in its microclimate but also in its owners; for despite its deceptively casual air it is a pleasure at every time of year, a testament to the imagination and care with which it has been both planned and maintained.

THE little pool and fountain add another aspect to this garden which, though small, is impossible to take in in one glance. On the contrary, as you walk round it you have the impression of visiting a much larger garden.

THE small conservatory built on the side of the house is not only filled with scent and colour in the winter months, but also in the summer, when pots of lilies, clematis, hydrangeas and fuchsias are brought within its cooler and shadier atmosphere.

A SECRET GARDEN

An unremarkable row of terraced houses on a busy road near Victoria Station displays to the world a series of doors and windows which on the surface are of no immediate interest. If you looked harder, however, you would realize that one of these doors is in fact a gate leading to a dark passage. And if you ventured through you would, like Alice, find yourself in a different world. The road is transformed into a narrow country lane, lined with cottage gardens surrounding small detached white stucco houses. Tall trees fill the skyline, blotting out any last vestiges of the surrounding city. After negotiating a twist in the path and a picket gate engulfed by vegetation you come upon John Codrington's extraordinary property.

Now in his nineties, John Codrington is the grand old man of British garden design. Yet he was a debutante in the field at an age when most people are planning their retirement. Over the past twenty years he has designed gardens all over the world, in Greece, India, Madagascar and Ethiopia – and of course England, where

ONLY a few splashes of colour stand out against the huge variety of foliage in John Codrington's London garden. Here a blood-red camellia overhangs a delicate bamboo, while an equally vivid rose clambers at will up the house wall and a neighbouring tree stump.

A NARROW path through a jungle of greenery leads to this secret garden, where plants are encouraged to grow freely, and nothing is trimmed or pruned. Plants are composed in such a way as to show off their natural shapes to best advantage.

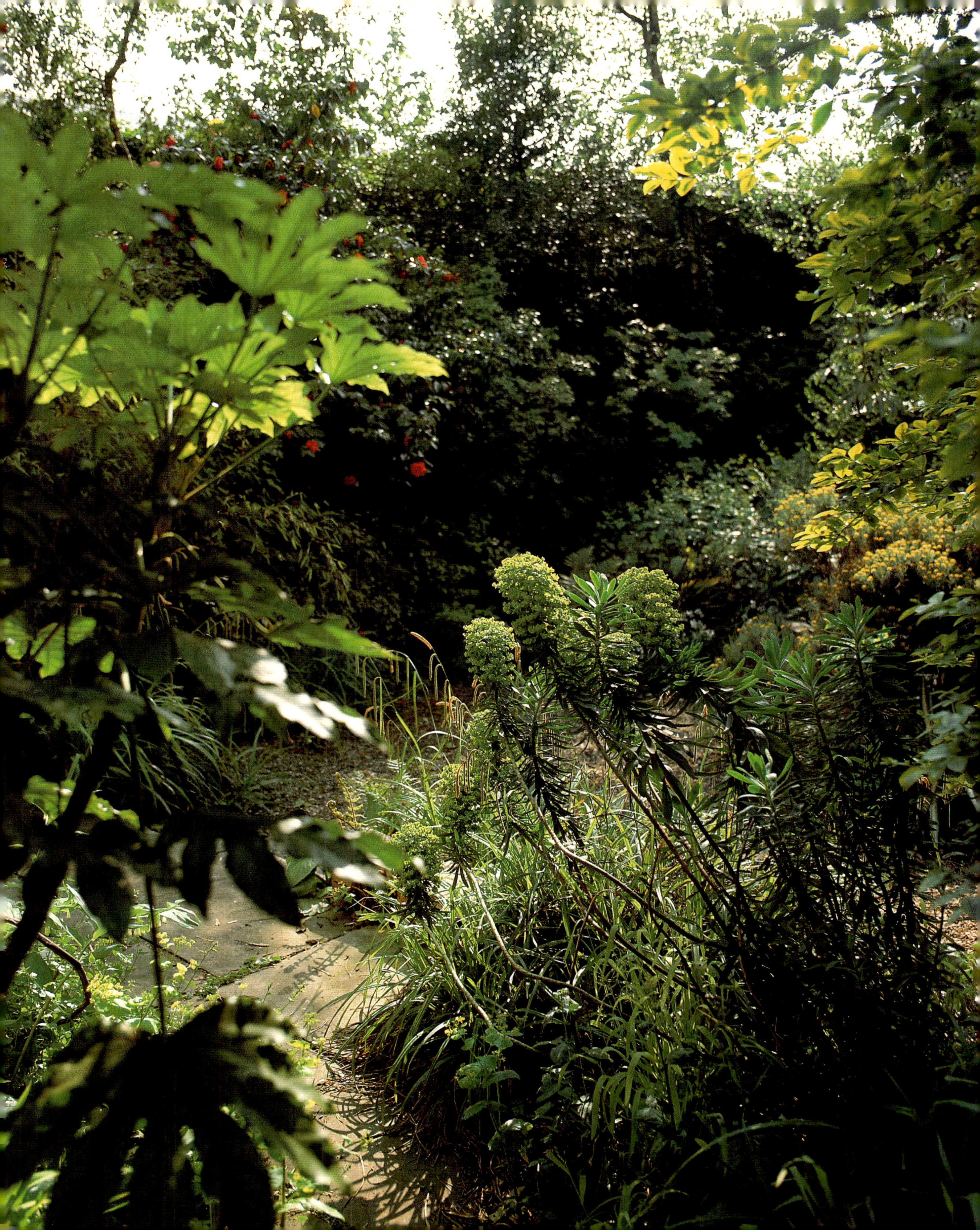

A JUNGLE of greenery surrounds the white stucco house: weeds and self-seeded plants are as welcome here as carefully nurtured rarities, if they contribute to the garden's extraordinary variety of leaf colour and shape.

most of his work is nowadays. Travel was not new to him, for as a professional army officer for some twenty years he had voyaged widely. His mementoes – shells, books (including an early edition of the Arabian Nights bought in Baghdad), furniture, hangings and more – fill his house, and into trunks and plan chests are crammed hundreds of watercolours. Mostly of landscapes and buildings, they are all his own work, dating to the early years of this century.

John Codrington is an accomplished artist who seems never to have travelled without his sketchbook; in his new career he put this skill to good use, offering his clients 'before and after' impressions of the gardens he is commissioned to improve. His magpie collecting instinct and his talent as an amateur botanist have led over the years to a collection of plants, seeds and bulbs brought back from far-flung places, which now grow in his country garden in Rutland as well as in his London garden.

Always observing with care the natural conditions in which plants thrive, he tries to provide a similar environment in his gardens; it is a simple formula but a successful one, for his plants flourish. Among other plants with interesting pedigrees, his country garden contains a forty-foot cypress which is the offspring of a seed brought back many years ago from the garden of Gethsemane in Jerusalem.

His gardens betray not only this natural sympathy with plants but also his artist's eye. They are composed rather than designed, for their merry profusion could not be more different from the structured formality preferred by some designers. His London garden is a jungle, with contrasting foliage and only a few splashes of colour to stand out against the tapestry of different greens. Behind a dainty bamboo, a blood-red camellia with polished dark leaves reaches up to meet a red climbing

The small raised brick pool is framed by clouds of *Allium triquetum*, lamium and wild cranesbill. The small misshapen stone set in the centre of the rim was once part of the medieval walls of Bermondsey Abbey.

rose, which grows unrestrained up the house and the ivy-clad trunk of an old tree. Below it is a collection of plants, ferns and grasses with leaves of different textures, shapes and tones of green.

A raised brick pool fed by water dripping from the rim of a mossy stone shell is the central feature of the garden. Set into the rim is an irregularly shaped stone with a history: during the Blitz John Codrington was walking through the shattered streets of Bermondsey when he came across some stones that were evidently medieval in origin. He concluded that a bomb must have unearthed them from the ancient foundation of Bermondsey Abbey, and resolved to give one of them a good home in the setting he felt it deserved. It has clearly delighted him ever since. The gravel beneath the pool plays host to *Allium triquetum*, lamium and wild cranesbill, while variegated and plain ivies spill over the steps and retaining wall, with euphorbias, fatsias and polygonums.

In John Codrington's philosophy plants are allowed to grow freely, and to create natural effects. Nothing is disciplined, pruned or contrived. He takes as much pleasure in plants which others might dismiss as weeds as he does in rarities: weeds and self-seeded plants are all welcome. Architectural shapes and compositions are achieved through careful positioning and observation of the plants' natural habits of growth. With his intimate knowledge of his plants, their origins and natural environment he is able to give them the conditions in which they will thrive and need little maintenance. John Codrington's secret garden in the heart of London shows not only his instinctive understanding and sympathy for plants and the principles of design, and his imagination and sensitivity in responding to the spirit of place; it also bears witness to the unusual and delightful warmth and humour of his character.

THE HILL, HAMPSTEAD: AN EDWARDIAN EXTRAVAGANZA

'Climbers, the jaunty prodigals of the garden,' wrote Thomas Mawson, architect of The Hill, '... are invaluable in almost every situation. ... Trained over verandahs, they form sheets of pleasing foliage, that delight the eye with their brilliantly coloured flowers on backgrounds of cool greenery; alongside the walks they form long bowers, where we can enjoy at sultry noon the coolness of declining day.' It only remains to add Sir George Sitwell's more impassioned supplication, 'Let climbing roses drop in a veil from the terrace and smother with flower-spangled embroidery the garden walls,' and you have virtually a blueprint for the intensely romantic combination of massive masonry and tangled foliage that is The Hill.

The pleasurable melancholy and unfocussed nostalgia now induced by his great colonnades and pergolas would have been a mystery to

STEPS lead down from the pergola to a gravel path bordering a round shrub border edged with yew. A large clump of hydrangeas spill over the sides of the hedge and behind an *Acer japonicum dissectum* forms a taller mass of fresh green filigree leaves.

IRONICALLY Mawson, who deplored unrestraint, would almost certainly have had difficulty in understanding present-day responses to the romantic melancholy of his overgrown and neglected colonnades. Picturesque as they are, they need extensive restoration work if they are to survive.

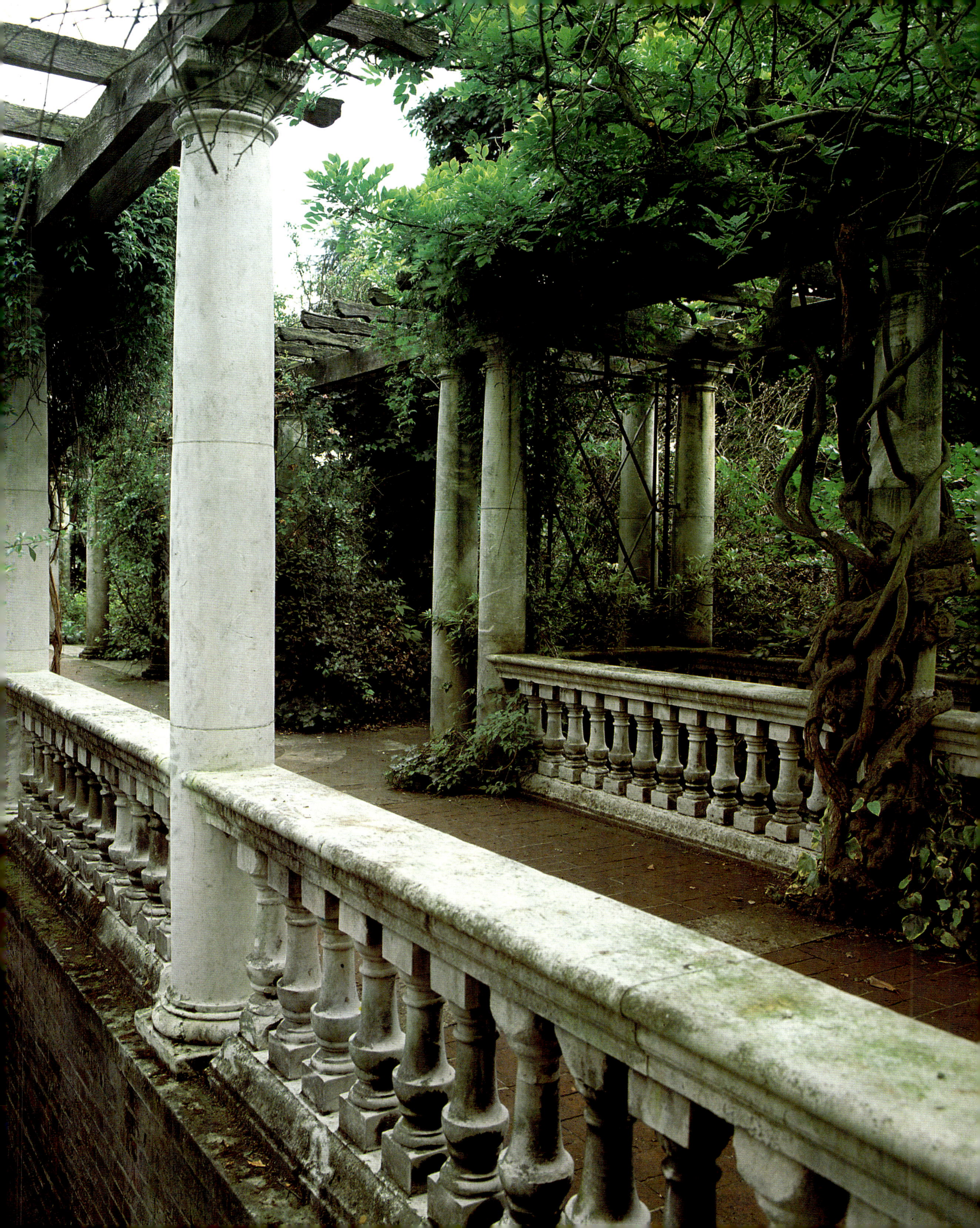

Mawson, however, who found 'unrestraint' regrettable. Photographs of the garden as it was when he laid it out for Lord Leverhulme at the beginning of the century – spruce, neat and with a hint of solemn pastiche – reveal the invaluable contribution that neglect and the passing years have made to this garden's charm. The gnarled trunks of octogenarian wisterias and roses clasp the stone pillars in a tight embrace, their branches writhe through crumbling balustrades, and their shoots and tendrils pry into every crevice. All this is not as Mawson intended, but it appeals greatly to the late twentieth-century imagination.

Mawson's intent was considerably more serious-minded. In his indigestible treatise *The Art and Craft of Garden Making*, in which he put forward The Hill as a model for 'A large town garden', Mawson described the role of the landscape architect in the following terms:

'This is his province, to infuse the drab necessities of existence with an inherent beauty, to divert the common crowd from low ideals by the elevation of their environment, and to cause those who never really loved art, and who resent it as a departure from their own level of mediocrity, to rise to more worthy aims. Filled with a right conception of the dignity of his art, and fired with a great desire for its advancement, he expresses out of his own soul his passion, and persuades his audience to see what he chooses by materializing his dream, using, as a medium to this end, architecture, verdure, flowers, and the other materials of his craft, weaving the whole into one rhythmic, harmonious composition.'

Both Mawson and Sir George Sitwell, whose *On the Making of Gardens* was published in 1909, were penning late contributions to a bitter war of words that started in the last years of the Victorian era. While the bemused gardeners of the land looked on, invective flew in the pages of books and the columns of newspapers and gardening periodicals. The adversaries in this battle were on one side the gardeners, championed with rude vigour by William Robinson, and on the other side the architects (or 'landscape architects', a term abhorred with a venom by Robinson), whose spirited defence was spearheaded by Sir Reginald Blomfield. The subject of their difference was the role of architecture, and architects, in garden design.

With his passion for wild flowers and cottage gardens, and his evangelical zeal on their behalf, William Robinson had already successfully challenged, virtually single-handed, the most treasured orthodoxies of Victorian garden design. His crusade against bedding out, 'pastry-work gardening', and anything to do with the Crystal Palace had been tireless, and the ideas of his New Landscape School became extremely influential. Through the work of his disciples, especially Gertrude Jekyll, English gardening was to be changed forever.

Robinson, as the prophet of 'naturalism', abhorred the meddling of architects in garden design, pouring scorn on those who 'call themselves "landscape architects" – a stupid term of French origin implying the union of two absolutely distinct studies, one dealing with varied life in a thousand different kinds and the natural beauty of the earth, and the other with stones and bricks and their putting together.' Among the shots in the architects' counter-attack was the publication of Sir Reginald Blomfield's *The Formal Garden in England* in 1892. Blomfield argued that garden design was work for architects, and was quite separate from (and, it was clearly implied, superior to) the sphere of the horticulturist. He

THE juxtaposition of this very regular pattern of paving with the lawn emphasizes the rectangular and formal water feature. Reeds, waterlilies and iris are reflected in the water.

also gave as good as he got: 'As to "nature" and "art"', he wrote in the preface to the second edition of his book, 'Mr Robinson is often florid. ... On the subject of clipt trees Mr Robinson becomes violent. ... It is sometimes difficult to see whether his perversions are wilful or merely stupid.'

Sir George Sitwell was more succinct: 'You can't hope to persuade us that nature built the house; why insult our understanding by pretending that nature made the garden?' he snapped. At Renishaw in Derbyshire Sitwell created a garden which probably owes more to the spirit of the Italian Renaissance than any other garden in England, and *On the Making of Gardens* was a passionately argued plea for the adoption of Italian Renaissance principles of beauty in English gardens. His son Osbert's less philosophical grounds for preferring the Italian style voiced an attitude that was perhaps closer to the roots of the style's success, and seem to capture the spirit of an age:

'*I think no English garden is as lovely as a foreign one. These gardens are created for rest in cool surroundings, for idleness and sauntering and imaginative thought, for love and a sense of mystery, but never for a show of tinkling tea-cups and hoarse cries of "Love-all". Physical action is inimical to the green lethargy we seek, and sweat is a mighty foe to peace.*'

As the 'golden afternoon' of the Edwardian era followed its languorous course, colonnades and pergolas, terraces and treillage, loggias and summerhouses multiplied in the gardens of the well-to-do. The Hill was an especially grand example. Mawson was commissioned to design entirely new gardens around the existing house, which Lord Leverhulme had greatly enlarged with the addition of sweeping new music-room and china-room wings. His brief included two contradictory requirements: firstly, the client wished his privacy to be protected from the adjacent knoll on Hampstead Heath which overlooked the whole of the grounds; and secondly this seclusion was to be obtained without obstructing the unique view to Harrow-on-the-Hill; and to add to his problems, as Mawson put it with some tact, 'Lord Leverhulme, with his usual enterprise and energy, was anxious that whatever was done should be done quickly.'

Mawson's solution was to enclose the garden with high walls, on which he laid out pergolas leading to domed rose temples. Potting sheds, gardeners' stores and the like were concealed underneath, and the covered raised walks offered views in all directions. A grand imperial staircase embracing a fountain basin and leading to an ornamental lily pond was laid out on axis with the south-western elevation; and when Lord Leverhulme acquired the neighbouring Heath Lodge this axis had hastily to be extended by a dog-leg over a bridge spanning a public footpath. Beyond the bridge were a garden temple and a colonnade leading to a belvedere.

The Hill is an extraordinary fantasy, grandiose in its heyday and touching in its decline. It is not any more, strictly speaking, a private garden as it is owned and managed by Hampstead Council and is freely accessible to the public; its atmosphere is, however, almost certainly more secluded and mysterious, more intimate and secret than ever before. Yet its fate seems to hang in a delicate balance, for romantic ruin may soon turn into complete destruction; some conservation work has been done, but more is urgently needed if these colonnades and pergolas are not to fall into irreversible decay.

THE gnarled trunk of this venerable wisteria clasps and entwines the stone pillars on the balustrade, its shoots wrapping themselves round each other and forcing themselves into crevices. The variegated ivy has crept up from the level below to form an attractive contrast to the ghostly trunk.

A VICTORIAN GARDEN

'Let me have something pretty to look at, and cheerful to walk in; let the outdoor apartment of my mansion, which we call "the garden", be always tasty, gay, and well furnished with seats and leafy alcoves for the ladies, – with fountains to serve as lustres, and their basins as mirrors, – with sun-dials instead of timepieces, – smooth carpet of verdant turf softer and more elastic than a Persian rug, – and everywhere that you can contrive to place them, well-chosen combinations of the brightest colours.'

So says an imaginary employer to his gardener in E. S. Delamer's *The Flower Garden*, published in 1859. Whichever Victorian gardener it was who laid out the garden of this villa in Barnsbury Square might – within the limitations imposed by a modest plot – have been following his instructions to the letter. A seat is set under a leafy alcove; a patch of soft lawn is surrounded by undulating herbaceous borders; serpentine paths meander round an island bed and under a rose arch; and a pretty fountain spills into a lily pond. Moreover one corner

THE soft patch of lawn surrounded by meandering herbaceous borders, serpentine paths running round an island bed and a pretty fountain spilling into a lily pond, a small gazebo, and even a tiny grotto shrouded in ivy, are some of the features of this enchanting Victorian garden.

THE pool and fountain are fed by a tiny waterfall which is sheltered by an ivy-shrouded grotto. The water is piped under the path, and pressure is provided by a pump hidden in the old coach house.

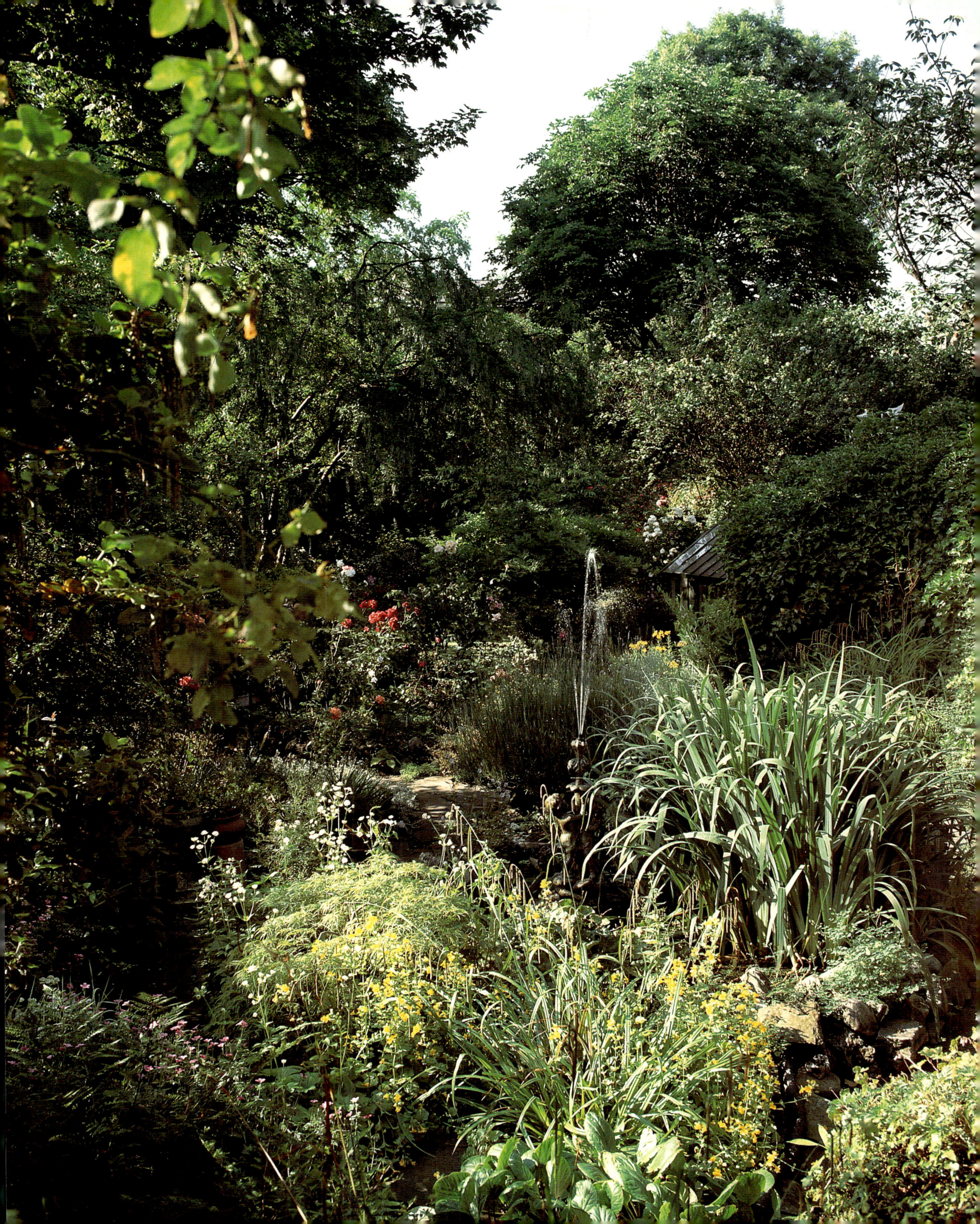

shelters a little gazebo with hints of chinoiserie; beyond the lily pond stands a little rustic greenhouse; and there is even a tiny rock-work grotto, romantically shrouded in ivy. All the elements required of a successful Victorian garden are to be found here; in fact, it lacks only a few crinolines and parasols, and perhaps the tap of croquet mallets.

Yet for years this garden lay untended; the present owner's grandmother bought the house in 1924, and as she grew older the garden fell into neglect. It was in 1964 that Mr and Mrs Gardner set about restoring it to its Victorian glory, a labour of love that was to last many years, and which Mrs Gardner was able to bring to fruition before she died early in 1989.

Preserved under the soil of Barnsbury lie the physical remains of millennia of London's history. Popular belief has it that Barnsbury Square was the site of a Roman camp during the revolt led by Boudicca, and even that this was the site of the British queen's last stand. Later tragedy and devastation are commemorated in a corner of the square, where there lies a plague pit, the mass burial place of countless plague victims who perished in the stifling summer of 1665, when London lost over a third of its population. By then a moated manor house stood on the site of Barnsbury Square, and the rural open spaces around had become a place of popular resort for city dwellers on holidays and for open-air political and religious gatherings. A spring called the White Conduit watered the fields, where dairy farms and market gardens flourished. By the end of the eighteenth century two notable botanic gardens were established here, one, in Liverpool Road, belonging to Jacob Harvey, and the other to Dr William Pitcairn, President of the Royal College of Physicians.

From the 1820s, however, rural Barnsbury succumbed to the great building boom of the nineteenth century, and its fields were dug for clay to make the bricks for new houses (often the clay was dug on site, the resulting hole becoming the basement of the house subsequently built with the bricks made from it). Thomas Cubitt, later to become famous for his speculations in Bloomsbury and Belgravia, was the builder here, a 'liberal benefactor ... of unassuming demeanour ... who bore his great prosperity with becoming modesty.' He laid out a rather loose and very attractive composition of stucco streets, crescents and open-cornered squares, of which Barnsbury Square is one of the prettiest parts.

It is possible that the White Conduit still flows through the square, though underground now, for there is certainly a stream running under the Gardners' garden: one of the supports of the arbour stands permanently in water, which bubbles up if ever the pole is moved. Water is a feature here, as it was of every self-respecting Victorian garden. Water, and the control of it with the new engineering skills then developing, became a mania. When Tsar Nicholas visited Britain in 1844, for instance, the Duke of Devonshire decided to mark the occasion by erecting the Emperor Fountain on his great estate at Chatsworth. The engineer Joseph Paxton, designer and builder of the Crystal Palace, was engaged for the work, and was instructed to do all in his power to outdo the spectacular *jeux d'eau* known to exist at the Russian imperial palaces. Paxton duly redirected a good number of the streams on the moors above the estates, constructed a couple of lakes and created sophisticated water systems in order to create the water pressure he required; using this, he was able to make the fountain spout to an astonishing 300 feet.

Such water schemes were the height of

LEAD cisterns are often used as ornaments or eye catchers, here this elegant one awaits its complement of summer bedding plants.

fashion, and were imitated on a humbler scale in the gardens of Victorian villas throughout the land. The fountain here is charming, made of mossy stone, it is supported by a small boy; its three jets spill down on to the leaves of iris and water lilies in the small rustic pond below, bathing with their spray the innumerable tiny frogs that bask on the lily pads. Frogs are now much less plentiful than they used to be, for the ponds where they lay their spawn have steadily disappeared or become polluted. City ponds such as this are therefore a welcome haven. Here the languid hush of a hot summer's afternoon is punctuated by a chorus of throaty croaks; and in the evening the frogs provide quite a spectacle. At eight o'clock sharp, according to Mr Gardner, they form up and process as one to the lawn, where, as if on a given signal, they scatter into the herbaceous borders to forage for food. As their diet includes slugs, snails and greenfly, Mr Gardner regards them with a benevolent eye.

Beside the pond is one of the garden's most remarkable features, the rock-work grotto, planted with ferns and ivy, of a type which was all the rage in Victorian gardens. Such decorative fancies echoed the taste for chinoiserie and the rococo which had flourished in the late eighteenth century; but to Victorian gardeners, obsessed as they were with doing things in the proper way in order to create the right impression, mere decorativeness was not enough. Controversy raged over the proper style to be adopted, and as usual contemporary writers adopted a didactic tone. 'The Chinese,' wrote C. M'Intosh in *The Flower Garden*, published in 1838, 'who are partial to imitations of the grander features of nature in miniature ... have rough shapeless stones thrown together in heaps to represent rocks.' Imitations of mountain scenery in suburban gardens tended to be absurd, however: 'It is by no means unusual, in our own suburban gardens, to see similar fanciful, and very incongrous, heaps of stones ... executed in the worst taste.' There then followed a few simple tips, no doubt intended to be encouraging: 'A dark cave, penetrating into the thickest part of the erection, is not very difficult to construct, and, when encircled with ivy, and inhabited by a pair of horned owls, which may be easily procured, it will form an interesting object.' Horned owls are sadly lacking, but otherwise this modest 'ferny grot' would surely have received Mr McIntosh's tight-lipped approval. It shelters an ingenious tiny waterfall, which flows into a large pipe laid under the crazy paving around the pool, and thence into the pond itself. Pressure for the fountain is nowadays supplied by an electric pump hidden in the old coach house beside the house.

Set into the crazy paving beyond is an island bed held in by tufa rocks and planted with Hybrid Tea roses: 'Crimson Glory', 'Peace', 'Blue Moon', 'Elizabeth Arden', and others so old their names have been lost. Beside the rose bed there stands a little glasshouse, another development of the Victorian era which owed much to the huge success of Paxton's Crystal Palace. Before the industrial processes which made possible the construction of this enormous glass and iron structure had been developed, glass was generally of poor quality. It was estimated that the 'green glass' used for horticultural purposes reflected as much as three-quarters of the light that fell on it; furthermore it could only be manufactured in small panes and it was subject to duty, and therefore very costly. As Mrs Beeton remarked

A LITTLE gazebo, with a chinoiserie roof, is sheltered in a leafy corner of the garden from which one can enjoy the view back to the house. A rambling rose gently embraces the pointed roof and other shrubs flank the paved path leading to it.

PRIVATE GARDENS OF LONDON

in *Beeton's Book of Garden Management*, published in the 1870s, 'Glass structures of even the smallest kind would, a very few years ago, have been considered a piece of great extravagance for any but the affluent.' After the Great Exhibition, restrictions on glass manufacture were lifted and processes improved, so that now a range of glass was available to suit most pockets. Suburban villas could have their own versions of the magnificent glasshouses of the great estates, designed and built by the army of firms which sprang up to meet the need. Others undoubtedly selected designs that were as grandiose as they could afford, but this one has a simple, cottage-garden charm.

In these glasshouses Victorian gardeners were able to cultivate the new plants now reaching Britain's shores from far-flung corners of the Empire, often transported in the miniature sealed greenhouses invented in 1829 by a London doctor, Dr Nathaniel Bagshaw Ward, and known as Wardian cases. Many of these plants were half-hardy annuals, and they gave rise to the new style of gardening called 'bedding out'. Herbaceous perennials were banished in favour of these novel introductions, which gave a superior demonstration of the gardener's skills, and which also, planted *en masse*, yielded the concentrated blocks of colour so beloved of bedding-out schemes. Petunias, clarkias, salpiglossis, salvias, schizanthus, alstroemerias and eschscholzias, among others, quickly became firm favourites for elaborate designs, which became known as 'mosaiculture'. As in virtually every other aspect of Victorian gardening, however, feeling ran high, and the bedding-out craze bred its own reaction in the person of William Robinson, who in his major works, *The English Flower Garden* (1883) and *The Wild Garden* (1870), set out his views with characteristic forthrightness: 'The genius of cretinism itself could hardly delight in anything more tasteless or ignoble than the absurd daubs of colour that every summer flare in the neighbourhood of nearly every country-house in Western Europe.' It was estimated that for any averagely ambitious scheme as many as 7000 plants would be needed.

Robinson insisted that his more informal style of gardening was better suited to small gardens, and his ideas became extremely influential. Followers of his New Landscape School were to include Gertrude Jekyll and Alfred Austin, who summed up their feelings when he wrote, 'I have seen one clambering rose, one lingering hollyhock glorify a cottage

LONDON's population of frogs is diminishing as their breeding grounds become polluted or disappear. This garden is a haven for them.

THE herbaceous borders have been restocked in an informal, cottage-garden style in the manner advocated by William Robinson and Gertrude Jekyll. Alfred Austin, another follower of Robinson, wrote, 'I have seen one clambering rose, one lingering hollyhock glorify a cottage home, arrest one's step, and prolong one's meditations, more than all the terraces of Chatsworth.'

home, arrest one's step, and prolong one's meditations, more than all the terraces of Chatsworth.' Clearly this was the school of gardening which most influenced Mrs Gardner as she re-stocked the herbaceous borders – though the hollyhocks of which there used to be so many simply disappeared one year, and have proved impossible to re-establish. Quantities of camellias, peonies and geraniums are here, while *Rosa* 'Paul's Himalayan Musk' grows through a tall *Cotoneaster lacteus* and a pink rambler scrambles up a crab apple tree.

A clematis arch under a laburnum tree, with a cherry beyond, marks the transition from the top half of the garden to the lawn and borders. Under the trees are *Rosa* 'Buff Beauty' and a *Syringa meyeri* 'Palibin', a dainty cousin of the ordinary lilacs with leaves the size of an old penny and minute mauve-pink flowers, and nearby is a bush wisteria which flowers at the same time as the laburnum, with breathtaking results. Much consternation was caused in 1987, when after the night of the hurricane the Gardners awoke to find a huge sycamore from next door sprawled across this part of the garden. Fortunately the damage did not turn out to be as serious as they feared: the tree had ripped a large bough off the cherry tree as it fell, but then had been supported by its own branches and so had not completely flattened everything underneath.

Halfway down one of the borders are a seat and white wrought-iron table, in the shade of an arbour of clematis, jasmine, ivy and rose 'Cerise Bouquet'. In the opposite corner of the garden stands the graceful chinoiserie gazebo, the perfect spot from which to enjoy the view back to the house. This garden is a commemoration not only of an era in garden design, but also of the considerable time and care devoted to its restoration by Mrs Gardner, who might have had in mind some words of Gertrude Jekyll: 'The purpose of a garden is to give happiness and repose of mind, which is more often enjoyed in the contemplation of the homely border ... than in any of those great gardens where the flowers lose their identity, and with it their hold of the human heart.'

THE glasshouse was an important innovation of the Victorian era: developments in the manufacture of glass meant that every suburban villa owner could build his or her own glasshouse, in which they could cultivate the many exotic and colourful new annuals reaching Britain's shores.

ON THE THAMES
AT CHISWICK

Strawberry House stands on the banks of the Thames at Chiswick, one of the beautiful Georgian houses that give Chiswick Mall its special character. In winter it is especially noticeable for the gnarled trunk of an aged wisteria, which clambers along the delicate ironwork of a first-floor balcony. The front garden, separated from the house by the road, stretches down to the river, which at high tides rises to flood it. The cherry tree that stands in the middle of the grass is frequently half submerged when in full bloom in spring, its froth of pink blossom emerging surreally from the grey waters. Behind, the horizontal lines of the willow-fringed island known as Chiswick Eyot make an almost monochrome composition of misty slate and ochre. In summer the road is lined with greenery, and the riverside

Two pyramids of clipped yew with skirts of small-leaved ivy stand on either side of the pond framing the view of the house with the white stucco bow windows. A small lead figure of a girl holding a goose rises from the centre of the small pond.

MAGNOLIA × *soulangeana* 'Lennei' and *M.s.* 'Alba Superba' in full flower shed some of their petals on the paving and water. Large camellias are covered in pale pink double blooms, their dark evergreen leaves making a good background for the magnolias in front. In the narrow canal and in the pond glow the bright yellow flowers of *Caltha palustris*.

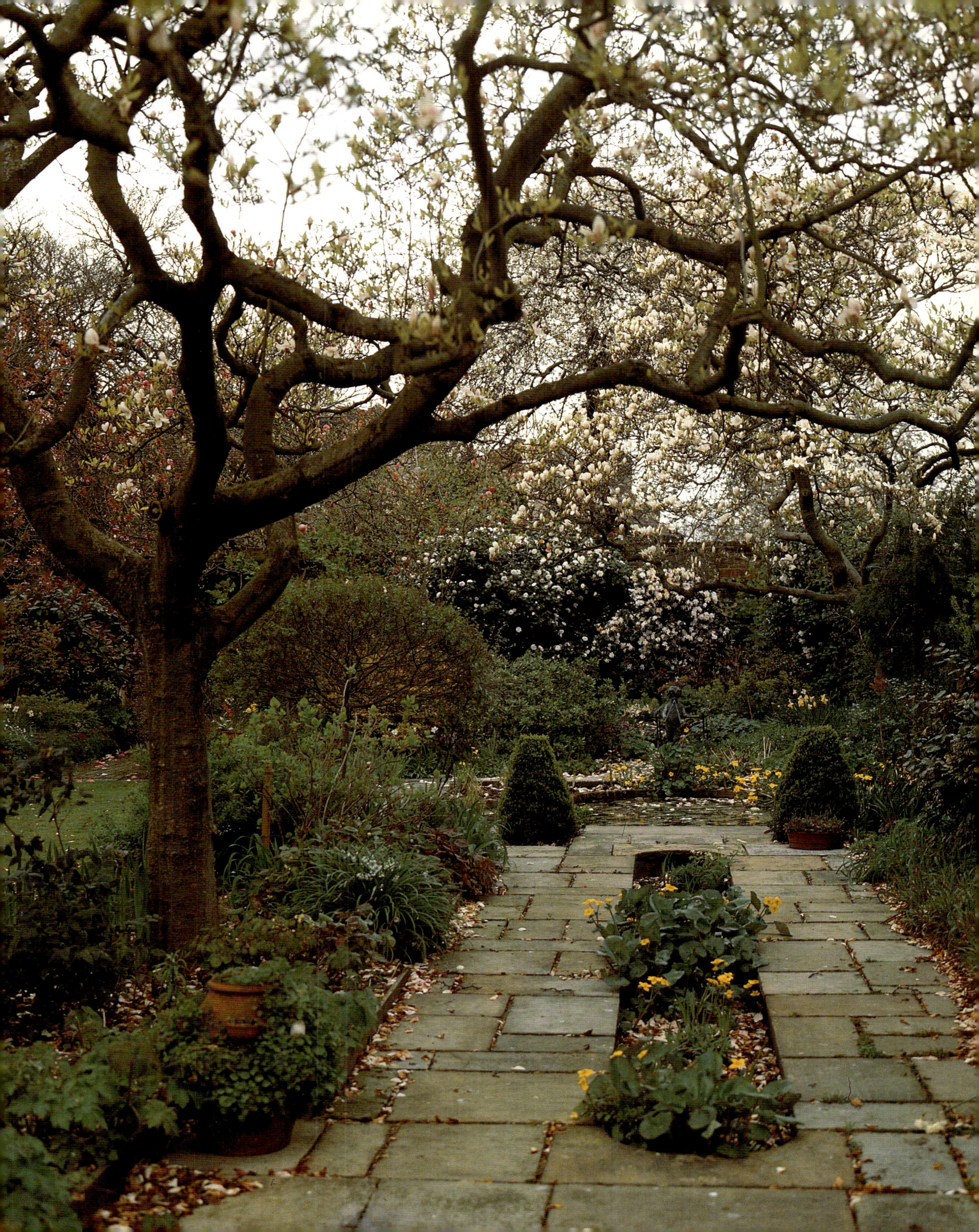

garden is filled with roses, peonies, buddleia and abelia among silver-leaved plants. Mallards, swans and coots waddle about in the shade of a tall weeping willow, dogwood and a *Salix babylonica pekinensis* 'Fortuosa' and the iron railings are covered with roses.

The back door of Strawberry House opens on to a York stone terrace, with the high walls of the neighbouring houses rising on either side. To the right a huge *Hydrangea petiolaris* climbs almost to the rooftops, and to the left is a magnificent blood-red camellia, one of the collection for which this garden is famous. There is another camellia in a pot, and a mossy stone trough decorated with carved arabesques stands against the left-hand wall.

Two brick buttresses topped with ball finials frame the view to the end of the garden, which covers about a third of an acre in all. A broad flight of steps sweeps up to them, and to the second terrace, with a small circular lily pond at its centre. The garden seems to form a green backdrop to this stone stage, and it comes as no surprise that the designer of this garden in its present form was a theatre designer, Norman Wilkinson, who laid it out in about 1924. Two pyramids of clipped chamaecyparus with skirts of small-leaved ivy stand to either side of the pond and just beyond it. A small lead figure of a girl holding a goose is placed symmetrically between them on the pond's margin, so that the swan's arching neck leads the eye directly to the garden's focal point, a statue in the depths of a shady pergola. A lawn, rectangular with rounded ends, runs from the chamaecyparus pyramids to the pergola, where a stone path continues the main axis.

Mixed borders flank the lawn, and two more run the length of the weathered brick walls that rise high on either side. Between these two parallel beds on the left is a stone path, and on the right, where the space between the beds is

A LARGE camellia with blood-red flowers is one of the collection for which this garden is famous. Another camellia inhabits a pot, while a mossy stone trough decorated with carved arabesques stands against the wall.

THE luxurious, huge leaves of *Lysichiton americanus* which are preceded by scented white flowers, are a focal point at the end of the pool. It delights in boggy conditions where it seeds itself readily. Rose-pink and white waterlilies flower in the summer, the rounded leaves floating on the surface of the pool.

rather wider, is a bog garden. A small paved area, screened by a yew buttress and a bank of camellias and *Viburnum × burkwoodii*, forms a sort of antechamber to the bog garden (and also reputedly served as the wings to Norman Wilkinson's stage), with a seat overlooking a small rectangular pool through mounds of lavender and red penstemons.

Between this pool and another at the further end of the garden, larger and with elliptical ends, runs a long narrow water channel known as the bog garden. 'It is probably in the smaller ponds and pools ... that most pleasures in water-gardening may be had,' wrote Gertrude Jekyll in *Wall and Water Gardens*; here *Caltha palustris* flowers profusely in April and May, its golden-yellow flowers shining against the deep green leaves, followed in summer by rose-pink and white water lilies, Cape figwort, pale blue *Iris laevigata* with their feet in the water, *I. ensata* on the margins, candelabra primulas, astilbes, alchemilla and a mass of other water-loving plants.

In spring the surface of the furthest pool is strewn with the pale pink petals of a magnolia, while the deep rose-pink petals of a *Magnolia × soulangeana* 'Lennei' near the pergola and a white *M.s.* 'Alba Superba' towards the house scatter the path and lawn beneath. A dainty *Azara microphylla* behind the larger pool bears its large sprays of vanilla-scented yellow flowers and a *Daphne odora* is even more fragrant.

This is the season when the garden is at its prettiest, when the blossom of two apple trees on the other side of the garden echoes the magnolias – my favourite tree – and the camellias are covered with their waxy perfect bloom in pure white and every shade of pink and red. In the camellia walk and woodland area at the bottom of the garden the rose-pink racemes of *Ribes sanguineum*, the crimson flowers and buds of *Chaenomeles speciosa* 'Apple Blossom' and white *C. × s.* 'Nivalis' tone with the pink leaves of photinia as the wisteria on the pergola prepares to flower. A neat mound of *Rhododendron* Cilpinense is covered with loose trusses of bell-shaped gleaming

A WOODEN pergola at the end of the garden is shaded by a magnolia whose flowers brighten the area on spring mornings. Camellias and ferns line the shady tunnel under the pergola where the ground is covered in self-seeded wild spurge from Kew.

A BROAD flight of steps leads up to this terrace with a circular pond at its centre. Two pyramids of clipped yew frame the view of the rectangular lawn and the garden beyond. Mixed borders flank the lawn leading to magnolias and apple trees whose blossom covers the branches in spring.

white flowers flushed with pink, and *Kerria japonica* blooms yellow against a dark backdrop of ivy, while hellebores, miniature daffodils and the forget-me-not flowers of brunnera cover the ground beneath. A mahonia fills the air with its scent under the knotty trunk of an old mulberry tree. This is reputedly a relic of the

PRIVATE GARDENS OF LONDON

mid-eighteenth century when, before he established the Botanic Gardens at Kew, Sir Joseph Banks would bring his ship right up the Thames on his return from his great plant-hunting expeditions, and plant his new-found species in nurseries on Chiswick Mall.

Camellias and ferns line the shady tunnel under the pergola, where the ground is covered with a self-seeded wild spurge from Kew. From here there is a view back along the main axis, past azaleas and two moss roses which bloom deep pink in summer and over the open lawn to the house. The shady beds that border the path running back to the house are filled with *Campanula portenschlagiana*, *Dicentra formosa*, bergenias, day lilies, ferns and other shade-tolerant plants spilling on to the narrow path beneath a large *Fatsia japonica*, ivy and more camellias. Although the garden is at its peak in spring, it is filled with such a variety of plants, and in such numbers, that every season has much to offer.

Even in winter there is always something of interest: *Lonicera purpusii*, mahonias in variety, winter jasmine, *Cornus mas*, smothered in small yellow flowers in February, *Viburnum × bodnantense* with its sweet-scented pink-tinged flowers, and numerous other shrubs including *Garrya elliptica* hung with long grey catkins, and *Abeliophyllum distichum*, bearing fragrant pale pink flowers in February. *Stachyurus praecox* bears long racemes of yellow cup-shaped flowers in March or earlier, and *Daphne odora* and *D. mezereum* produce their sweet-smelling flowers from February. Beneath the shrubs snowdrops and *Helleborus orientalis* have naturalized in drifts, with winter aconites, winter heliotrope, violets, bergenia and delicate lavender-blue *Iris unguicularis*. This – by no means an exhaustive list of plants of interest to be discovered here at this most unpromising time of year – perhaps gives an indication of the remarkable richness of the planting in this garden. Camellias in abundance – among many others the weeping *C. japonica* 'Akashi-gata', considered one of the best of all camellias with its large, semi-double peachy pink blooms – then magnolias steal the limelight, ushering in the luxuriance of late spring and summer.

Even more remarkable, perhaps, is that so many plants, shrubs and trees should be fitted into a comparatively small space with such apparent ease, and without disturbing the restful balance of the conception as a whole. This is an elegant garden, Edwardian in feel, and of exquisite taste. Like many of the best English gardens it is full of interesting plants, both old-fashioned and rare, while remaining quite simple. Soft, informal planting is contained within an architectural framework the contours of which have been weathered and cushioned by time. Under its patina of moss and lichen, with its ancient trees and magnificent camellias, the garden at Strawberry House has the air of settling into graceful and gentle maturity.

IN spring the petals of the garden's numerous magnolias, ranging in colour from pure white to deep rose pink, strew lawns and paths. The waxy blooms of the camellias, in every shade from white to crimson, complement them perfectly.

FROM the camellia walk a narrow shady path leads back to the house; it is lined with *Campanula portenschlagiana*, *Dicentra formosa*, ferns, bergenia and other shade-loving plants.

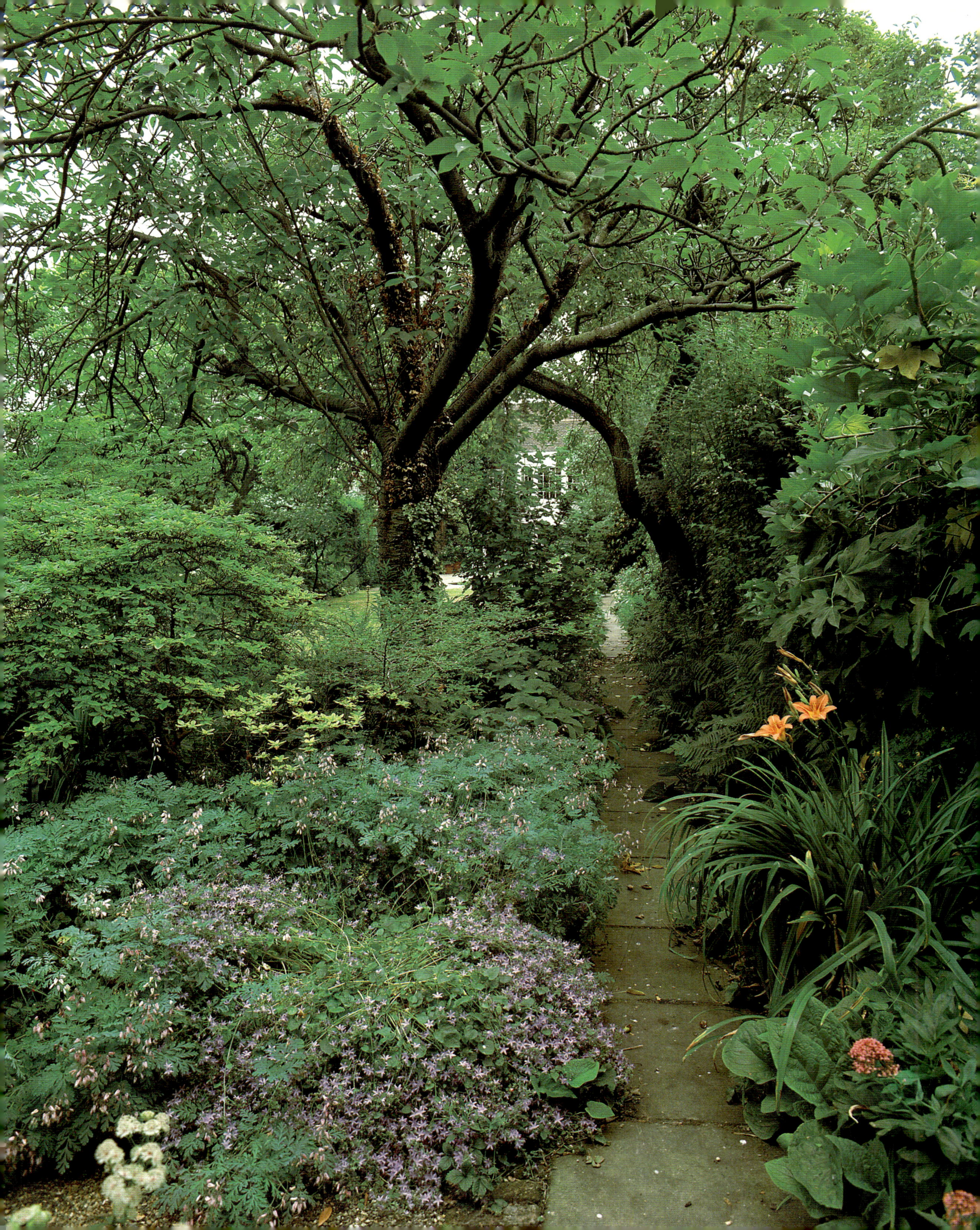

THE VINEYARD

Behind its eighteenth-century façade, with its pretty Regency chinoiserie porch, The Vineyard is probably the oldest house in Fulham. The ground floor is early seventeenth-century and reputedly stands on the foundations of a Tudor monastery. The first floor, constructed out of ships' timbers, was added at the beginning of the next century, and the façade was last of all.

Surprisingly few records have survived of this long history: in 1660 there was a smallholding here with a few farm buildings, which grew vegetables for the local community and perhaps also for Fulham Palace, the manor house of the bishops of London. Until well into the nineteenth century Fulham remained a collection of scattered settlements, dotted with fine houses and surrounded by nurseries and market gardens, and it was known as the 'great fruit and kitchen garden north of the Thames'. There were also vineyards here, for a nineteenth-century his-

CYNARA *cardunculus* is one of the most magnificent of all herbaceous plants. The long, deeply-divided silvery leaves are extremely elegant and make bold architectural shapes in the front of the border. The purple thistle heads are borne on stout grey stems and are extremely decorative in flower arrangements.

POTS of all shapes, sizes and colours are a great feature in this garden. In the spring some hold deep burgundy tulips, and others are filled with white agapanthus, marguerites and petunias for a summer show.

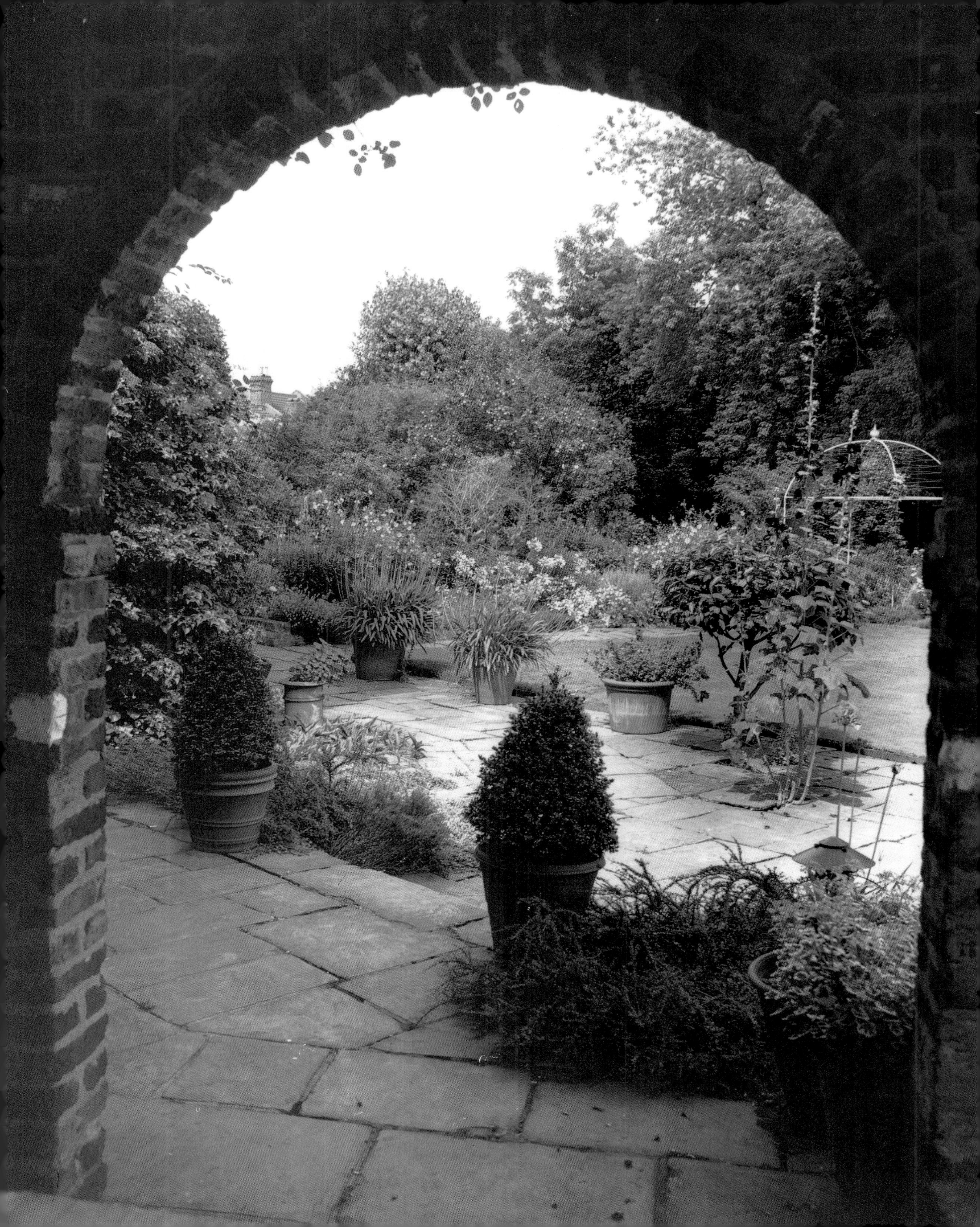

PRIVATE GARDENS OF LONDON

tory noted a record showing 'that in a vineyard at Parson's Green some Burgundy grapes were ripe in October 1765, and that the owner of the vineyard was about to make wine from them, as he did annually.'

The only traces that now remain of the generations of occupants that the house has seen over the centuries (apart from a quantity of Victorian toys that were found in the attic by the present owner) is in the fabric of the structure itself, and its successive alterations. It is often by chance that such details emerge, as, for instance, when following a fire the plaster was removed from the study, which had been thought to be a Victorian addition. As the plaster fell off, however, the rough-hewn timbers of a barn that was as old as the ground floor of the house were revealed. It had been preserved under the later additions, which were stripped away to reveal the original beams, nails and pitched roof.

Perhaps the most colourful period in The Vineyard's history started in 1918, when the house and its acre of garden were bought by Lord Beaverbrook, first of the great press barons. It was to be a halfway house between his town house overlooking Green Park and his country house in Leatherhead, and it was also to be the scene of political intrigue and power-broking on a grand scale. Here for over thirty years he hosted the famous meetings and dinner parties which could turn the tide in the careers of politicians and statesmen. It was at The Vineyard, according to his own account in his autobiography, that Lloyd George's downfall was engineered. Kept in power after the 1918 election by the post-war coalition of the Liberal and Conservative parties, the Liberal prime minister was increasingly resented by a growing number of Tory MPs. In 1922 their restiveness came to a head when the nucleus of this influential group – the origin of the 1922 Committee – met at The Vineyard with Lord Beaverbrook as host. By October of that year

WILD flowers grow freely in the islands of long grass around the trees and fringe the smooth-mown lawn in front of a green and white wendy house. A large black pot stands surrounded by the beautiful but invasive cow parsely; beyond you can see *Rosa* 'Albéric Barbier' growing on wooden pillars and chains suspended above the herbaceous border.

HOLLYHOCKS have colonized the paving round the house; here its large leaves can be seen at the foot of a brick arch. Through this is the front garden where a parthenocissus smothers the wall and falls over a border of the ferns which run the length of the shady street wall.

Lloyd George had been replaced by Andrew Bonar Law, sometimes described as the forgotten prime minister, who held office for only seven months before succumbing to ill health.

Lord Beaverbrook was a formidable man with a fascination for power that was legendary. When he bought the *Daily Express* in the early 1920s – with the avowed aim of influencing public opinion – its circulation was tiny; by 1930 it had the biggest circulation of any newspaper in the world. The Vineyard became a gathering place for men of influence and power, including Winston Churchill, who during the Second World War appointed Beaverbrook as minister for aircraft production (a task which he approached in his usual swashbuckling fashion, sweeping aside red tape and bureaucracy in order to obtain the aluminium that was so desperately needed for aircraft manufacture). In the dining room at The Vineyard, behind some curtains, was a cinema screen on which Beaverbrook and Churchill would vet wartime propaganda films, and also watch the feature films for which Churchill had a passion. His staff would often have to sit late into the night, through several hours of the latest feature films, before he was ready to go into conference. It was not unusual for work to start at one in the morning and go on until four – leaving them three brief hours to sleep before going on duty again.

In the grounds Lord Beaverbrook built two tennis courts and laid out park-like gardens in the fashion of the day, with straight, formal flower beds packed with serried ranks of bedding plants. His sister who succeeded him in the house was an enthusiastic gardener who laid out more formal beds and filled them with battalions of hybrid tea roses and irises. The garden has not changed in shape since Lord Beaverbrook's day (although part of the front garden disappeared in 1930 when the road was widened from a narrow lane), and apart from a few that have died of disease or old age has retained many of its trees, which in their maturity perpetuate its appealing countrified atmosphere.

The present owner, granddaughter of Lord Beaverbrook, has always been a keen gardener, but only after her marriage to her present husband, an architect, did the garden begin to take on proper shape. A series of different areas was defined so as to provide variations of pace and mood, and changes of focus and perspective were contrived with eye-catchers and vistas. Their first move was to extend the York stone paving round the house and to divide the garden into three main areas. The sitting room windows look out through a rose-covered arcade and across the terrace to a wide rectangular lawn which occupies the centre of the garden. To the left it is bordered by a raised herbaceous bed with a trellis of roses festooned on chains slung from posts, and beyond this are an orchard, a vegetable garden and a wild garden. To the right, behind a brick colonnade and an autumn border, both cutting diagonally across the space, is a spring woodland garden, with a bee garden in the far depths. Here six beehives are placed behind a trellised pergola which runs along the end of the garden, so as to deflect the bees' flight path. The shrubs and herbaceous plants have been chosen for their pollen and nectar, and the family collects the honey. At the back of the lawn, parallel to the house, is a path linking the autumn borders with the raised herbaceous bed. On one side of it are roses, shrubs and ground cover, and on

FROM the orchard and wild garden there is a vista along the brick path which cuts across the whole width of the garden, past the Ali Baba pot which acts as an eye-catcher on the garden's main axes.

the other terracotta pots of marguerites sitting in a narrow border planted with thyme.

In spring the colonnade is covered with the white flowers of a *Clematis armandii*, which are followed later in the season by the mauve racemes of a *Wisteria sinensis* and, from May to October, by the great purple bells of *Cobaea scandens*. Through the branches of a white magnolia you can glimpse the flowers that carpet the woodland garden early in the year. Hellebores cover the ground beneath the camellias, while the brilliant blue star-shaped flowers of *Anemone blanda* are strewn through drifts of the white daffodil 'Mount Hood'; these are followed by the nodding bell-shaped flowers of *Fritillaria meleagris*, spotted with rose-purple, which flourish in the shade of an ancient horse chestnut, a lime tree and a graceful acer which colours beautifully in autumn.

The woodland garden shades into the autumn borders, where a *Clerodendron bungei* is a highlight in August and September, its dark stems bearing corymbs of rose-red fragrant flowers against the large heart-shaped leaves. An artichoke towers next to the delicate blue spires of *Perovskia atriplicifolia*, both rising from a variety of lower shrubs and herbaceous perennials, including the pale pink daisies of osteospermum tucked behind the steely blue *Ruta graveolens* 'Jackman's Blue'. The rampant cerastium, *Iberis sempervirens*, *Alchemilla mollis* and many other spreading plants smother the raised edge.

The present owners have planted a number of trees, which with the existing ones hide the few distant houses to be seen and give the garden its rural feel. As well as fine specimen trees there are also some simple groupings of great charm: to the left, for instance, is a small orchard of apple trees, with roses clambering through their boughs, and near by a blue wisteria grows through a purple-leaved acer. Wild flowers grow freely in the long grass that forms islands under the trees and fringes the smooth-mown lawn in front of a green and white Wendy house. Standing on the mown grass against a dark yew hedge is a curved stone seat. From here there is a vista down the full width of the garden: your eye is drawn along the herringbone brick path, down some steps and through a white metal pergola, past a large

A GARDEN of this size could not be without beehives. One of six, this hive is positioned in a sheltered part of the garden where plenty of forage is available. The shrubs and herbaceous plants nearby were chosen for their pollen and nectar.

THE herringbone brick path cuts across the whole width of the main lawn, dividing it from the woodland borders. More terracotta pots filled with bush marguerites are placed inside a narrow border, with thyme planted between them, to form a carpet around them. On the other side *Stachys byzantina* spreads its woolly leaves under lilies and roses.

Ali Baba pot set in a pattern of cobbles and finally to another seat and a table tucked into a trelliswork pergola.

The path is edged with a soft colour scheme in shades of mauve, purple, pink and white. At the far end two standard *Pyrus salicifolia* 'Pendula' grow out of hedge-like mounds of *Ceanothus thyrsiflorus* 'Repens', beneath a double-flowered purple lilac. A large *Rosa* 'Penelope', covered in semi-double almost white flowers, makes a restful contrast before the deep rose-pink cloud of a tamarisk. Beyond this is a collection of David Austin's modern roses, which have the scent and shape of old-fashioned roses but also flower the whole summer through. Silver and aromatic plants are everywhere: *Stachys byzantina* on one side under the roses, and rosemary on the other.

Rosa 'Albéric Berbier' smothers the chains that are suspended above the herbaceous border. This is a true old-fashioned border, filled with peonies, delphiniums, regale lilies and a very good form of the tree mallow *Lavatera thuringiaca* 'Barnsley'. Artemisias, santolinas and lavenders lighten the colour scheme with shades of grey and silver.

A pileostegia, with evergreen leathery leaves and creamy white flowers in summer and autumn, grows up the north-east-facing house wall, and a *Clematis montana* drapes an old wall on the terrace. Here two standard Portuguese laurels growing out of the paving are on axis with the sitting room windows, the Ali Baba pot and the potting shed beyond. Bluebells and lily of the valley have colonized the crevices, along with corydalis, ajuga and hollyhocks. Pots of all shapes, sizes and colours are a great feature not only on the terrace but throughout the garden. In the spring some hold deep burgundy tulips, their velvety petals shading to white at the edge, and others are filled with white agapanthus or dark mauve petunias for late colour.

Through the arcade is the front garden, where ivy and *Solanum crispum* spill over the brick wall, nearly touching the York paving beneath, where the cracks are colonized by the white valerian, *Centranthus ruber albus*. A simple but pretty dog kennel is swamped by a huge clump of *Mahonia* × *media* 'Charity', its spine-toothed lanceolate dark green leaves contrasting with an enormous bed of ferns running the length of the shady street wall. A jasmine has twined its gnarled trunk through the trelliswork of the porch, and to either side of it are pyracanthas clipped into columns. A blue wisteria is trained up the ochre house wall, and a newly planted selection of Mrs Smallwood's favourite silver plants and cistus grows beneath.

The garden at The Vineyard is so full of unexpected features and plant combinations that it would be an impossible task to try to describe them all. With its woodland walks, its wild flowers and its bees it is like a country garden in the middle of London, and it receives care and attention on a similar scale. So imbued is it with the atmosphere of the country that when you step into it you leave urban life behind you. This is a garden which seems to dictate a pace of life far removed from the bustle of the city.

A *CLEMATIS montana* drapes an old wall on the terrace; below it a *Cotoneaster salicifolius* spreads its slender branches studded with small deep green leaves.

A TROPICAL JUNGLE IN THE EAST END

There are no limits to what an imaginative mind can create, given space, vision and a knowledge of plants. Who would suspect that behind the unassuming façade of this Victorian terraced house in London's East End there lies a magical subtropical garden, where as you follow the little winding path to the forest pool at the bottom your elbow is brushed by the huge leaves of tropical plants; where above your head huge stems bearing myriads of tiny flowers reach for light; where your senses are assailed by the exotic sights and scents of the rainforest?

'Magic, mystery and drama are the most important qualities in a garden', says Myles Challis with feeling. In his view a well-designed garden – however small – should be endlessly surprising, to be discovered little by little as new vistas open up and treasured plants are revealed. Add to this his passionate love for jungle plants, for huge leaves and exotic flowers, and you have the essence of his garden.

It all began when, at the age of seven, he visited the Aroid House at Kew Gardens. He was already fascinated by jungles and the mystery that pervaded them. Then, delighted and mesmerized by the tropical atmosphere of the giant hothouse and the extraordinary shapes and sizes of the leaves, he resolved to start his own collection. Fortunately he was blessed not only with a large heated conservatory at his family home in Hampstead, but also with a globe-trotting butterfly collector uncle, who encouraged his nephew by sending him fine specimens from exotic climes. In a few years the young Myles had assembled a collection of some of the world's most beautiful tropical foliage plants. Sadly it was not to last. The oil crisis came and with it prohibitively high heating bills, which meant that the collection had to be disbanded and sold off. Myles was devastated.

All hope was not lost, however. In his desolation he consulted all the books he could find, and discovered that not all exotic-looking plants needed cosseting in subtropical temperatures; indeed many of them did not need a greenhouse, and would grow outside even in the British climate. Having experimented in his

WHILE the plants in this garden are chosen on the whole for the beauty of their foliage, which also provides a great variety of colour, a few flowers are admitted for the extreme beauty and drama of their shape and colour. This is the flame-red flower of *Canna generalis* 'Wyoming'.

THE narrow path that winds down to the forest pool is virtually engulfed by huge exotic leaves. To the left, behind the beautiful scented flowers of a *Datura cornigera*, rises a fine Indian horse chestnut which flowers late in the season and has glossy pinnate leaves.

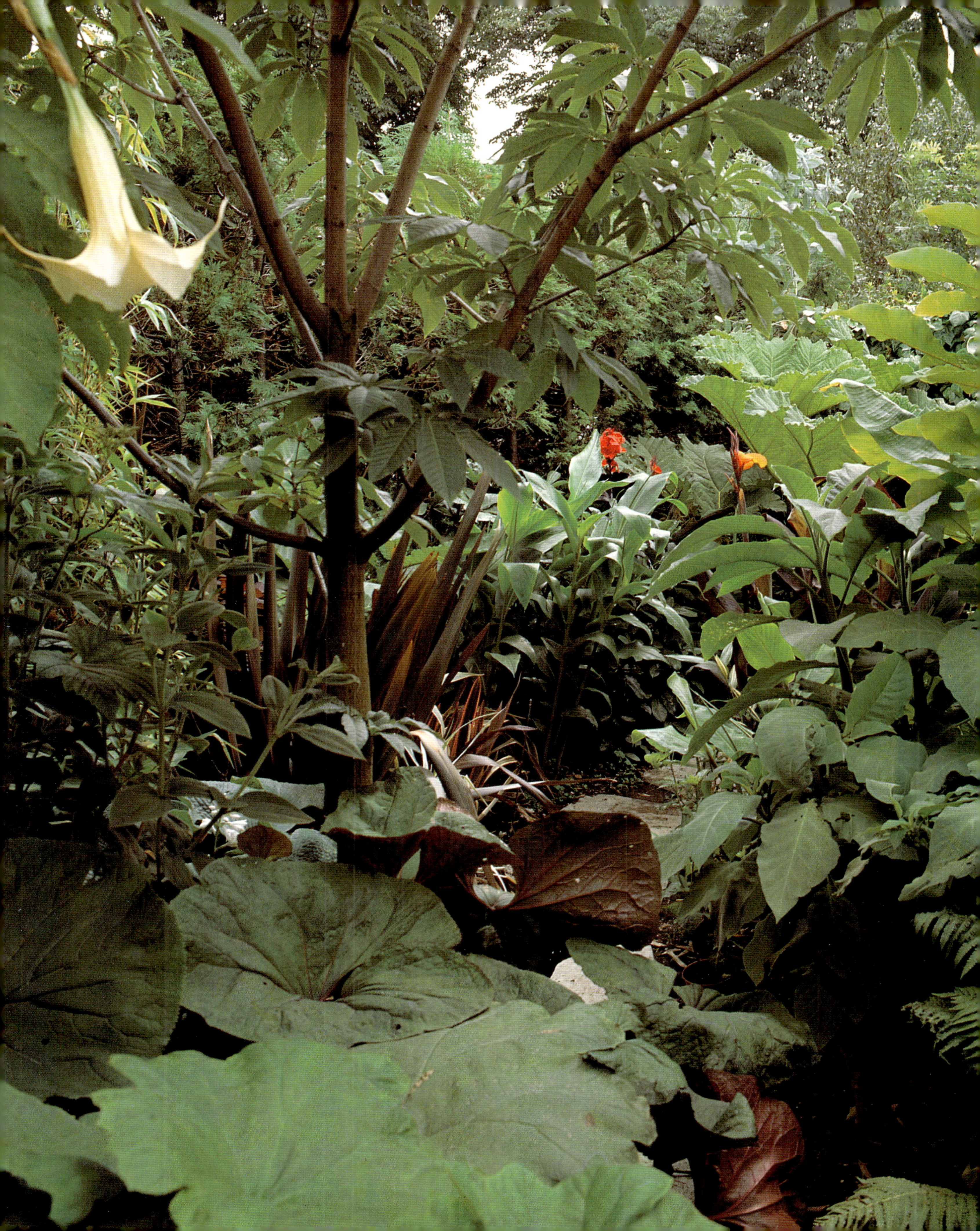

PRIVATE GARDENS OF LONDON

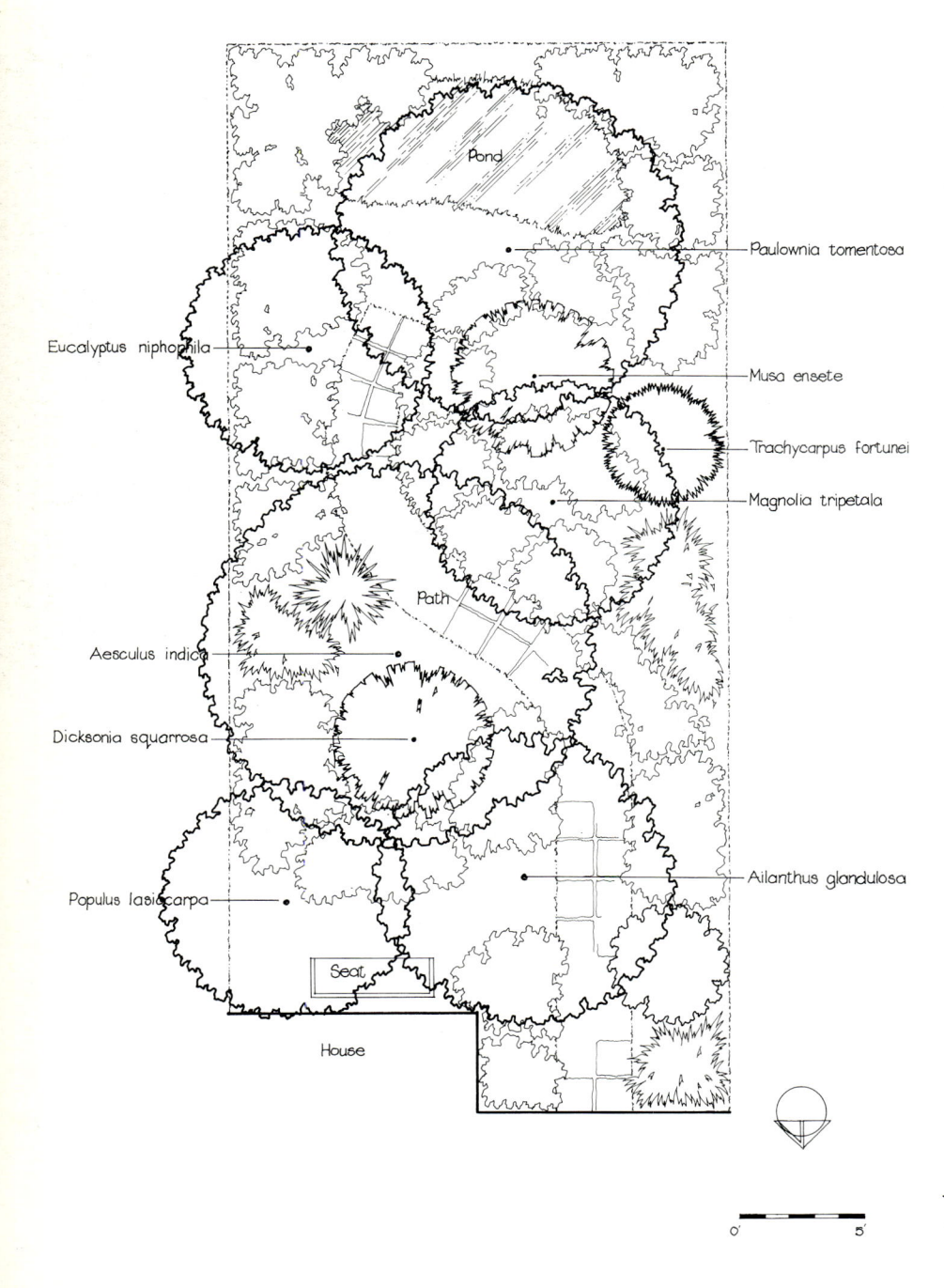

This planting plan shows how much the owner has succeeded in packing into a restricted space and how the curving path appears to increase the garden's length.

garden with bamboos and a palm he was still dissatisfied. Then it was that he discovered a book by Henry Cooke, a Surgeon-General in the Indian Army who, on his retirement to England at the turn of the century, set about realizing his dream: in the unlikely setting of a Gloucestershire valley he embarked on the creation of a garden which would evoke the tropical splendour of the gardens of India. Undeterred by mundane considerations of what might be possible or practical, he planted quantities of ferns, palms, bamboos, orchids, yuccas, cannas and innumerable other exotic plants, most of which flourished to create a veritable jungle. His proudest possessions were his Abyssinian banana palms, of magnificent proportions, 'under whose spreading arches an elephant might stand for shade'. In winter these tremendous plants, with sail-like leaves up to fourteen feet long, had to be uprooted and moved into glasshouses with the help of six men and a team of horses. The indomitable Henry Cooke was to become Myles Challis's great mentor and inspiration, and Cooke's book, *A Gloucestershire Wild Garden* his bible.

About seven years ago he moved to Leytonstone, where behind a typical London house he found an equally typical London garden, small and narrow, measuring about twenty feet by forty. It was ideal. Having removed an old apple tree, the garden's sole occupant, he set out to create his own exotic dream. Most people feel their garden needs one or more trees to provide a framework and to break up the skyline. Myles Challis's first choice was the Chusan palm, *Trachycarpus fortunei*. Of Chinese origins, it is perfectly hardy, though he recommends protecting the crown with straw or bracken for the first few winters, and it eventually grows to some twenty feet. He also planted an Indian horse chestnut, *Aesculus indica*, which he prizes for its beautiful red-stemmed leaves and its late-blooming delicate pink flowers, a *Paulownia tomentosa* (syn. *P. imperialis*) and a tree of heaven (*Ailanthus altissima*). These last he pollards annually, an extraordinary practice with magical results. Each winter he cuts both

A TROPICAL JUNGLE IN THE EAST END

THERE is nothing to equal this majestic waterside plant; the rough leaves of *Gunnera manicata* are sometimes six feet across and are borne on equally high stalks. It likes its fleshy roots near the water, is a hungry feeder and needs protection in the winter. Here it is planted at the edge of a little pool, and together with *Petasites japonicus giganteus*, *Darmera peltata* and a lysichiton hybrid all assume giant proportions.

almost to the ground, allowing just one shoot to develop. This will bear leaves far larger than normal: three to four feet long in the case of the tree of heaven, and two to three feet wide in that of the paulownia, or 'foxtail' tree. The pinnate, almost palm-like leaves of the ailanthus make a fine contrast with the paulownia's downy, heart-shaped leaves. He believes the ailanthus is one of the easiest trees to grow (and it will grow to a hundred feet if allowed to), actually preferring poor soil; paulownias are fussier, preferring rich, moist soil in a sunny, sheltered position.

To these trees he has added a *Populus lasiocarpa*, 'by far the loveliest of all the poplars' with heart-shaped red-veined leaves a foot long, and a *Eucalyptus niphophila*, the hardy 'alpine snow gum', which in maturity has beautiful flaking bark of marbled grey, green and cream. But his pride and joy is his Abyssinian banana, *Ensete ventricosum*, 'the crowning glory of the exotic garden, the largest in leaf and most magnificent of plants that we can grow in the open air in this country'. In its native habitat it grows on the lower slopes of mountains, and it is therefore stockier than other species of banana, and its stupendous leaves less vulnerable to laceration by the wind. It likes full sun, and in summer will drink copious amounts, for the rate of evaporation from the vast surface area of its leaves is very high. This remarkable plant needs to be overwintered under shelter, and will happily turn into a houseplant for the winter. If they become unmanageably big (and they are prodigious growers, reaching as much as nine feet from seed in eighteen months), Myles Challis finds it relatively simple to replace them with new plants grown from seed.

Between and around these trees he has woven a sinuous path, for he believes that a path should wind and twist around strategically positioned shrubs or clumps of bamboo, so that there arises a feeling of mystery and an air of expectation. The end is never in sight until you are almost upon it – for 'if you can see clearly what lies at the end of the path, why should you want to follow it?' On this shady forest path, under its canopy of exotic leaves, you pass bamboos and gingers, tree ferns and magnolias, cannas and daturas, each seemingly more choice and rare than the last. The moisture-loving bamboos, an essential part of any exotic

DATURA *cornigera* is another tender plant which requires shelter during the winter months. Its huge, white fragrant pendulous flowers, some eight to ten inches long, are among the most beautiful. It can be grown as a shrub or as a single stem when it will produce many more flowers from April through to October.

167

garden's 'bones', are not only extremely graceful but also very useful for screening (and hiding such things as compost heaps). Here they include the large-leaved palm-like and very distinctive *Sasa palmata*, rampant and thicket-forming, which contrasts beautifully with the small-leaved, black-stemmed *Phyllostachys nigra*, the purple-green canes of *Pleioldastus viridistriatus*, the tall pale green canes of *Phyllostachys viridis* and the vigorous and hardy *Semiarundinaria fastuosa* (which has the added advantage of being edible: the shoots are delicious when eaten young).

Between the bamboos to left and right is a densely luxuriant growth of large, handsome foliage of every variety, including the gingers, *Hedychium gardnerianum* and *H. forrestii*, beautiful both in leaf and in flower, the former (the more spectacular) bearing ten-inch spikes of fragrant yellow flowers with orange stamens in late summer; the shade-loving *Astilboides tabularis*, with pale green circular leaves as much as three feet across and tall spikes of small ivory flowers; and *Melianthus major*, one of the choicest foliage plants, here grown with the purple canna, *Canna × generalis* 'Wyoming', a spectacularly successful combination. The majestic fronds of a tree fern, *Dicksonia squarrosa*, cast their shade over a *Ligularia wilsoniana*, with slightly triangular leaves a foot across borne on angular hollow stems, and a handsome *Fatsia japonica*, a much underrated shrub in Myles Challis's opinion. Under a *Magnolia delavayi*, with long, grey-green leaves, a *Hydrangea aspera* spreads its sumptuous velvety leaves and beautiful deep pink lacecap flowers, while further down the garden whorls of long *Magnolia tripetala* leaves shade the brilliant golden foliage of *Hosta* 'Sum and Substance'.

CANNA 'Firebird' has flame-red flowers and fresh green leaves, here growing together with the huge banana-like leaves of *Canna iridiflora* 'Ehemannii' the largest and loveliest, which has magnificent three foot-long leaves and delicate rose-pink blooms. These plants need to overwinter in a frost-free place till May when they can be planted out.

When the plants in a garden are chosen for the beauty of their foliage, the period when the garden is looking at its best is automatically greatly extended. When gardens that rely for their beauty on the blooms of annuals and perennials are already beginning to look straggly and jaded, the exotic garden still looks fresh and lush. As so much colour is provided by foliage – purple, yellow, silver, pink, orange, scarlet, cream and white, as well as all shades of green from soft grey-green to aquamarine – flowers may be selected for the drama or extreme beauty of their colour, form and scent. Among this garden's loveliest ornaments are undoubtedly its cannas and its daturas. Cannas, with their banana-like foliage and exotic flowers, look splendidly appropriate in this informal tropical jungle setting: *Canna* 'Firebird' has flame-red flowers and fresh green leaves; *C. × generalis* 'Wyoming' has purple leaves and apricot-orange flowers; and *C. iridiflora* 'Ehemannii', the largest and loveliest, has magnificent three-foot-long leaves and delicate rose-pink blooms. Even the gorgeous cannas' limelight is stolen, however, by the daturas, whose huge, fragrant, pendulous flowers are the height of exoticism. The long, white semi-double blooms of *Datura cornigera* and the peachy cream single blooms of *D.* 'Grand Marnier' are quite breathtaking in their beauty.

In this garden even the more commonplace plants take on a tropical aspect. As the path opens on to the forest pool at the end of the garden a *Darmera peltatua* and a lysichiton hybrid seem to assume giant proportions, sharing the limited space with a huge *Petasites japonicus giganteus* with kidney-shaped leaves up to three feet across ('not recommended for small gardens', notes the owner wryly) and a positively gargantuan *Gunnera manicata* ('lovely big rhubarb', a passer-by was heard to remark). Water, in Myles Challis's view, is indispensable, even in a small garden, for it is one of the easiest ways of achieving those sought-after qualities, magic and mystery. On the wall behind the pool he has erected one of his own sculptures, a Medusa mask, forever dribbling a trickle of water, constructed according to a method he has invented. Dissatisfied with the statuary and sculpture generally available, which he found too small, too costly and too rigid in character for his style of gardening, he developed a method in which he builds up layers of cement on a chicken wire frame to create the large, baroque and sometimes grotesque forms he seeks. Durable, relatively light and with the inestimable advantage of looking instantly weathered, his sculptures are a splendidly imaginative complement to the exotic garden. Those who saw the silver medal-winning garden that Myles Challis created at the Chelsea Flower Show in 1986 will not easily forget his sculpture of Neptune.

Being a passionate and knowledgeable plantsman means that Myles Challis is able to experiment with some tender plants which are beyond the average gardener's reach: he believes, for instance, that he has this country's only specimen outside Kew Gardens of the Mexican *Wigandia urens*, which grows to ten feet and bears huge racemes of mauve flowers – and, unfortunately, stinging hairs. But he believes that no plant is worth cultivating if it does not put on vigorous growth, and insists on the practical as well as the aesthetic advantages of exotic gardening. Despite their aura of mystery, these temperamental-looking plants are on the whole quite simple to cultivate. A professional garden designer and author of *The Exotic Garden*, Myles Challis approaches his subject with infectious enthusiasm and an almost evangelical fervour. Perhaps the last word should be left to him:

'The exotic garden has many virtues and no particular vices. Its season is long, its maintenance low, its interest abundant and its restful qualities unparalleled. It concentrates on plants which have something to offer at all seasons of the year, and it makes full use of the innate beauty and grace of the design nature has bestowed on them. Above all, it is a relaxing place, both subtle and dramatic, varied and harmonious, a place which ideally should remind us of warmer, more restful climes.'

ECCLESTON SQUARE

London's leafy squares are the envy of other European capital cities. The grandest of them – Belgrave, Cavendish, Grosvenor and the rest – were designed as the focal points of fashionable new suburbs. Belgrave Square, for instance, was one of the most desirable addresses in Belgravia, a loose composition of stuccoed crescents, avenues and squares laid out on reclaimed marshland by Thomas Cubitt between 1810 and 1825. So successful was this venture that in the following decade Cubitt decided to extend it southwards over the marshlands of Pimlico, then owned by the Grosvenor Estate. There was a brewery on the marshes, some osier beds which supported a basket-making industry, some market gardens and a good deal of waste land. Cubitt lost no time in acquiring the lease and managed the scheme with brilliant opportunism: the bricks were made on site from London clay excavated from beneath the gravel, and the land was levelled with rich black loam brought by river from St Katharine's Dock, which was then being excavated.

Pimlico was a success both commercially and architecturally: designed for rather less illustrious occupants than the houses of Belgravia, the stuccoed streets and squares were substantial and imposing without rivalling their nobler neighbours. Contemporary society was extremely sensible of the difference, moreover, as faithfully recorded by Trollope. For Lady Alexandrina, newly married in *The Small House at Allington*, the acme of happiness would be that coveted address in Belgravia: 'If indeed they could have achieved Eaton Square, or a street leading out of Eaton Square – if they could have crept on to the hem of the skirt of Belgravia – the bride would have been delighted.' This proving unattainable and her knowledge of the geography of Pimlico being imperfect, she is saved from a hideous error by a

VICTORIAN ropestone edging the path is one of the square's legacies from its early days, when it was planted with irreproachably respectable and rather dull shrubberies and lilac groves. Fashionable hostas now line the path.

ONE of the attractions of Eccleston Square is its variety. This shady corner shelters a patch of woodland where narrow paths meander through sweet-smelling long grass, hostas and lush ferns, and ivies clothe the tree trunks. Shade is provided by the tall London planes that surround the square.

TWO hundred or so residents look over this leafy view so peculiar to London squares; not only can they walk and sit in this communal garden but they can play tennis and take their children to the play area. The planting and layout have been designed by one of the residents.

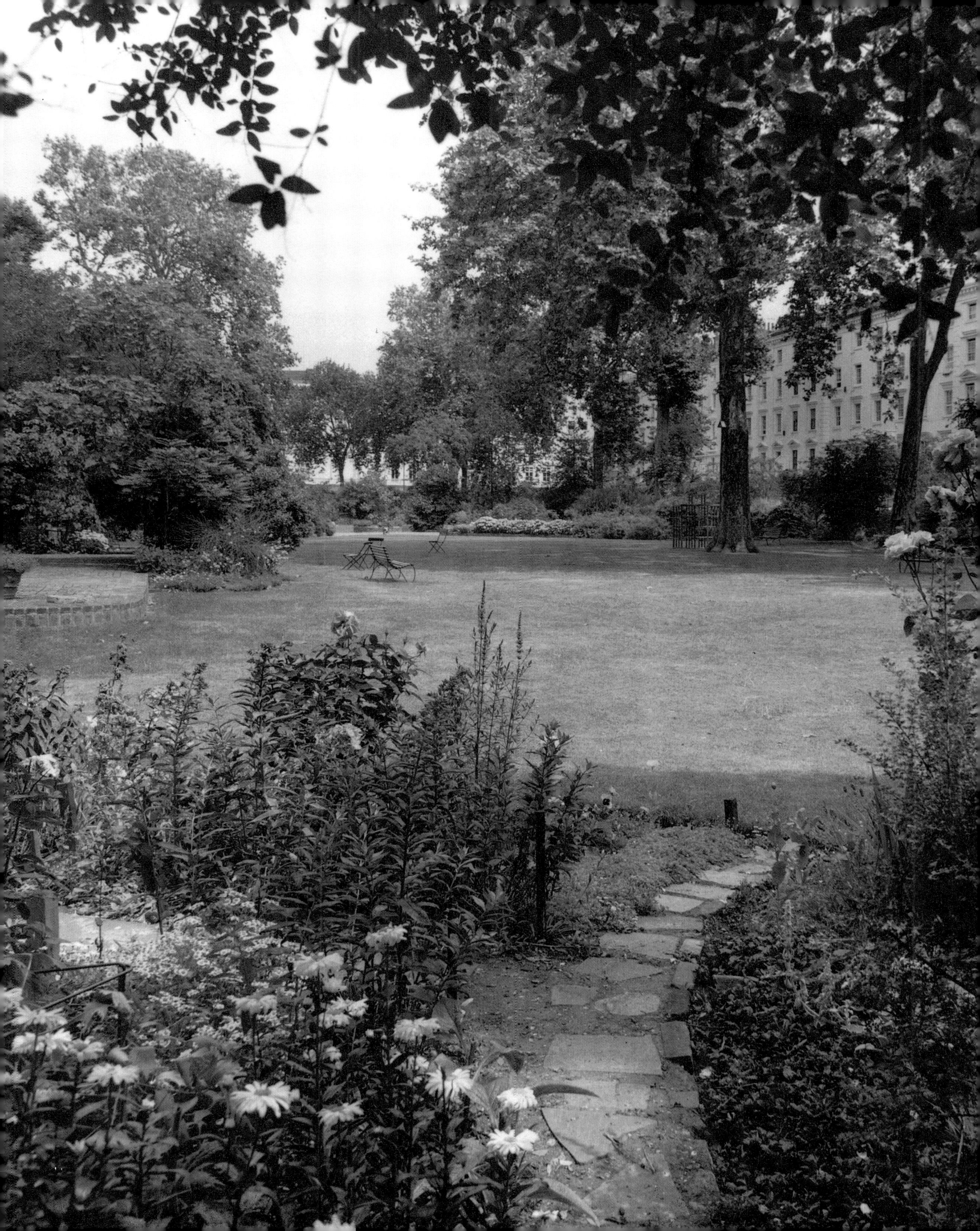

concerned friend: 'For heaven's sake, my dear, don't let him take you anywhere beyond Eccleston Square!'

In the manner of the grander estates, Eccleston Square was the focal point. Elegant iron railings were erected around the 'area' to each house, and the square overlooked by their windows was planted with eminently respectable shrubberies and lilac groves, as well as the London planes which by then had virtually become a standard furnishing of the city's streets. A hybrid of the oriental plane, introduced in the sixteenth century, and the western plane brought back from Virginia a century later by John Tradescant the younger, the London plane had established its credentials as a hardy survivor within another century. Pollution of the city's air did not start with the industrial revolution, and by the middle of the eighteenth century it was becoming clear that not all trees could cope with the soot and smoke produced by thousands of coal fires. Perhaps because they are continually shedding the outermost layer of their bark, planes proved able to withstand such grimy deposits in apparently unlimited quantities. As they were attractive in summer and winter alike, with their golden fruits in winter and their dappled bark, they quickly became one of the most widely planted trees in London.

Such arrangements of houses around a communal square gave rise to one of those congenial arrangements peculiar to London. In Eccleston Square the two hundred or so residents not only look out on a leafy view, but they can also walk and sit there, play tennis in them, and take their children to the play area in them. And all this they can do without getting their hands dirty, because a gardener's salary is included in their local rates. Over the years, however, like many other open spaces in the city, the garden in Eccleston Square had ossified into a kind of genteel sterility. Then eight years ago things started to change: Roger Phillips, a resident for some years, was made honorary manager of the garden by the committee, and he had strong views about how it should be used: 'London is absolutely full of squares and many of them are totally neglected'.

Roger Phillips is not a professional gardener nor a trained botanist, yet he is the author of a very successful series of plant-identification books aimed at the layman and catalogued according to his own system. The system, based on flowering season rather than any more complicated botanical classification, is typical of his refreshingly undaunted approach. Few things apparently give him greater pleasure than the debunking of commonly believed myths, for instance the 'universal truth', well known to all gardeners, that it is impossible to make leaf mould out of the leaves of plane trees as they do not rot. Leaf mould was needed in quantities here, for the city air is constantly depositing an impermeable layer of grime and grease on the soil, which needs frequent turning and digging with leaf mould so that it can absorb precious water. Funds were limited and huge quantities of plane tree leaves were available, so Roger Phillips used them – with complete success.

Mr Phillips gave himself and the square's gardener, Arthur Heppell, an ambitious brief in setting out to bring the square back to life, for he was very aware that he needed to take into account all its functions, and to cater just as much for children and joggers as for sitters and strollers and armchair gardeners. Faced as he was with three acres of 'urban desert', as he saw it, his most urgent need was to fill the empty beds with ground cover and to find shade-tolerant plants that would grow under the broad canopies of the plane trees. His limited budget dictated patience and ingenuity: years of painstaking dividing and propagating have brought the garden to its present well-furnished state. This is the backdrop against which he now has the well-deserved luxury of experimenting with new ideas.

As you walk round the square you quickly become aware that the planting has been designed with the eye of an artist (Mr Phillips has an artist's training and it shows) rather than with a horticulturist's precision, and arranged according to an informal, asymmetrical planting scheme where surprise is of the essence.

Serpentine paths ensure that the garden unfolds before you as you walk, and it is with a pleasurable sense of discovery that you come upon corners of specialist planting or encounter a sudden change of mood. In spring, among the thousands of indispensable bulbs, you may find a drift of hellebores or a mass of camellias, which Mr Phillips finds useful as they resist both drought (always a problem under the spreading trees) and frost. In early summer peonies make a glorious show of rich pink and crimson, and the garden is becoming celebrated for its sea of tall bearded irises, which again strike a practical note as they are tolerant of the damp winter conditions and dry summers. Terracotta pots filled with pelargoniums and fuchsias, nasturtiums and herbs stand on a brick terrace used for summer barbecues, and more herbs in impressive numbers and variety crowd the surrounding beds. A walk across the open lawns brings you to a thicket of bamboo, where narrow tunnels wind through a jungle of tall stems and the airy foliage waves gracefully above your head. Another secluded corner shelters a romantic wilderness of long grass, ivies and lush ferns, where shady paths meander through the greenery and the sweet woodland smell carries you far from the heart of London.

Mr Phillips is a gardener of enthusiasms, always open to new ideas and not afraid of bold statements. If he sees a combination he likes in another garden he is likely to take it one stage further, and by enlarging the scale of the planting and transposing it to a broader canvas he frequently creates remarkably successful effects. He may notice a particularly good association – the pastel pinks of lavateras and poppies above white alyssum, perhaps, or the intense violet-blue of bluebells against pale variegated foliage – and expand it to fill a whole bed. He is equally eager to cherish happy accidents: a knot of larkspur which seeded itself by the tennis court has spread to make an arresting splash of brilliant blue under the climbing roses planted to hide the wire fence. Seeding itself more diffusely in a nearby bed, it also looks good among sweet williams.

There is a pleasantly spontaneous feel to the garden, which is clearly meant for enjoyment. Mr Phillips has an admirable magnanimity of approach: his is the burden (willingly shouldered) of general planning and budgeting, of organizing the pruning and digging, the painting of the railings and the repair of the sheds; yet he does not seek the copyright on creative ideas. Residents are encouraged to get involved at every level (they turned out in their scores to clear the debris after the hurricane of 1987), and several have their own plots within the square. One – a particularly pretty tapestry of delphiniums, foxgloves, lupins, antirrhinums and other cottage-garden flowers – typifies the 'lived in', homely feel that is such a feature of the square. Within an overall unity of design is a patchwork of small, discrete pockets and corners, more intimate in scale and more easily digestible than grander, more formal planting. At the same time, only a few yards away, an ambitious wisteria walk has just been completed, which in future years will be of the utmost elegance and distinction.

Roger Phillips and Arthur Heppell's respect for the square's history is clearly evident in the discretion they have used in its design and planting, but they have also managed to give it a flavour of the twentieth century. Thanks largely to the energy and imagination of a few individuals, Eccleston Square is now not only the focal point of a gracious architectural conception, but also a valuable retreat offering welcome peace and seclusion to all its residents.

WHERE the space to be filled is greater than the funds available, self-seeding and spreading varieties are especially welcome. New ideas and effects are also encouraged here, and broad statements suit the unusually large scale of the garden. If an *ad hoc* association – such as this combination of sweet williams in different shades of pink, mauve-blue campanulas and self-seeded larkspur – is thought to be particularly good, it may be expanded to fill a whole bed.

COLOUR IN THE GARDEN

'*What is needed for doing of the best gardening is something of an artist's training ... for gardening, in its best expression, may well rank as one of the fine arts. But without the many years of labour needed for any hope of success in architecture, sculpture, or painting, there are certain simple rules, whose observance, carried out in horticulture, will make all the difference between a garden that is utterly commonplace and one that is full of beauty and absorbing interest. Of these one of the chief is a careful consideration of colour arrangement.*'

Reacting against the garish and insensitive bedding-out designs and the quest for bright colour at all costs which characterized Victorian gardening, Gertrude Jekyll used her artist's eye and training to mix palettes of softly harmonizing and complementary colours in her borders. These borders, chosen with care for gradations of shape and size of plant, of foliage texture and seasonal flowering, were the antithesis of the flat geometrical patterns of harsh and often clashing colour that still dominated the world of gardening when Gertrude Jekyll, greatly under the influence of William Robinson, was developing her theories. But colour was the one single factor of the greatest importance in her schemes, where she tended to design discrete compartments, each dominated by a single colour, and all separated by evergreen hedges.

Her influence on gardening was comparable to that of the Impressionists on painting, and her techniques were based on some of the same understanding of the colour spectrum and the way it is perceived by the eye. Her gardens were like canvases on which she built up pictures as an artist might compose a painting, giving due attention to the balance and structure of the overall design, and of the effect of light and shade, of smooth and rough textures, of round and pointed shapes – and above all of colour. 'Any experienced colourist knows that the blues will be more telling – more purely blue – by the juxtaposition of rightly placed complementary colour', she noted famously in *Colour Schemes for the Flower Garden*, and she put theory into practice by prefacing blue or grey borders with beds filled with plants with yellow flowers and gold or variegated foliage, or placing a spot of vivid colour against a drift of muted shades. So profoundly have such ideas influenced English gardening, and so dear are they to the hearts of gardeners, that it is hard to imagine that they were once new.

MRS CAPRON views her garden as an extension of her drawing room. The colours of the planting on the terrace and round the steps are carefully chosen to tone with the interior decoration and the rest of the colours in the garden are chosen with equal discrimination.

A SMALL statue nestles in the shrubbery at the far end of the garden, where the lime trees take most nutrients and moisture out of the soil. There are conifers, mahonias and euphorbias to the back and drifts of iberis fall over the edge at the front.

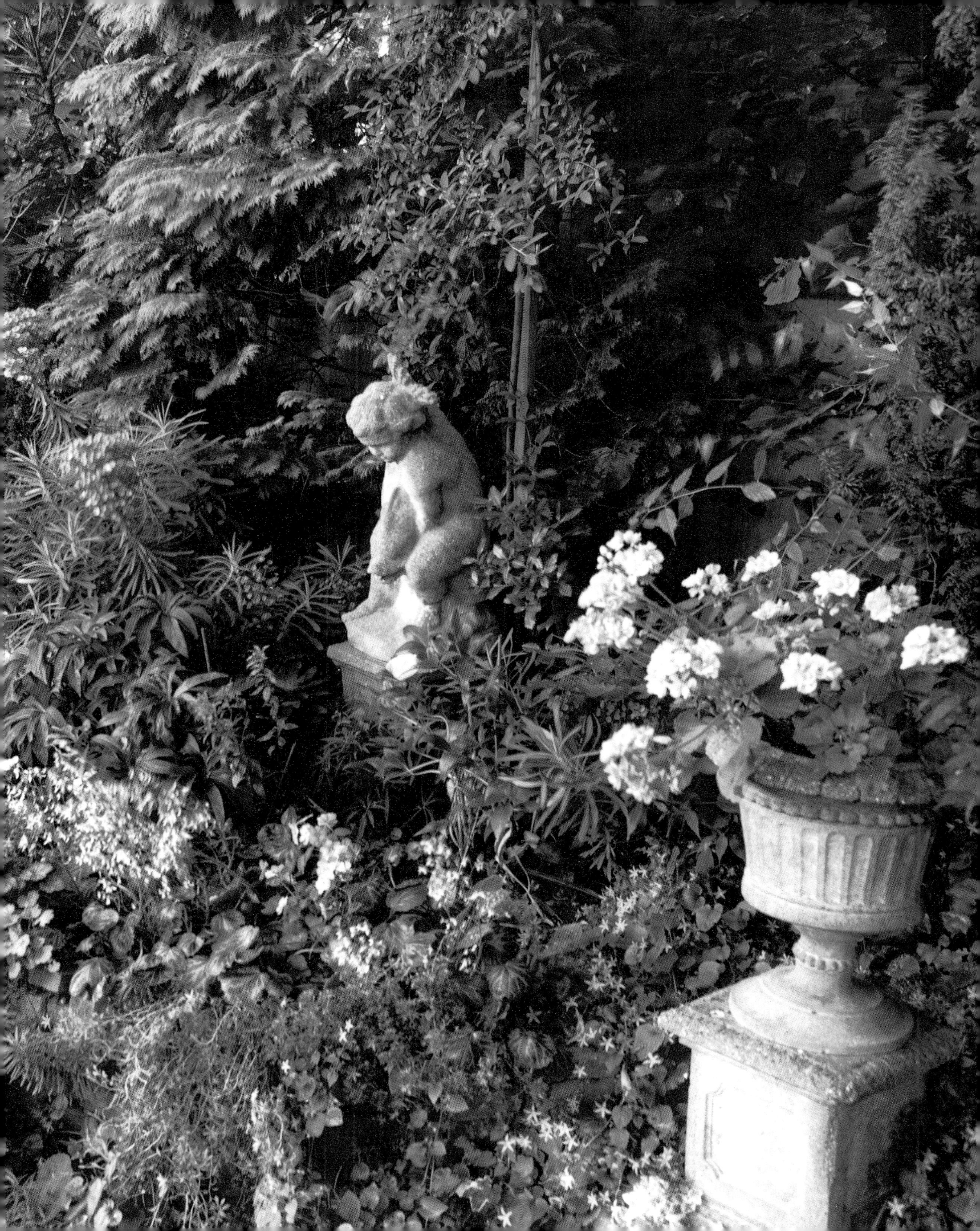

THE spectacular *Abutilon* 'Canary Bird' is covered in lemon-yellow flowers virtually throughout the year.

It was not only in her theories that Gertrude Jekyll linked the worlds of art and of gardening. The great and fierce argument that raged in the late Victorian gardening world between naturalists, represented by William Robinson, and architects, championed by Sir Reginald Blomfield, was resolved only by the partnership of Gertrude Jekyll and the young architect Edwin Lutyens. Between them they evolved a style of gardening which for the first time reconciled formal design with natural planting, thus making peace between architects, gardeners and craftsmen. A devotee of the Arts and Crafts movement and of the ideas of William Morris and John Ruskin, she infected Lutyens with her concern for the artistic unity of house and garden.

Mrs Deirdre Capron's Kensington garden reflects similar enthusiasms, for in it she uses colour to blur the distinction between landscape and interior design. Mrs Capron views her garden – literally and metaphorically – as an extension of her drawing room. From the large French windows she looks out over a foreground of coral pink, cream and light blue (chosen to pick up the colours of the interior decoration) to a study in gradations, shadings and harmonies of colour: purples merging into soft pinks, blues and white on the left; yellow and white on the right. For Mrs Capron plants her garden with an interior designer's attention to colour; but where interior designers consult colour cards and bundles of swatches, Mrs Capron refers to nursery catalogues and her own expertise and enthusiasm as a plantswoman, which has taken her as far as the Caucasus on horticultural trips.

The coral, blue and cream scheme starts on the little York stone terrace directly outside the drawing room window, where pots of coral and red pelargoniums and terracotta urns of brick-red *Begonia pendula* mingle with the perfect blue flowers of *Felicia amelloides*, under the branches of a wisteria, a sweet-scented *Trachelospermum jasminoides* 'Variegatum' and a *Jasminum polyanthum*, which twine up the whitewashed wall behind. A Banksian rose climbs up the back of the house, with blue- and red-flowered *Lathyrus sativus* 'Azureus' (grown from seed) weaving their tiny sweet-pea-like flowers through its lower branches. On the other side of the windows *Camellia japonica* 'Adolphe Audusson' adds a note of blood-red early in the year, while later coral and carmine fuchsias flower around the little goldfish pond, merging with the soft pinks and violets of verbenas and petunias. A raised bed behind the pond echoes the colour scheme, with 'Super Star' roses and 'Chattahoochee' phloxes underplanted with violas and a host of other dainty ground-cover plants.

Semicircular brick steps lead up to a smooth green lawn surrounded by meandering herbaceous borders. These are filled with plants chosen with care so that one part of the colour spectrum should merge softly into another, against the high green backdrop of four mature lime trees. On the left the coral, cream and pale blue border gives way to a palette of mauves and purples, which in turn shades into pinks,

COLOUR IN THE GARDEN

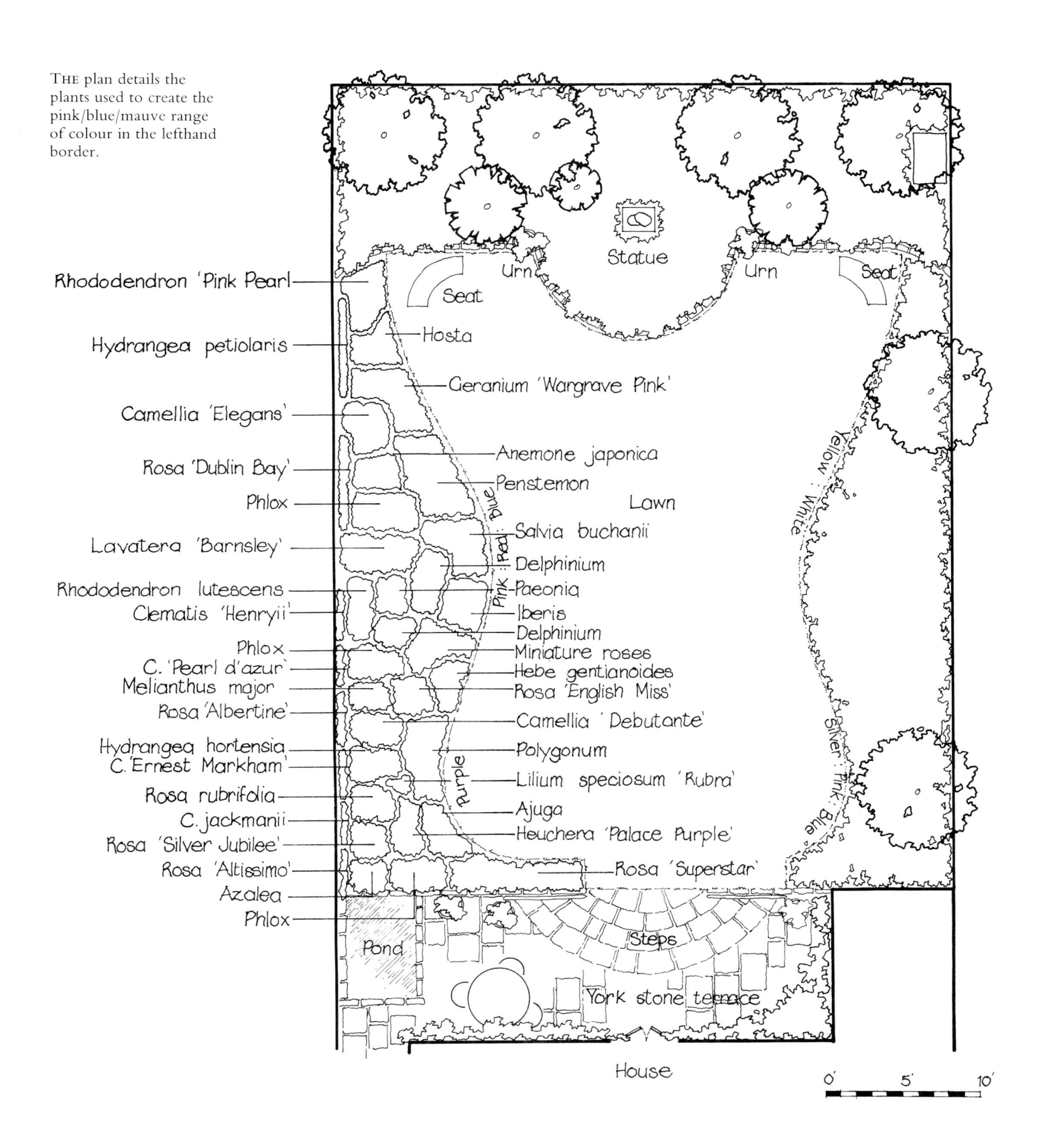

THE plan details the plants used to create the pink/blue/mauve range of colour in the lefthand border.

- Rhododendron 'Pink Pearl'
- Hydrangea petiolaris
- Camellia 'Elegans'
- Rosa 'Dublin Bay'
- Phlox
- Lavatera 'Barnsley'
- Rhododendron lutescens
- Clematis 'Henryii'
- Phlox
- C. 'Pearl d'azur'
- Melianthus major
- Rosa 'Albertine'
- Hydrangea hortensia
- C. 'Ernest Markham'
- Rosa rubrifolia
- C. jackmanii
- Rosa 'Silver Jubilee'
- Rosa 'Altissimo'
- Azalea
- Phlox

- Hosta
- Geranium 'Wargrave Pink'
- Anemone japonica
- Penstemon
- Salvia buchanii
- Delphinium
- Paeonia
- Iberis
- Delphinium
- Miniature roses
- Hebe gentianoides
- Rosa 'English Miss'
- Camellia 'Debutante'
- Polygonum
- Lilium speciosum 'Rubra'
- Ajuga
- Heuchera 'Palace Purple'
- Rosa 'Superstar'

Seat — Urn — Statue — Urn — Seat

Pink : Red : Blue

Purple

Yellow : White

Silver : Pink : Blue

Lawn

Pond — Steps — York stone terrace

House

0   5'   10'

POTS of all sizes clutter the steps in front of a small raised fountain. *Camellia japonica* 'Adolphe Audusson' in the larger pot adds a note of blood red early in the year, while later coral and carmine fuchsias flower, merging with the soft pinks and violets of verbenas, petunias and geraniums.

blues and white; opposite, meanwhile, tones of yellow mingled with white merge back into silver, pink and blue nearer the house. At the far end, under the limes, two Irish yews stand sentinel on either side of an apsidal bed, and in the shade of the trees is a soft woodland planting of *Helleborus orientalis* and *H. argutifolius*, polygonatum and *Euphorbia characias wulfenii*. To the right a *Kerria japonica* and an *Elaeagnus pungens* 'Maculata' standing next to a *Mahonia japonica* signal the start of the yellow border.

Here ferns and ivy form an evergreen background to the pendulous pale yellow flowers of *Forsythia suspensa* and the apricot-gold blooms of *Rosa* 'Buff Beauty', emerging from clumps of lemon-yellow irises and alstroemerias and hostas. A white-flowered abutilon rises behind the golden-leaved *Philadelphus coronarius* 'Aureus', which in July and August is starred with the large pure white blooms of a *Clematis* 'Marie Boisselot' growing through its branches. A spectacular *Abutilon* 'Canary Bird', covered in bell-shaped lemon-yellow flowers virtually throughout the year, forms a dramatic composition with graceful *Lilium* Green Magic and *Rosa* 'Golden Showers', which bears its fragrant honey-gold double flowers almost continuously throughout the season. A buttercup-yellow *Fremontodendron californicum* and *Azalea mollis* with rose 'Sanders' White Rambler' behind, *Lilium regale* 'Alba', *L.* 'Mont Blanc', *L.* 'Apollo', *Hemerocallis* 'Kwanso', *H.* 'Flore Pleno', a white peony and white penstemons seem to play infinite variations on the theme of yellow and white. Beneath them yellow pansies, primulas, cyclamens, *Stachys byzantina* and alchemilla are just some of the innumerable toning ground cover plants that the indefatigable Mrs Capron has managed to assemble here.

The short walk across the lawn (the garden is some 64 feet by 40 in all) entails a leap virtually to the opposite end of the spectrum, where a silver *Rosa glauca* underplanted with *Heuchera* 'Palace Purple' marks the beginning of the purple border. Claret-coloured *Clematis* 'Ernest Markham' drapes itself over hydrangeas, with phlox and indigo-flowered *Ajuga reptans* in the front of the border, while the violet-purple flowers of *Clematis × jackmanii* are especially rich in combination with *Lilium speciosum rubrum* and *Polygonum amplescicaule*.

With the pale blue clematis 'Perle d'Azur', white *C.* 'Henryi' and the coppery pink rambler rose 'Albertine' this bed flows into a soft pastel palette of pink, white and blue. Pink peonies, *Rhododendron* 'Pink Pearl' and *Lavatera thuringiaca* 'Barnsley'; pale blue delphiniums and azure *Salvia patens*; creamy white *Hydrangea petiolaris* and almond-white *Anemone × hybrida*; and penstemons in every shade of pink, crimson and mauve rising from drifts of paper-white iberis, mauve aubrieta, coral heuchera, *Geranium endressii* 'Wargrave Pink' and violet-

COLOUR IN THE GARDEN

blue *Campanula carpatica*, make one of the garden's prettiest set-pieces.

Secluded in the corner beyond is a curved stone seat set under a white hydrangea and pink foxgloves, with the glossy leaves of a large *Fatsia japonica* rising above it and a mass of campanula, heuchera and variegated ivy at its feet. With its matching pair in the opposite corner it flanks two stone urns, filled in summer with salmon-pink pelargoniums, and a central stone statue of a boy with a dolphin.

One of the more remarkable things about this garden is that its colour schemes are more or less consistent throughout the spring and summer, for from January to May the beds are full of spring flowers and bulbs which anticipate the colours of summer: pale yellow auriculas and winter aconites; golden daffodils, white narcissi and creamy white hyacinths; brilliant blue gentians and *Iris reticulata* and delicate violet-blue wisteria; deep pink cyclamens and camellias and palest pink cherry blossom. As the seasons unfold so do new colour combinations in apparently endless variety, but always within the palette chosen with such care by Mrs Capron.

WHEN *Prunus × subhirtella* 'Autumnalis Rosea' is in flower, from November to March, the whole garden is pervaded with the sight of the thousands of small pale pink flowers covering the slender branches. It is one of the most delightful trees.

CANONBURY HOUSE

In the north-east corner of Canonbury Square in Islington there rises Canonbury Tower, built in 1509, a relic of the days when Islington was a country village surrounded by fields; the area that we now know as Canonbury was a tiny hamlet clustering around the buildings of a priory. Built on ancient, pre-Roman foundations, the tower has a curious history, in which kings and bishops, attainder and treason, mad poets and elopements all play their part; and a potent atmosphere – owing perhaps to the twenty-four ley lines which are reputed to pass through the site. In its shadow, on the site of the priory gardens, is a venerable mulberry tree with a history of its own. Nearly 500 years old, it was planted by a former tenant of Canonbury House, who lived here from 1616 to 1625: Sir Francis Bacon.

It was while he was living here that Bacon – statesman, philosopher, essayist, member of parliament and attorney general – was accused of political and judicial corruption, a charge of which he was palpably and flagrantly guilty. Tried and convicted, he spent a few days in the Tower of London until he was released at the personal request of James I, whereupon he retired to his house at Canonbury and to his books. Banned from holding public office or sitting in parliament, he devoted himself to study and writing – and, it may be assumed, to the cultivation of his garden.

Tenants who followed Sir Francis Bacon after the Civil War (and who presumably also enjoyed the shade and the fruit of his mulberry) included Oliver Goldsmith, who wrote *Vicar of Wakefield* there and whose rent was subsidized by Samuel Johnson, the poet Christopher Smart, Washington Irving and Ephraim Chambers, compiler of the first encyclopedia.

It is tempting to imagine the contribution that each of these singular men might have made to the gardens here. An elegant new house was built under the tower in about 1770, but parts of the garden go back to the early seventeenth century and perhaps earlier. The mulberry now stands in a courtyard bordered on one side by the tower and on another by a small theatre used by the repertory company that now inhabits a part of the tower. On summer nights the area around the mulberry sometimes comes alive with people in unusual costumes, as actors from the company make their entrances across the courtyard.

When the present owner came here fourteen years ago the garden was derelict. Peter Coats' help was enlisted and the quarter-acre site was replanted, with more replanting two years ago.

THE main part of the garden can be viewed from this elegant York stone terrace. It is slightly raised above the lawn and is large enough to take tables and chairs. Just below it is a narrow bed planted with apricot-yellow roses and bordered with *Stachys byzantina* and lavender. Box balls mark the end of the border.

SIR Francis Bacon planted this ancient mulberry, which now stands in a small courtyard on the left hand side of the main garden. A rectangle of random York stone paving was laid on the ground beneath it when its roots surfaced and spoilt the smooth surface of grass.

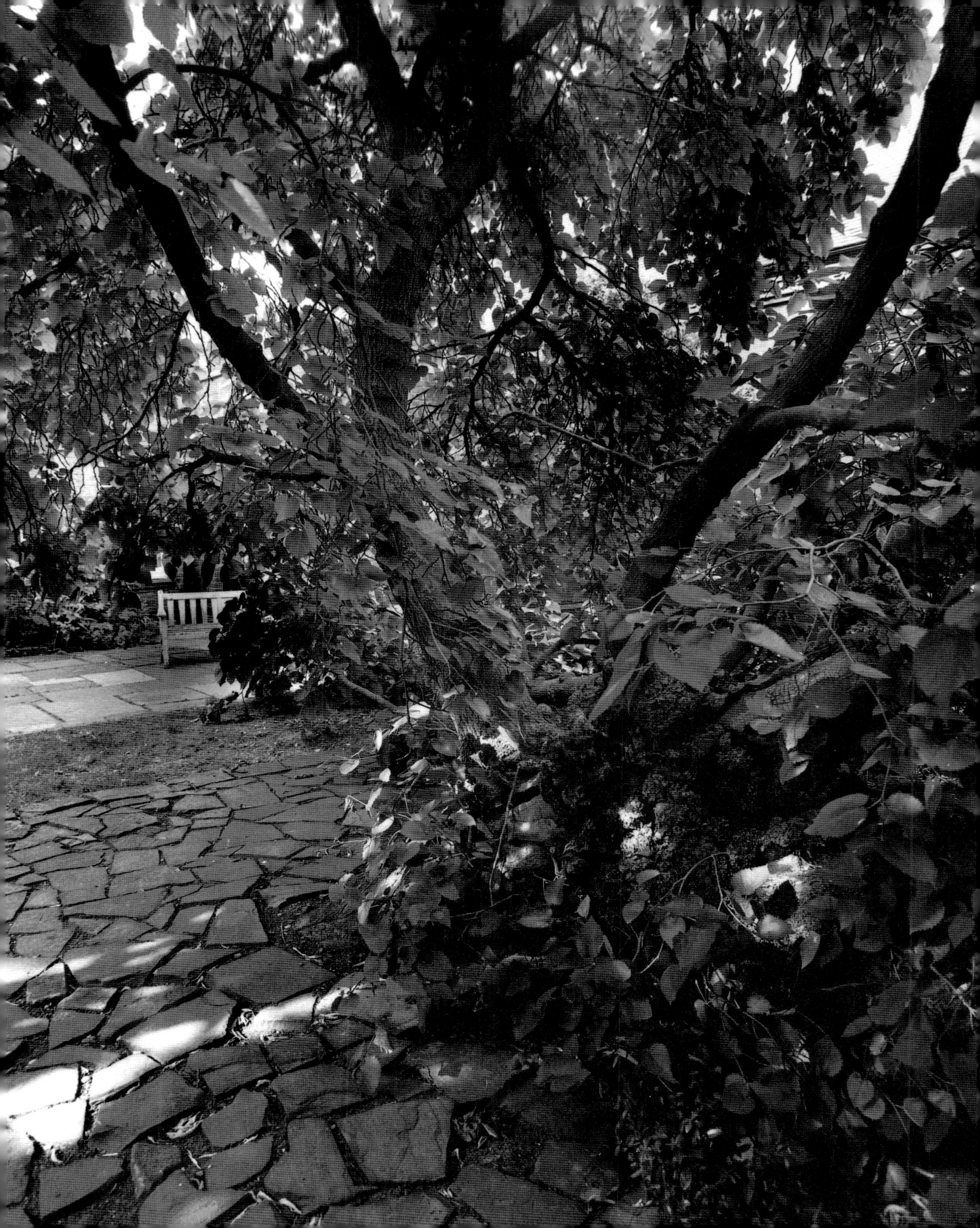

RED hollyhocks and red brick make a successful and daring combination. Hollyhocks line the path which runs under the windows of the theatre building, that forms one side of the courtyard in which the mulberry stands. On summer nights actors in costume sometimes flit across the courtyard to make their entrances, making unusual *tableaux vivants* under the ancient mulberry.

The design is at once fresh and restrained. An elegant York stone terrace, slightly raised above the main lawn and large enough easily to take tables and chairs, runs along the back of the house and under an old Georgian arch smothered in the violet-purple flowered *Clematis* 'Vyvyan Pennell', climbing rose 'Iceberg' and *Solanum jasminoides* 'Album' to the mulberry courtyard. Beyond the arch to the left is a large whitebeam, *Sorbus aria*, with its distinctive silver leaves, and on both corners of the red brick theatre building to the right stand tall bay trees. Planted along the wall are bright red hollyhocks, a daring and successful combination, while the red is picked up by some scarlet pelargoniums under a white rambling rose. The random, straight-coursed York paving continues alongside the borders beneath the buildings, surrounding on three sides the green square of lawn from which the mulberry rises. As the roots of the ancient tree have surfaced over the years and spoilt the smooth surface of the grass, a rectangle of random York paving was laid around the base of the trunk. The neutral background given by the use of stone and grass enhances the beauty and antiquity of the tree, while the occasional spots of carefully chosen colour – blue scillas and *Anemone blanda* – complement the leafy green spectrum of this shady courtyard.

To the other side of the terrace lies another shady retreat, this time more intimate in its proportions and its planting. Here there is more random paving, with deep borders on either side edged with Victorian tiles. Iris, tree peonies, pyracantha, ivy, philadelphus, busy lizzies and other shade-tolerant plants fill the borders, and lilacs, camellias and buddleias meet overhead to form a tunnel. At the far end, where the path opens out, the cool green shade gives way to bright sunlight, which floods in unhindered. A white-painted Victorian seat, placed so as to stop the eye as it travels down the path, takes full advantage of the sunshine, while beside it in the shadows there stands a statue of a young boy in cool and shady retreat.

The interplay of light and shade is a feature of this garden, as is the contrast in atmosphere between the formality of the lawn and its surrounding borders and the more lighthearted intimacy of the small pool and the planting around it. The approach to the pool is formal in mood: a narrow border under the terrace, planted with apricot roses and edged with *Stachys byzantina* and lavender, turns a right-angled corner to follow the path which leads to it. Two steps lead down from the terrace to this path, which lies on axis with the back door to the house, and the angle is marked by a box ball. The planting at the other end of the pool and behind it is much more luxuriant. Variegated water irises (*Iris pseudacorus* 'Variegata') and free-flowering marsh marigolds (*Caltha palustris*) bloom together in early summer at both ends of the pool, their leaves providing effective contrasts of texture and shape for the rest of the summer.

In the raised bed against the retaining wall behind, five *Hebe subalpina* form soft evergreen cushions, interplanted with grey-green mounds of rue, also evergreen, and the rampant *Campanula portenschlagiana*, which makes a curtain of violet-blue in summer. 'Iceberg'

roses grow at the back with taller campanulas, while *C. portenschlagiana* has been allowed to seed itself freely in every nook and cranny, and especially between the paving stones. The dainty fountain, with two basins for the birds, is of lead, a material which in colour and texture is particularly well suited to this garden. Square lead containers also stand along the theatre wall and the margin of the terrace and are filled in winter with variegated ivies and in summer with tall apricot lilies.

The main borders, more stately in mood, form a semicircle around the end of the lawn, under the canopy of two mature horse chestnuts and a London plane. Magnificent as they are, these trees rob the borders below of both light and moisture, and the abundance of shrubs planted here have had to be selected with this in mind. Philadelphus, rhododendrons, camellias, *Fatsia japonica*, hollies plain and variegated, mahonias, berberis, *Sambucus nigra* 'Laciniata', pink-flowered deutzia, *Rubus* Tridel, cotoneaster and hellebores all thrive here, with a ground cover of *Euphorbia amygdaloides robbiae* under the trees. In the one sunny border, against the wall of the theatre, clumps of aquilegias and deep blue delphiniums grow beneath four large *Magnolia grandiflora*, with low-growing potentillas in front.

The refined architecture of the façade of Canonbury House, its blind arcading disappearing under wisterias and ivy and its ground-floor windows decorated with window boxes of white pelargoniums, magenta petunias and lobelia, serves as an apt introduction to the garden within. Could it have been this garden, perhaps not so different from its present incarnation, which prompted Sir Francis Bacon's famous opening to his essay 'Of Gardens'? 'God Almighty first planted a garden. And indeed it is the purest of human pleasures. It is the greatest refreshment to the spirit of man.'

THE lead fountain stands in the middle of a formal rectangular pool. Both ends are planted with water loving plants such as *Iris pseudacorus* 'Variegata' and *Caltha palustris*, their leaves contrasting effectively throughout the summer. In the background a square lead container is planted with tall yellow lilies.

THE LANNING ROPER
MEMORIAL GARDEN

'*Time present and time past*
Are both perhaps present in time future,
And time future contained in time past....
Footfalls echo in the memory
Down the passage which we did not take
Towards the door we never opened
Into the rose-garden.'
T. S. Eliot *Four Quartets*, 'Burnt Norton'

Timelessness is a quality of gardens. The gardener's anticipation of the full-grown tree which will grow from a sapling telescopes the decades, and the passing of the seasons becomes a promise of renewal, and of increasing beauty as plants reach maturity. The fact that this garden is so central to Trinity Hospice – both literally and metaphorically – and is available

THE spreading boughs of a magnificent horse chestnut tree cast their shade over the lawns of Trinity Hospice. When new landscaping work – inspired by Lanning Roper – began in 1983, the mature trees were the only reminder of the garden's former grandeur.

A MODERN and original interpretation of the traditional semicircular seat, this interesting example was designed by Charles Verey. Placed in the dense shade of a large horse chestnut, it views the garden from a good vantage point.

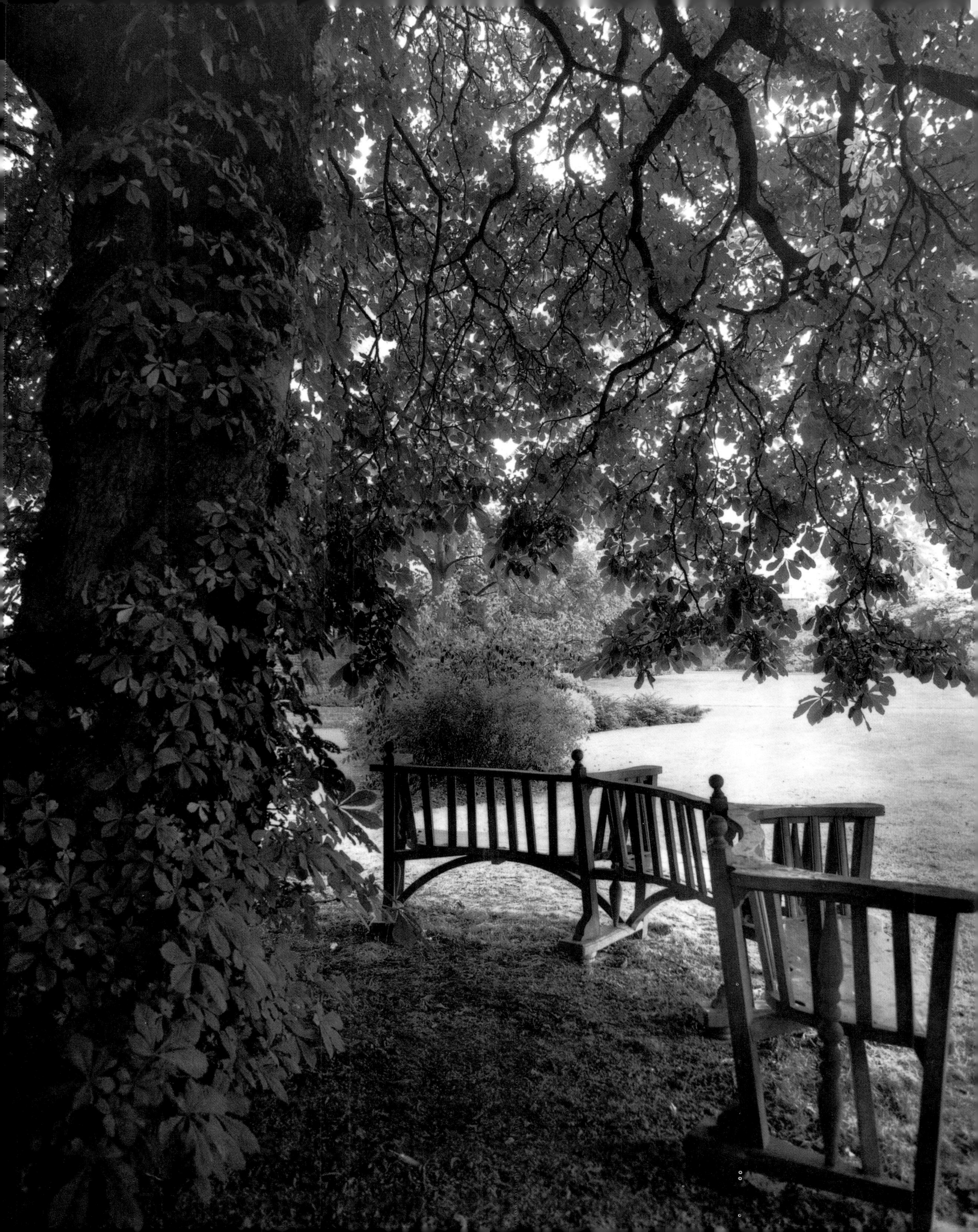

WIDE herbaceous borders line either side of the curved brick path. *Hosta* 'Honeybells', *Achillea* 'Moonlight', and *Lavandula* 'Hidcote' grow in front of the taller shrubs and spill over the path. *Rosa* 'Charles Austin' with its double apricot-yellow flowers, which become pale pink with age, stands upright above a clump of dianthus.

for the enjoyment and comfort of patients, visitors and staff, must surely contribute to the remarkable atmosphere of tranquillity and happiness that pervades the Hospice.

It is poignant that this should have been one of the last gardens on which Lanning Roper worked before he died. By this time of course he had scaled the pinnacles of garden design, had carried out innumerable commissions in grand and celebrated gardens, and had acted as garden consultant to the National Trust and the Prince of Wales. It was early in 1980 that he went to look at the gardens of the four houses overlooking Clapham Common (one of them with a fine eighteenth-century façade) which made up Trinity Hospice, a charitable hospital for the care of those with advanced cancer. The site had a noble history, for Clapham Manor once stood there, and in the seventeenth century Samuel Pepys used to retire there to take the country air. The buildings, though of a later date, retained an air of distinction, but the grounds were sadly dilapidated. The only reminders of former grandeur were some fine trees: two mulberries, a catalpa, a swamp cypress, a weeping ash, a horse chestnut and a plane. It was to these, the 'skeleton' of the gardens, that Lanning Roper first turned his attention. When a purple beech near the pavilion had to be felled because it was dangerous it was replaced in 1981 by another, planted by Her Majesty Queen Elizabeth the Queen Mother, patron of the Hospice.

He also advised on the early stages of the restoration of the gardens, suggesting paths and contours which would lend the flat, two-acre site interest and character. But then essential building works intervened, and by the time these were finished in the autumn of 1982 (leaving the gardens looking rather like the landscape of the moon) Lanning Roper was too ill to continue, and the work was taken over by John Medhurst and David Foreman. The major landscaping that followed in 1983 was inspired by Lanning Roper's ideas and principles of garden design as well as by the specific advice he had given, and the work was made possible by the generous response of his friends to an appeal for gifts of money and plants with which to make a garden in his memory.

It is clear as you approach the Hospice from Clapham Common that the gardens are both well designed and expertly tended. Clever planting means that they are both pretty and practical, for maintenance has necessarily to be kept to a minimum, as the gardens are in the care of just one full-time gardener, Anne Wood, and a team of volunteers. The choicest plants are in the sunny borders under the Hospice's windows: 'Buff Beauty' roses are the main feature in the two borders on either side of the entrance, with lavender in front and *Osmanthus delavayi* behind. Clothing the walls are the sweet-scented *Jasminum officinale affine*, and a superb wisteria on the eighteenth-century façade, *Clematis* 'Lasurstern', with purple-blue flowers from June to October. Along the boundary with the street sycamores, holm oaks and crab apples provide shade and an effective barrier against the noise of the busy traffic. Underneath them is a dense screen of more everyday plants, several species of mahonia, yew, cotoneasters, euonymus and elaeagnus, relieved by the golden *Sambucus racemosa* 'Plumosa Aurea' and a graceful arundinaria.

Strange as it may seem, once within these

leafy confines it is easy to forget the traffic that thunders past, and to allow yourself to be taken over by the peace and quiet of the Hospice. The garden is reached through a little exhibition area, where plans and photographs of its evolution are displayed. From the York stone terrace there is a sweeping view over spacious lawns, herbaceous borders and shrubberies. Mature trees offer height and shade, and some have welcoming seats around their great trunks. Throughout this garden there is thoughtful provision for seating: a pergola and pavilion contain beautifully simple wooden furniture designed by Charles Verey, and elsewhere more seats form an intimate circular sitting area overlooking the pool at the end of the garden, and yet more are dotted liberally along the paths. These paths provide a firm footing for patients and where there are changes of level ramps are provided for access by wheelchair and even by bed.

Skilful placing of trees and shrubs and serpentine paths ensure that the garden cannot be taken in at a glance, and that there is a constant element of surprise – a quality which is attractive in most gardens, and which here, where the desire for privacy and solitude is always respected, is essential. Paths meander through lawns and shrubberies, past sitting areas and pergolas, to the secluded meadow garden at the far end, hidden behind a curving beech hedge. Wild ducks have made their home on the pond here, to the delight of patients and staff, and several families of fluffy

THE paved circle is reached by a path which runs between two herbaceous borders, and is engulfed by romantic planting in soft pastel shades. Height is given by *Rosa* 'Iceberg', *Rosa* 'Mme Hardy' and *Buddleia* 'Lochinch'. Under these are cushions of pink lavender, nepeta and salvia.

187

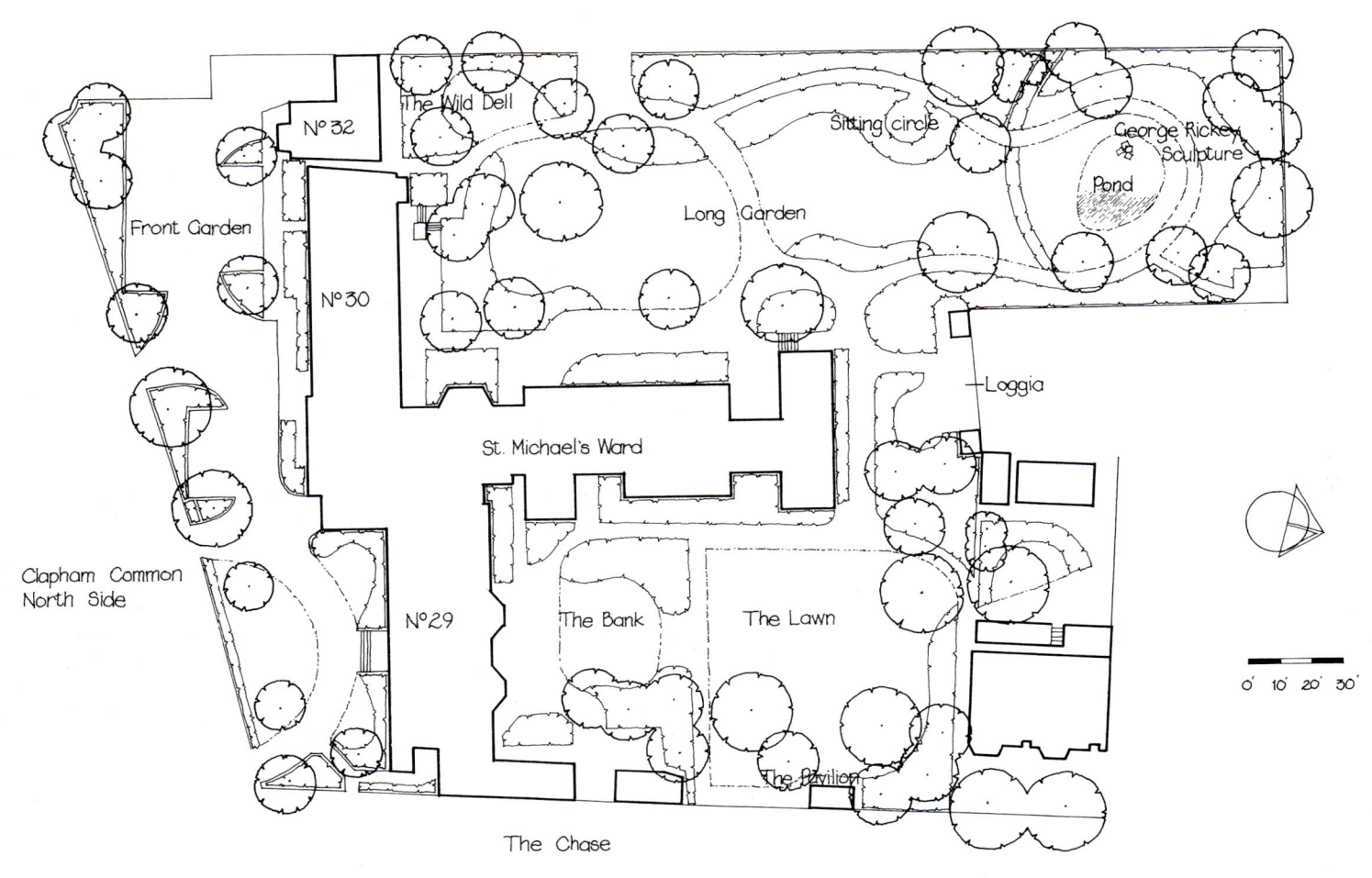

ALTHOUGH more have been planted since, the trees in this garden were the bones from which Lanning Roper developed his scheme.

ducklings have been reared among the long grass and wild flowers at the water's edge.

The garden is enclosed on all sides by high brick walls, where rambling roses flourish, 'Sanders' White Rambler' and 'Toby Tristram' making a very pretty combination with *R. filipes* 'Kiftsgate'. Roses are everywhere in this garden, and Lanning Roper would surely have approved:

'When I let my thoughts wander to the perfect garden, roses are the first flower that always comes to mind. How I love them ... in all the gardens ... including the cottage gardens of country lanes, where climbers and bushes grow over the sheds and walls, through the trees and even in the hedgerows.'

Beneath are planted shrubs carefully selected to go together, among them *Rosa* 'Königin von Dänemark' with *Geranium psilostemon*, underplanted with *Artemisia ludoviciana* 'Silver Queen', agapanthus and *Scabiosa* 'Butterfly Blue', set in front of *Viburnum vitifolium*. Such colour combinations of soft pinks, blues and silver were among Lanning Roper's favourites.

The path then leads you on, beside a carefully planted border with a 'spine' of taller plants all along its length, to a circle where curved stone seats are engulfed by a romantic planting, again in soft pastel shades. Height is given by *Rosa* 'Madame Hardy', lavatera, *Abelia × grandiflora* and *Buddleia* 'Lochinch'. Under these are cushions of pink lavender, purple sage, blue nepeta and the yellow *Achillea* 'Coronation Gold', followed later in the season by *Perovskia* 'Blue Spire', which flowers at the same time as the lavatera.

Beyond this the curved beech hedge conceals the wild garden, where a meadow of wild flowers surrounds the pond. In spring cowslips, fritillaries and orchids bloom under the lilacs and apple blossom, giving way in summer to tall grasses and dog daisies, with wide swathes of comfrey under the trees. Here the soothing, hypnotic effect of water is enhanced by a kinetic sculpture, 'Four Open Squares Horizontal Tapered', by the American sculptor George

Rickey. Four hollow brushed stainless steel frames move constantly and silently with the gentlest breeze, their reflections rippling and dissolving in the water.

A great mulberry tree overhangs the path as it turns back towards the building. The route now goes past a glazed loggia hung with *Wisteria sinensis* and the Chilean glory flower, *Eccremocarpus scaber coccineus*, which shelters inviting wooden seats, and on to a plane tree with its great trunk half encircled by another seat. Beyond the loggia garden the character of the planting changes from sunny border subjects to shade-loving woodland shrubs, which fill the deep border and increase the sense of seclusion. In winter the bare branches of *Hamamelis* 'Pallida' are smothered with clusters of pale yellow, sweetly scented flowers, silhouetted like miniature fireworks against the evergreen foliage of cotoneaster, fatsia and aucuba. In summer these evergreens make a dense backdrop to philadelphus, hypericums and *Hosta sieboldiana*. Other hostas here, 'Thomas Hogg' and 'Honeybells', are particularly good in association with *Osteospermum jucundum*, *Iris pallida*, *Rosa* 'Graham Thomas', *Hemerocallis* 'Golden Chimes' and *Calamintha nepeta nepeta*, which Lanning Roper once remarked to me was one of his favourite plants.

Straight ahead now, beside the parthenocissus-shrouded pavilion, is a yellow border, backed by large free-flowering roses with large single blooms in shades of creamy white, pale yellow and honey gold: 'Nevada', 'Frühlingsgold' and 'Golden Wings'. In front of them is a great cloud of *Alchemilla mollis*, broken by clumps of *Hosta fortunei aurea* and hemerocallis, while the variegated leaves of the taller philadelphus and physocarpus add to the golden scheme, which is thrown into relief by evergreens behind.

It is tempting to sit a moment in the pavilion and look back over the lawn to the house, which rises above a densely planted bank buttressed by a retaining wall. Here, beneath cherries and a large *Magnolia × soulangeana*, grow plants which prefer dry sunny conditions. 'Hidcote' lavender, *Agapanthus* Headbourne Hybrids, *Geranium × riversleaianum* 'Russell Prichard' and *Ceanothus thyrsiflorus* 'Repens' together make another wonderful kaleidoscope of blues, mauves and magentas.

No single epithet can describe this garden: it has romance in the intimacy of the sitting circle; cottage-garden arrangements in its nursery beds, with its wigwams of sweet peas and its clumps of pinks and lavender; botanical interest in the plants donated by Kew Gardens and others; architectural interest in its sculpture and pavilions; the thrill of secrecy in the wilderness area; formality in its clipped hedges; and more. Nor can it be called a 'spring' or 'summer' garden, for it has been designed with every season in mind: wild flowers, bulbs and blossom in spring; roses, of course, in summer; cyclamen, amelanchier and Virginia creeper in autumn; and in winter the evergreens come into their own. Better perhaps simply to enjoy it then, rather than attempting to pigeonhole it, and to remark and remember the influence of Lanning Roper, who sadly did not live to see the garden finished.

THIS modern sculpture by the American George Rickey hovers just above the water, the hollow stainless steel frames move constantly and silently with the breeze.

MALVERN TERRACE, BARNSBURY

'The smallest garden may be a picture, and not only may we have much more variety in any one garden, but, if we give up imitating each other, may enjoy charming contrasts between gardens.' William Robinson, champion of the 'natural' school of gardening against the well-drilled excesses of high Victorian ornamentalism, would surely have approved of the gardens of Malvern Terrace; for modesty, simplicity and charm, the qualities that he recommended most highly in gardens, are to be found here in abundance.

A picturesque cobbled lane overlooking a leafy square, Malvern Terrace has somehow retained some of the rural atmosphere of old Barnsbury, before the stuccoed streets and crescents were laid out. This row of a dozen or so houses was built in the late 1830s on a part of the site of Thomas Albion Oldfield's dairy, chinoiserie teahouse and cricket ground, to which the burghers of London, their servants and apprentices used to flock at holiday times towards the end of the eighteenth century.

When building this simple country terrace

THIS small garden has a cool, shady feel about it, like a small courtyard. The pretty palmate leaves of *Acer shirasawanum* 'Aureum' crowd the flat branches of this small tree in the foreground, its only disadvantage being that is is very slow to grow to any size. A small form of *Acer palmatum dissectum* at the back forms a small mound against an Irish yew.

the builders did not see the need to impose the rigid uniformity expected of the grander terraces in towns. Instead a general unity of architectural style was imposed rather loosely, and within this each two-storey slate-roofed house plays a variation on a theme. A white-painted string course runs the length of the London brick terrace, and all the window frames and their facings are painted white. The ground-floor windows are elegantly arched, and each front door is topped with a pretty fanlight echoing the rounded shape. Beyond this the houses have their individual character: some have a white-stuccoed ground floor, others are all brick; the grandest are double-fronted with three bays, the smallest a minuscule one-up one-down cottage with barely room to squeeze the front door in beside the window.

The gardens show a similar approach, pleasantly relaxed and yet also aware of an aesthetic scheme which seems to encompass them all in a larger whole. Varying in size from small to tiny, they all have elegant wrought-iron railings, with a gate opening from each garden on to the cobbled street. Each is individual, serving the differing needs of the occupants, but nothing jars. None of the houses has more than a tiny yard at the back, so this is where all the outdoor living goes on. Some have paddling pools and children's toys on patches of lawn; some have terraces set with tables and chairs; and everyone has to find somewhere to put the dustbin.

The planting of the gardens also shares this agreeable balance of harmony and individuality. Most have paths with herbaceous borders on one or both sides, which tend to be filled with old-fashioned cottage-garden plants. One simply has 'Iceberg' roses growing against the railings, with violas growing through them and alpine strawberries as ground cover; others are a billowing mass of foxgloves and lavender, geraniums and hollyhocks, acanthus and verbena, with clematis and climbing roses everywhere. Some have hedges covering the railings, others have climbers delicately twisting through them; some houses are decorated with neat windowboxes and pots below; others are engulfed by honeysuckle or clematis, jasmine or ivy, wisteria or a *Rosa banksiae*. Most have an open, sunny feel; one is a cool shady courtyard, where the boughs of trees and shrubs meet over mossy cobbles and pebbles to make a bower of green. Together they make not only a delightful prospect, but also a fascinating lesson in the marriage of individual expression and discreet cooperation.

Having begun with William Robinson it seems appropriate to finish with his disciple Gertrude Jekyll. Less evangelical and more philosophical in her approach, though she would undoubtedly have been equally charmed by the gardens of Malvern Terrace she might have reflected upon them: 'The size of a garden has very little to do with its merit. . . . It is the size of [the owner's] heart and brain and goodwill that will make his garden either delightful or dull.'

THE gardens of Malvern Terrace complement its architecture perfectly. This row of small cottages overlooking a cobbled lane takes the visitor back to the days before the great Victorian building boom which covered the fields of Barnsbury with stucco. Just as the houses all vary slightly, so the gardens combine a harmony of style with individuality of character: most are extremely pretty variations on a simple cottage-garden theme.

THE small path leading to the house, gently curves towards the front door leaving enough space for a border on the right and a generous lawn edged by another border on the other side. Here may be found roses and lavender and other plants such as geraniums, foxgloves and alpine strawberries.

A LOW-MAINTENANCE GARDEN

Grand in an eccentric manner, this evergreen and gold garden manages to be at once imposing and slightly frivolous. Solemn conifers and the rather sombre planting of the Victorian shrubbery frame the broad expanse of lawn in an apparently conventional fashion – yet the more you look the more you become aware of its original shapes and planting combinations. Halfway down the lawn, for instance, is a spreading yew, from the midst of whose arching fronds there rises, quite unexpectedly, a giant hogweed; and further down are scattered asymmetrical blocks of golden and variegated box. The effect is of an open-air hall of living sculpture in every shade of green, mannerist and occasionally surreal in conception. The topiary and closely planted shrubs create optical illusions, distortions of perspective and scale, as though a child had been playing with giant building blocks of soft green leaves.

The house, built in 1832 on meadowland then attached to Fitzroy Farm, stands on the highest point in London, and shares Cob Stenham's magnificent views over Hampstead Heath (see pp. 70–77). A fine hornbeam hedge screens the front garden, while at the back of the elegantly proportioned house pretty bowed windows seem to preside watchfully over this wayward garden. Since the present owner moved in in 1951 the half-acre of garden has, as she puts it, 'just grown'. She admits to no design, but planned it for year-round interest and minimum upkeep, as she looks after it all herself. When she arrived the garden was laid out with rose beds and herbaceous borders, with a large kitchen garden at the bottom. All this was to go, to be replaced by an encyclopedic array of evergreen and variegated trees and shrubs. With no herbaceous border, no vegetables and only three roses, this is a garden dedicated to leaf colour and texture, and to architectural shapes.

A few steps lead down from one side of the terrace to the path below, which lies parallel to it, bordered by a raised bed planted with many different species of thyme. Here great blocks of golden yew posted like sentinels at the corners of the lawn act as points of alignment, imposing a strong sense of balance. For you are drawn automatically to the mid-point between the two, where you find yourself on axis with the house and garden, and gazing directly at the focal point, a *Magnolia* × *soulangiana* 'Alba Superba' rising from a circular bed. In former times this was a pond, which had been filled in by the previous owner for the safety of his young children. Now the magnolia is underplanted with several species of ivy, glossy dark green and variegated, and ringed with asymmetrical blocks of variegated yellow box (*Buxus sempervirens* 'Marginata').

The graceful fronds of innumerable different conifers, including a large collection of junipers, stretch out to each other across the

IN the former kitchen garden meandering paths twist away in all directions through layers of greenery, overhung by the boughs of old apple and pear trees.

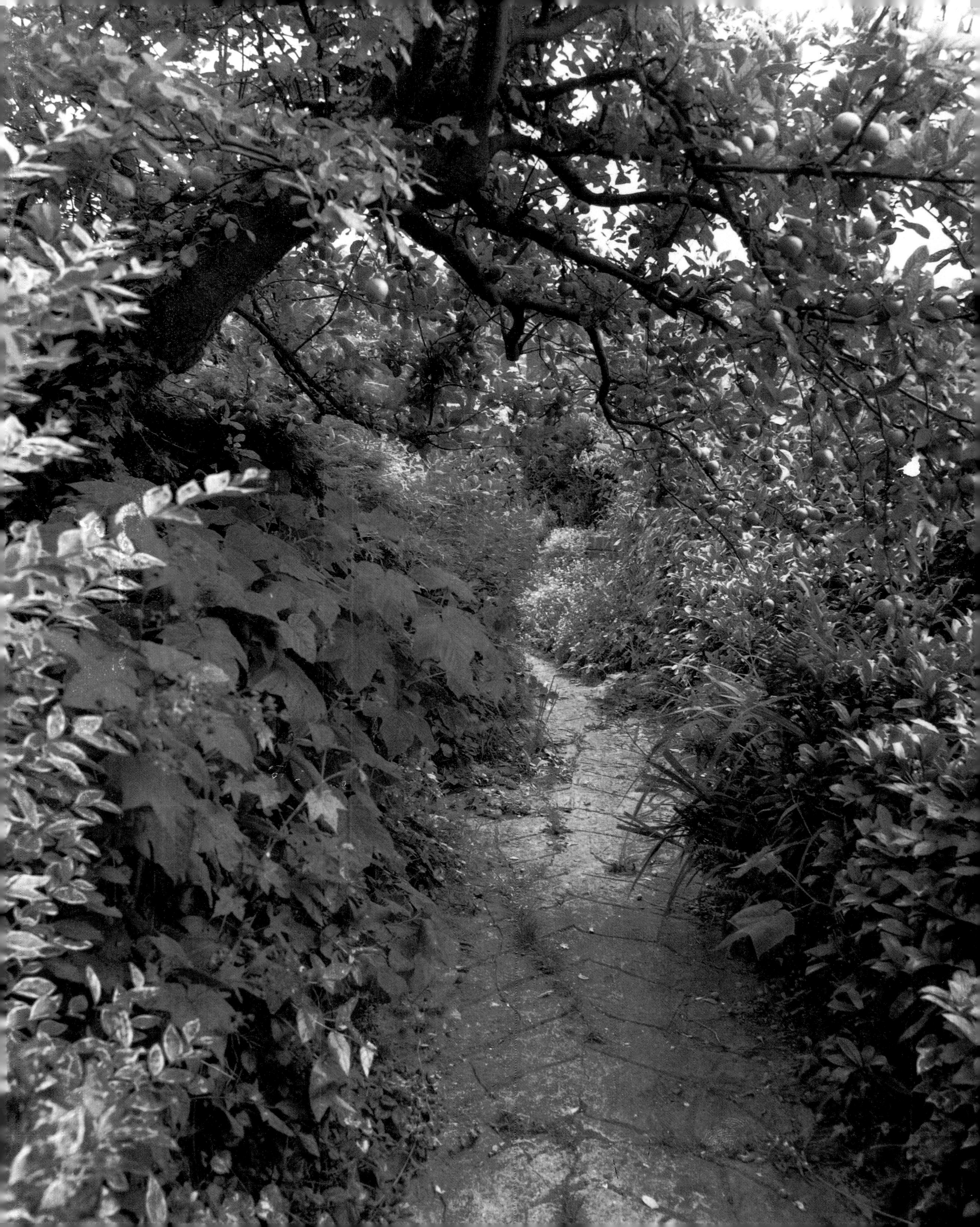

CONIFERS rise from the dense planting. *Bergenia cordifolia* is used here as an edging to the narrow border along the brick colonnade. Self-seeded *Euphorbia characias wulfenii*, *Iris sibirica* and cotoneaster are planted near a narrow stretch of water which runs parallel to a lichen-covered stone path.

A WALK through the shady green tunnels that flank the lawns becomes a voyage of discovery, with every fork or bend promising new interest: an old church pew under the boughs of a silver juniper, a statue emerging from the undergrowth, a mossy stone balustrade in a pool of sunlight – or a cat enjoying the cool shade.

lawn. Perhaps the most dramatic of these is the *Taxus baccata* 'Dovastonii Aurea' whose spreading branches cradle the giant hogweed during the summer months. This specimen, now approaching middle age (it was among the first things planted by the present owner) has yellow margins to its leaves which, as they hang gracefully from the long weeping branchlets, seem to hold the light, as though permanently lit by a low autumn sun.

The lawn gives a deceptive impression of openness, for it is flanked on both sides by shady tunnels like the transepts of a vegetable cathedral. The tall brick boundary walls are clothed with a jungle of greenery: one small section contains a fig tree, a wisteria, a *Vitis vinifera* 'Purpurea', an akebia, and some of the numberless ivies growing in the garden (at one time there were well over thirty different species). A walk through these green tunnels becomes a voyage of discovery, with every fork or bend promising to reveal a little clearing or a new vista. You may come across an old stone balustrade, shrouded in moss and ivy, where sunlight suddenly penetrates the cool shade; a little seat, hidden from sight but overlooking the lawn; a statue half-hidden in the undergrowth; or an old church pew under the swaying branches of a silver juniper. Every contour is shaded by overhanging branches and softened by clematis, loniceras and other climbers. Every corner seems to hide another nook or enclave, aromatic with the scent of box, where a seat thoughtfully placed tempts you to linger a while and contemplate the view.

Under the shade of towering yews, cypresses, junipers and thujas wild strawberries have seeded themselves among the ivies and periwinkles that spread underfoot, and in summer the deep green is dotted with the yellow of Welsh poppies and splashed with white iberis in drifts. The lower 'walls' of the tunnels are formed by a multitude of shrubs, many of them evergreen or variegated, or both. A *Cornus stolonifera* 'Flaviramea', with young shoots of yellow or olive-green, grows through the most dashing of the spotted laurels, *Aucuba japonica* 'Crotonifolia'. Nearby stands a *Symphoricarpos orbiculatus* 'Foliis Variegatis', with yellow-margined leaves, behind an unusual hedge of *Stephanandra incisa*, with its distinctive zig-zag stems. The north-facing wall behind is clad with a huge *Hydrangea petiolaris*, below which camellias flourish in white and all shades of red and pink, interspersed with graceful self-seeded ferns. In autumn the feathery heads of Aaron's rod poke through among the pretty dried flower heads of the many hydrangeas, and the cotinus are eye-catching in warm, brilliant shades of ochre, burnt umber and deep purple. Meanwhile a pyracantha heavy with close-packed orange berries contrasts well with the white 'snowballs' on the bare branches of some large symphoricarpus.

Beyond the camellias, in a nook formed by the tall boundary wall and a brick colonnade that crosses the garden at the foot of the lawn, is a golden corner. Here *Euonymus japonicus* 'Ovatus Aureus', *Ligustrum ovalifolium* 'Aureum' and *Hedera helix* 'Buttercup' flourish beneath a bust of Cicero, over whom there is set a wartime inscription from the walls of the present owner's husband's office. It is somehow an appropriate introduction to the next part of the garden, for beyond this point you enter a different realm.

As they pass under the arches of the colonnade the narrow paths snake out of view, meandering and multiplying to form a labyrinthine wilderness. Here the delicate balance of power between man and nature seems perilously close to being tipped in nature's favour. There is a sense of mystery and excitement in the air, and it is no surprise to learn that children adore it here. The tiny woodland paths twist away in all directions through the dense undergrowth: geraniums, ivies and lamium stroke your ankles as you pass, occasionally spreading right across the path to detain you further, while clematis and loniceras catch at your hair and shoulders. The tide of greenery seems to be advancing in soft waves, submerging seats, sheds and paths, while tall shrubs, trees and terracotta chimney pots bearing plants aloft emerge from the swell.

The division between these two worlds is marked by the brick colonnade, its crevices colonized by corydalis and ivy-leaved toadflax and its pillars 'buttressed' with unclipped box. Parallel to it and just behind is a long, narrow water garden bordered by lichen-covered stone slabs – laid in the days when, as the owner recalls, 'you could simply go to the local dump and collect them'. The idea was inspired by her memories of working in Persia before the war, where she was particularly struck by the system of tiny canals that ran round and even through

A VIEW from above reveals the remarkable variety of colour and shape in this evergreen garden, achieved mainly with conifers: the effect is like an open-air gallery of living sculpture. Beyond, the magnificent view over Hampstead Heath sweeps away to the horizon.

195

A BRICK colonnade crosses the garden at the foot of the lawn. Its pillars are buttressed with unclipped variegated box and its crevices and cracks are colonized by ivy-leaved toadflax and corydalis. Through the openings you glimpse a path meandering away and multiplying to form a labyrinthine wilderness.

the houses. Here grows the variegated form of the yellow-flowered true water iris, *I. pseudacorus* 'Variegata', surrounded by self-seeded euphorbias, bergenia, *Cotoneaster horizontalis* and even a yellow-flowering fremontodendron. Ivies, ever-present in this garden, here form soft hummocks and smother the foot-high walls that border the paths, and the water is overlooked by a green marble seat in the deep shade of an ivy arch which echoes the shape of the colonnade. Under one of the brick arches meanwhile, against a backdrop of snakebark maple and topiary yew, lies another seat, which overlooks a small grove of berberis, variegated osmanthus (*O. heterophyllus* 'Aureomarginatus'), ilex and a spreading picea. And to one side, in the lee of the great buttress wall and raised on a three-foot-high platform reached by crumbling steps, this thoughtful garden provides yet another seat, this time for the contemplation of the incomparable view westwards over the Heath. It is framed in the foreground by drifts of rampant *Campanula portenschlagiana*, corydalis and clove-scented pinks, which have seeded themselves in every cranny and crevice and spread along the wall.

Below lies the wilderness, its floor in summer a sea of the pink flowers of *Geranium endressii* and the yellow of *L. galeobdolon*, whose evergreen, silver-flushed leaves turn bronze in winter. A spreading clump of the ivy-like *Asarum caudatum* has recently begun to produce its exotic, orchid-like flowers, and in autumn fragile-looking cyclamens flower deep pink. Among the host of shrubs that form the virtually impenetrable undergrowth are a delicate, slender-leaved indigofera, a pretty *Corylus avellana* 'Contorta', with its corkscrew foliage, an unusual *Ligustrum ovalifolium* 'Argenteum', the variegated buddleia 'Harlequin', a beacon for butterflies, and *Hebe* 'Midsummer Beauty', which flowers well into November. And of course there are several varieties of box: yellow-leaved (*Buxus sempervirens* 'Latifolia Maculata'), narrow-leaved (*B. s.* 'Angustifolia'), and the rare blue-leaved variety. Above this rises a tall yew hedge with an archway cut through it, and nearby are some gnarled apple trees, 'John Downie' with *Clematis macropetala* scrambling through its branches, a Bramley clothed in the long, evergreen leaves of *C. armandii*, and a Siberian crab, laden in autumn with beautiful gold and scarlet fruit. They are a reminder of the days when this was the kitchen garden – indeed the chickens once kept here may be partly responsible for the evident fertility of the soil. At the far end rise two ghostly eucalyptus trees, their smooth bark mottled in buff and silver.

Among its many unusual qualities this garden combines three which are rarely found together: plantsmanship, practicality and intriguing design. It is a connoisseur's garden which of necessity largely looks after itself: thus ferns and euphorbias, cotoneasters and corydalis, ivy-leaved toadflax, lamium and geraniums have naturalized and seeded themselves among the strong architectural framework provided by the conifers. A designer's eye, unafraid of risks and eccentricity, was needed to conceive the strong shapes that echo and frame each other; the myriad combinations of colour and texture; and the audacious asymmetry of the topiary, constantly held in check and balanced by the symmetry of the overall conception. The gaiety that in other gardens is provided by flowers here is found in leaf colour and texture; and when the delicate woodland flowers bloom their colours assume their true value against the broad backcloth of shady greens and soft golds.

A HIGHGATE GARDEN

Mrs Sue Whittington's Highgate house, which dates from about 1760, has the spacious proportions of the Georgian era. It has been a hospital in its time, and an old plaque in the kitchen describes it as a 'House of rest and recreation for women and girls' – a description which takes on a note of irony in the light of the great amounts of time and energy that Mrs Whittington clearly devotes to her garden, packed with complex planting chosen and maintained entirely by herself.

In the early nineteenth century the gardens, then more extensive, were laid out in the Italian manner then in vogue, as expounded in an article which appeared in *The Gardener's Magazine* in 1828. The author, who signed him or herself 'An Amateur', while a professed admirer of the groves and lawns, shrubberies and 'gaudy flower-beds' of English gardens, felt they were unsuited to the English climate:

FROM the top of the steps the path leads down the slope to a woodland walk where roses and clematis cascade down from the tall trees. *Elaeagnus pungens* 'Maculata', pyracantha and camellias are planted beneath and ivies cover the ground and grow up the trees where allowed.

'What are they for the greater part of the year? Do dripping shrubs, do wet grass, and swampy ground, and flower-beds, known only as beds for flowers by their dingy mould, contrasted with the yellow lawn, do all, or any one of these, invite us into the open air? Do we not rather turn our backs upon them, stir up our fire, resume our book, and sit at home?'

An Italian garden, on the other hand, while foreign in every sense of the word to English habit, would solve all these problems:

'A plot of ground, of one acre only, attached to the mansion, laid out in the Italian manner, with its terrace, steps, balustrades, vases, fountain, and rectangular gravel walks, will add more to the cheerfulness of both the exterior and interior of that mansion ... than five times the quantity of land laid out according to our present English style of gardening.'

The terrain here lent itself perfectly to such a scheme, for a level terrace outside the house fell away steeply to the east, as if waiting to be clad with steps, balustrades and waterfalls. It was a style of gardening which, except when attached to the grandest buildings, was doomed not to survive much beyond the First World War, however. For it was of the labour-intensive school for which Robert Barr, co-founder with Jerome K. Jerome of *The Idler*, had some tips at the turn of the century: 'The best way to get real enjoyment out of the garden is to put on a wide straw hat, dress in thin loose-fitting clothes, hold a little trowel in one hand and a cool drink in the other, and tell the man where to dig.' Such gardens faced a long slow decline as social conditions changed.

Mrs Whittington has been here for eleven years. Within the formal framework that remained of the Italian garden she has added a tremendous number and variety of plants, encouraging them to spread and seed themselves at will, and to clamber over and through each other in romantic profusion. Her passion for plants is immediately evident as you step on to the York stone terrace, where creeping thymes, lavender, pinks, sisyrinchium and clouds of pale pink *Erigeron karvinskianus* have colonized the crevices. The rare *Hieracium villosum* adds touches of silver with its salvia-like felted leaves, and delicate diascias and *Pelargonium* 'Frank Headley' grow in pots, as do intoxicatingly scented lilies.

The white-fading-to-pink daisy flowers of erigeron, which seeds itself like a weed in conditions that suit it, fringe the steps leading up to the elegant stuccoed porch. Cushions of cistus flank the smooth white pilasters, the hardy *C. × corbariensis* on one side, with pure white flowers opening from crimson buds, and on the other *C. ladanifer*, with crumpled white petals stained brown at the base. *Rosa* 'Mme Grégoire Staechelin', which does not mind a north wall and bears magnificent large loosely formed pink flowers, grows up the house with a purple clematis, and the richer, darker blue flowers of *Ceanothus* 'Burkwoodii' extend the flowering season into the autumn.

Beneath its carpet of flowers this terrace is the formal part of the garden: a vista extends from the porch, across the stone flags and through an arch in a high beech hedge, where your eye is drawn down some steps to a graceful Victorian statue. Flanking the terrace at right angles to the beech hedge is a tall hedge of pyracantha, and in

The woodland path crosses over a small pool fed by a waterfall from a smaller pool above. The moist and cool borders are planted with low-growing *Acer japonicum*, *Juniperus sabina* var. *tamariscifolia*, abelia, hosta, fuchsias, foxgloves and ferns.

combination with the weathered stone these walls of green make a strongly architectural framework. This formality is emphasized by the symmetrical arrangement of four rectangular flower beds, set into the terrace to either side of the main axis and parallel to it.

The planting which fills the beds in lax profusion provides an equally strong counterpoint to the formality: 'Iceberg' and crimson roses, mingling with *Artemisia* 'Powis Castle' and *Phygelius* 'Winchester Fanfare' and the great round flower heads of allium, are densely underplanted with *Euphorbia amygdaloides* 'Purpurea', *Fuchsia magellanica*, *Alchemilla mollis* and a mass of other old-fashioned plants, while under the beech hedge *Campanula portenschlagiana* romps through all the cracks in the paving stone.

Under the pyracantha hedge to the right is a cool, shady spot where Mrs Whittington has plans to build a rose pergola. On the other side of the terrace the ground falls away steeply, and your eye is carried over the tapestry of green that covers the slope to the horizon beyond. At the edge of the terrace, behind the rose bed, is another parallel bed where a large *Rosa* 'Canary Bird' is silhouetted against dark conifers and the sky. Beside it is the purple-green foliage of a *Rosa glauca*, and in front are the white tiers of a *Viburnum plicatum* 'Mariesii' and a low mound of sculptural sea-green acanthus leaves. In the cracks below, lamium, helianthemums, hellebores and lychnis (campion) mingle with ever-present erigeron. Composed with care for balance, proportion and colour, this is one of the many telling combinations for which this garden is notable.

From the top of the steep path that leads down the slope the eye is caught by a pretty combination of a *Robinia pseudoacacia*, *Pyrus salicifolia* and a delicate variegated cornus, all in shades of palest green and soft silver-grey. Clustered together at the bottom of the slope, they act as a focal point at the same time as screening the building behind. Hidden to the left is the greenhouse sheltering Mrs

EVERY crevice in the York stone terrace has been colonized by thymes, lavenders, pinks, sisyrinchium and clouds of *Erigeron karvinskianus*. The wide borders are filled with crimson roses and *Rosa* 'Iceberg' is densely underplanted with hellebores, ruta, diascias and *Erysimum* 'Bowles' Mauve'. In the far border the purple grey-green foliage of *Rosa glauca* and a purple berberis are well combined with a large *Rosa* 'Canary Bird' and the silver pear in the back, in the front is a handsome *Viburnum plicatum* 'Mariesii'.

On this side of the terrace, a path falls away steeply, stepped at first and then curving down the slope. Clumps of herbaceous peonies, senecio, skimmias and azaleas form interesting rounded shapes to either side.

CLEMATIS montana clambers to the pinnacle of a giant silver chamaecyparis only to cascade down again like a liana. Iris send their tall pointed leaves through an azalea, below them and around them hostas, pulmonarias, ferns and variegated brunnera thrive in the cool woodland air.

Whittington's many seedlings and cuttings, and at the top of the slope, in full sun, is an alpine garden. There are very many species here, all growing in terracotta troughs for want of space anywhere else, and growing up the basement wall behind are peachy apricot *Rosa* 'Climbing Lady Hillingdon' with soft tangerine *Abutilon* × *milleri*. Honeysuckle reaches up to twine round the alpine troughs, and more pots contain pineapple sage, saxifrage and the unusual *Sauromatum venosum*.

The descent of the hill below is a catalogue of imaginative associations: the eye is drawn hither and thither as you pass *Rosa* 'The Fairy', covered in clusters of small pink rosettes, and *R. glauca*, both underplanted with the graceful tall grass Gardener's Garters and with shell-pink *Clematis* 'Hagley Hybrid' growing through them, followed by the deeply fragrant *R.* 'Ferdinand Pichard', with flowers striped in red, pale pink and white, above the blue-green leaves of *Hosta sieboldiana* 'Elegans'. Euphorbia, *Ribes sanguineum* 'Brocklebankii', golden philadelphus and the pyrus form groups of silver and yellow foliage with touches of pink, while a white azalea is eye-catching against dark skimmias and viburnums. Beyond, crimson-flowered *Clematis* 'Kermesina' winds through an old lilac, and a rhododendron glows red beneath. Near by one of Mrs Whittington's favourite roses, 'Mrs Oakley Fisher', bears large, very simple single blooms in shades of apricot and pale ochre.

Narrow cobbled and stone paths twist off to left and right and as the foliage closes over your head you become aware of the sound of falling water. Round a pool fed by a waterfall from a smaller pool above is a cool, moist area planted with *Juniperus* 'Blue Carpet', white variegated, hostas, fuchsias, foxgloves and ferns, with carpets of pale pink *Geranium endressii* underfoot. In this secluded woodland glade, home to a host of frogs, newts and dragonflies, the change of mood from the sunny, open, architectural terrace is complete.

Below the pool is a seat from which to enjoy the refreshing shade, the soothing sound of water, and the view back up the densely planted slope. Tall dark conifers grow here, their outlines softened by climbers growing through them: a Scots pine is smothered in an old white rose, and a *Clematis montana* clambers to the pinnacle of a giant silver chaemacyparis. Along the woodland path that winds past them the emphasis is on foliage plants. Outstanding among these is *Melianthus major*, its deeply serrated glaucous leaves, beautiful and rather subtropical, spreading under the coppery foliage of *Prunus cerasifera* 'Pissardii', with fresh green philadelphus and the large velvety leaves of *Hydrangea sargentiana* beneath.

Meandering past the knotty roots of trees, the path brings you on to a shady lawn, climbing gently all the time until you reach the garden where the statue stands. Green walls rise ahead and on both sides: the beech hedge on the right and on the left the pyracantha hedge which frames the statue, while a *Clematis viticella* 'Purpurea Plena Elegans' winds round its niche. A herbaceous bed beneath the beech hedge is full of late-flowering cottage-garden plants: pale pink penstemons under feathery bronze fennel; salvia with deep rose-pink lychnis against the aromatic grey-green foliage and blue flowers of caryopteris; lobelia, violas and *Nepeta nervosa* under hebe; and soft pink *Clematis* 'Comtesse de Bouchaud' behind.

The scope of this garden is enormous: taking full advantage of London's benign microclimate and soil it gathers together a great variety of species and genera, and yet manages to unite them in a cohesive and aesthetic whole. It is also a garden of changing rhythms and moods, soothing and stimulating in equal measure; and a similar opposition is to be found in the contrast of romantic planting and the grandeur of formal vistas and clipped hedges. Sue Whittington has combined her skill as a designer and her enthusiasm as a plant-lover to make a garden that wears its considerable botanical interest lightly. Concentrating on the contriving of graceful and expressive combinations of plants, she displays rare specimens and old favourites alike in a new light, which serves to reveal their special qualities with a fresh clarity.

WHITE variegated hostas, planted on either side of the narrow cobbled path, brighten this shady corner together with *Iris foetidissima* 'Variegata'. Behind, an escallonia gracefully surrounds the sculptural trunk and branches of *Pyrus salicifolia*.

A VISTA extends from the porch, across the stone flags and through an arch in a high beech hedge, where your eye is drawn down some steps to a graceful Victorian statue.

A WHITE GARDEN

The white stucco houses of a street in central London are set back from the street, so that in spring and summer their gardens merge into one another. In spring they virtually disappear under a froth of pink and white cherry blossom, punctuated by magnolias, lilacs and camellias, and in summer the borders spill over with cistus, roses and a mass of other flowering shrubs.

One house, on the shady side of the road, displays a rather different approach, more restrained though equally attractive. A thirty-foot standard bay tree fills one side of the drive, and on the other I planned pleached limes to screen the house, a sort of high-rise hedge on stilts. Beneath, a pattern of closely planted box hedges and balls covers the bare earth completely and makes a layer of sculptured green; and between the two, winding up over the fence and the gateposts, is the evergreen *Rosa* 'Mermaid', shade-tolerant and extremely vigorous, with fragrant single creamy yellow

Bupleurum fruticosum spills over the raised border below the drawing room terrace, its greeny-yellow flowers smothering the grey-green leaves. A white marguerite is planted in a pretty terracotta jar against the trellis.

THREE steps lead from the octagonal brick terrace up to a York stone terrace. Perppermint scented *Mentha requienii*, *Veronica gentianoides* creep along the cracks, while sysirinchiums and tightly clipped santolianas give a little height where necessary.

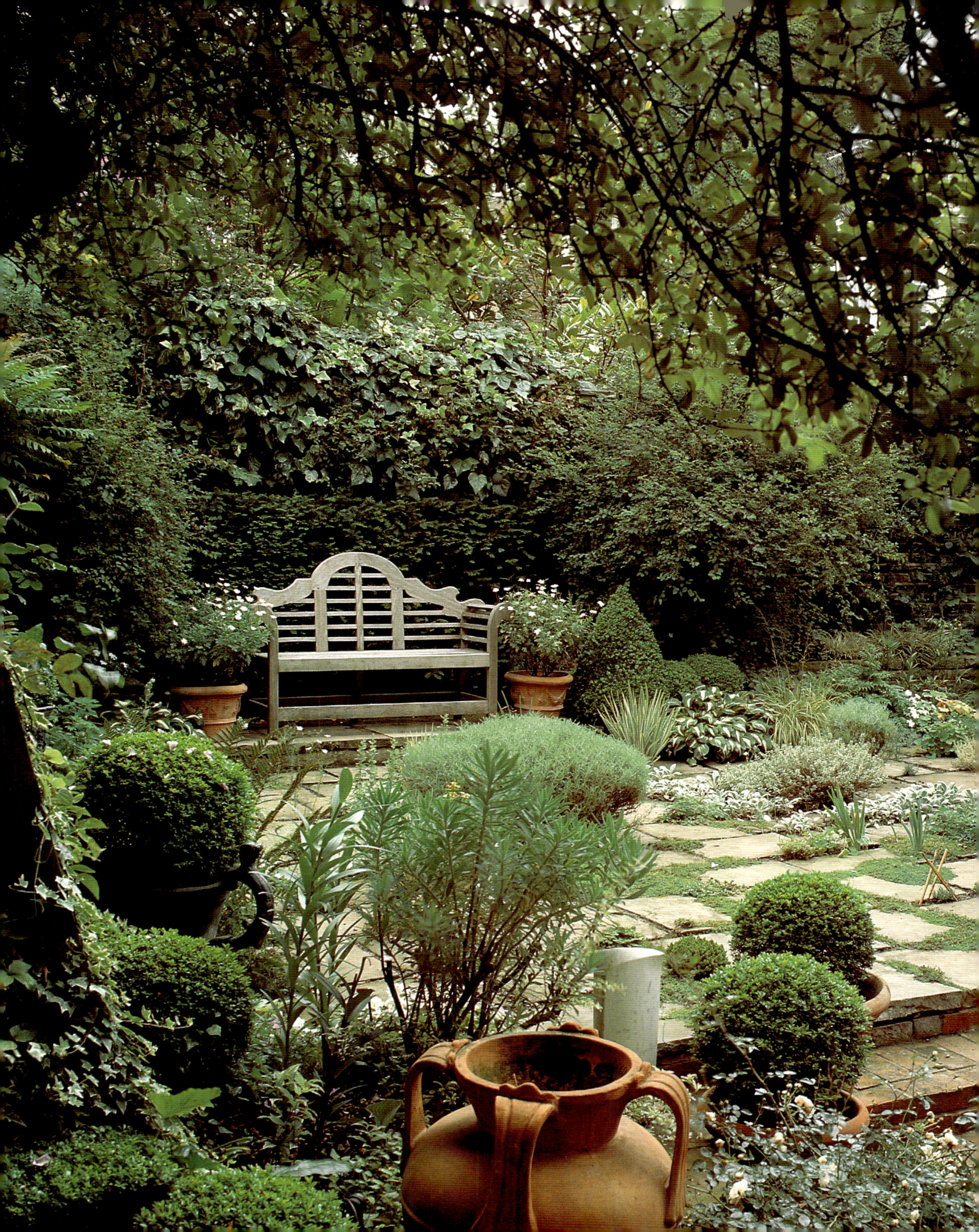

A WHITE GARDEN

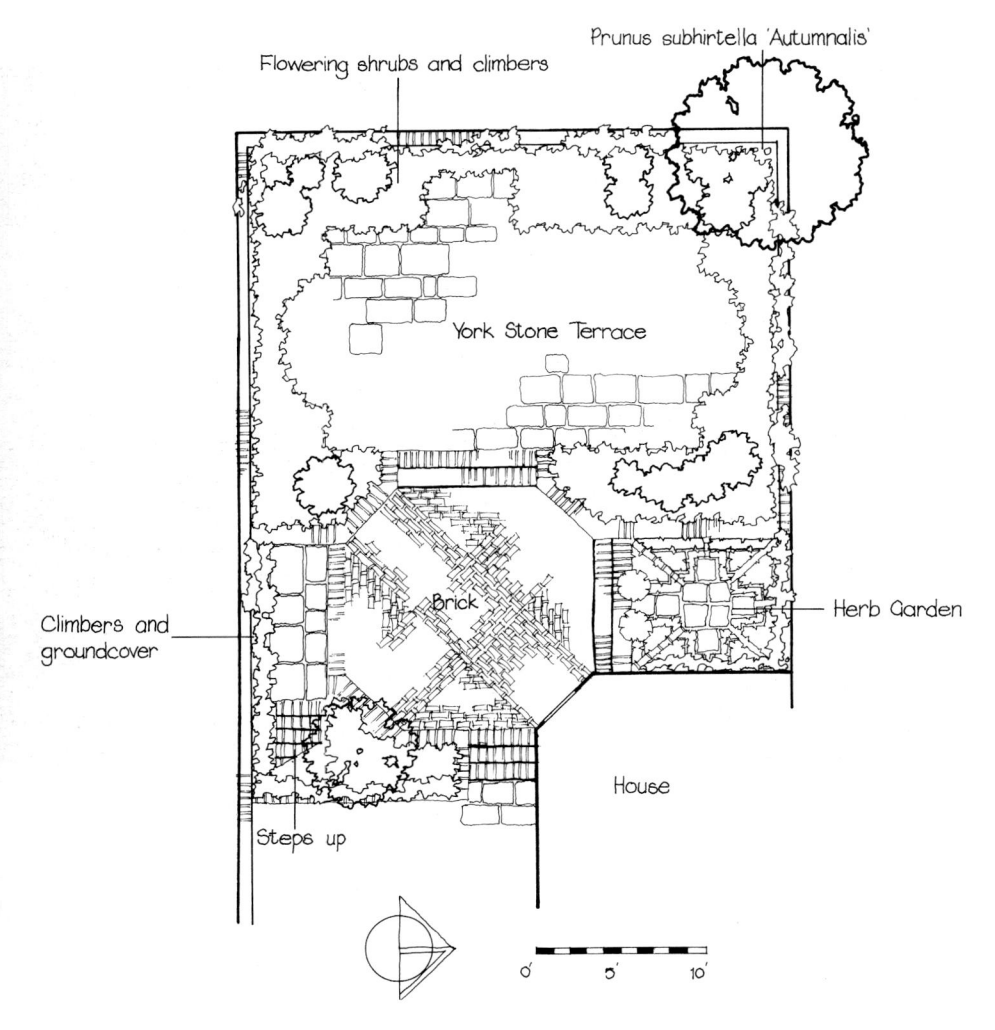

Labels on plan: Prunus subhirtella 'Autumnalis'; Flowering shrubs and climbers; York Stone Terrace; Climbers and groundcover; Brick; Herb Garden; House; Steps up

PLAN showing the main elements of this elegant white garden, which makes the most of a relatively confined space.

The house is tall, like many London houses, and looks out at the back over a garden at basement level which is a sea of greenery. It is reached from the first-floor drawing room, down a wrought-iron staircase spanned by iron hoops covered with *Wisteria floribunda* (syn. *W. multijuga*) 'Alba', the lovely Japanese variety with graceful white racemes up to three feet long. *Clematis armandii* and *Rosa* 'Seagull' were planted to clothe the house wall, and in summer the first thing that catches your eye as you come down the steps is a large pyracantha engulfed by the enormous scented white trusses of *R.* 'Kiftsgate'.

White is the keynote of this garden: the brief given to me stipulated no grass, no colours except for white and a smattering of blue, and plenty of flowers at all times. The design was conceived with the shape and geometry of the house in mind, and the steps now lead down to a sunken octagonal terrace of pale terracotta bricks set with a table and chairs. Three more steps, centrally placed, lead up to a York stone terrace, where the slabs are set on sand and soil with wide joints in between.

These provided the opportunity for one of the garden's prettiest features, as a large variety of small and creeping plants was coaxed into the cracks: *Ajuga reptans*, with spirals of white flowers in high summer; tiny white *Arabis ferdinandii-coburgii*; white thrift; silver-grey *Artemisia schmidtiana* 'Nana'; peppermint-scented *Mentha requienii*; lemon-scented *Thymus × citriodorus* 'Silver Queen; other thymes including the white-flowered form of the wild variety, *T. serpyllum albus*; black trefoil; pale-blue *Veronica gentianoides*, white violets and edelweiss are among the ground-hugging plants that fight for space beneath slightly taller ones. Mounds of dwarf white lavender and clipped santolinas and the more vertical outlines of aquilegias, the variegated form of *Sisyrinchium striatum* and hostas make a delicately pretty display against the weathered stone throughout the year, a mass of dainty bulbs appears in spring, and in summer the creeping thymes and mints release a bouquet of Mediterranean scents when crushed underfoot.

flowers. A *Rosa banksiae* 'Lutea' grows up the street face of the house, and in only a few years has already reached the second floor. As long as it is kept warm and sheltered and is pruned with care, as the flower buds form on the second year's shoots, this rose is very generous with its flowering, and when well established is smothered with clusters of tiny pale yellow flowers during May and June. Even though it has no scent I find this rose quite irresistible and think that no garden should be without it. Perhaps this is because it conjures up childhood memories of my home in Rome, where the sight of a *Rosa banksiae* weaving through a very old blue wisteria, practically filling a large courtyard between the Spanish steps and a palazzo nearby, took my breath away every year.

A WHITE GARDEN

The borders surrounding the paving are also planned to escape that fallow time of year when everything looks so dull. Thriving in the shady border among native ferns are *Hosta* 'Thomas Hogg', *Dicentra spectabilis alba*, with delicately cut leaves and white heart-shaped flowers in early summer, and the enchanting *Brunnera macrophylla* 'Dawson's White', which has more cream on its leaves when planted in the shade and bears sprays of forget-me-not flowers in May and June. Above them rise a standard *Viburnum carlesii*, studded with intoxicatingly fragrant white flowers in late spring, a variegated holly and the graceful and vigorous *Spiraea × vanhouttei*, its branches crowded in June with dense umbels of white flowers. The pretty silver-striped dead nettle, *Lamium maculatum* 'Album' brightens a sombre corner and is also used as ground cover, together with *Pulmonaria saccharata* 'Alba' and the variegated miniature ivies to be found tucked under the shrubs and trees. A mahonia has found its way into the garden, and despite its yellow flowers has been allowed to stay because of its irresistible perfume and its architectural evergreen leaves, and another, more muted yellow interloper also thrives here, in the semi-shade of another border. The interesting evergreen *Bupleurum fruticosum* makes a medium-sized shrub with grey-green leaves and flat yellowish flowers from July to September which, though discreet, brighten the entire bush.

Mounds of *Phlomis fruticosa* (regularly shorn of its yellow flowers when they appear in June and July) and *Euphorbia amygdaloides robbiae* spill on to the steps at either side. Clumps of white 'Yvonne Rabier' roses, iris and white campanulas fill the border nearby to overflowing, while the white *Clematis* 'Henryi', which bears large creamy-white flowers in May and June and again in August and September, and 'Iceberg' roses rise behind a tall *Abutilon vitifolium* 'album'. A variety of the silver plants which are now so popular is dotted around, adding to the ethereal feel of the planting, while pyramids and balls of clipped box form sculpted groups of more formal, rather mannerist inspiration.

The overall design would not have been complete without a small formal garden, and an ideal spot was found to the right of the brick paving. At the top of a few steps is a miniature knot of box hedging, filled originally with culinary herbs, which proved rather wayward and were replaced with dainty white *Viola cornuta*. A particular favourite with children and adults alike, the formal garden has a strength of atmosphere quite out of proportion to its size.

This garden owes its success to its owner's unswerving determination to limit its colours to whites and muted pastel blues, with very occasional touches of pale yellow. Impulse buys are strictly prohibited, and every new plant is positioned with meticulous care. Each has its allotted space and size, and those that threaten to overstate their presence are pruned so that they once again merge into the whole. The integrity of the design is living proof of one of gardening's greatest paradoxes: that the most delightfully artless and natural of effects are almost invariably those that require the most rigour and discipline from the gardener.

A SMALL formal garden designed with staggered box hedges has borders filled with *Viola cornuta alba*. Standard box balls rise above and give height. Behind, a white rose grows next to a white *Wisteria floribunda* 'Multijuga' and one day will cover the wall. Rosemary planted against the wall of the house acts as a hedge.

A FLORAL DECORATOR'S GARDEN

To Kenneth Turner his garden is really almost more important than his house: he deliberately blurs the distinction between the two, for he sees the garden as an 'overflow' for the house, with spots for eating and drinking, for curling up with a book and for chatting with friends. It should be restful and decorative, interesting and welcoming; and above all it should be a source of inspiration and ideas.

Kenneth Turner's stylish flower arrangements are evidence not only of extremely artistic taste and an unusual sensitivity of approach, but also of a highly ingenious and original mind. His spectacular compositions took the public by surprise and caught their imagination at a time when the Constance Spry school of arrangement was beginning to look rather hackneyed. His passionate love of plants and flowers, his sensitivity to their shape and architecture and his understanding of their individual habit and character combined to produce floral decorations which were not quite like anything that had been seen before.

Bright colours do not frighten him – he

THE wooden table on the York stone terrace just outside the conservatory is the perfect place for entertaining on a summer evening. Overhead, the boughs of the old apple tree are weighed down with a romantic tangle of roses, clematis and honeysuckle.

LUXURIANT profusion is the keynote of this garden, with plants encouraged to grow up, over and through each other. The effect of casual abandon is not achieved without a gently guiding hand, however: here a rose is being helped to climb into the branches of an old fruit tree.

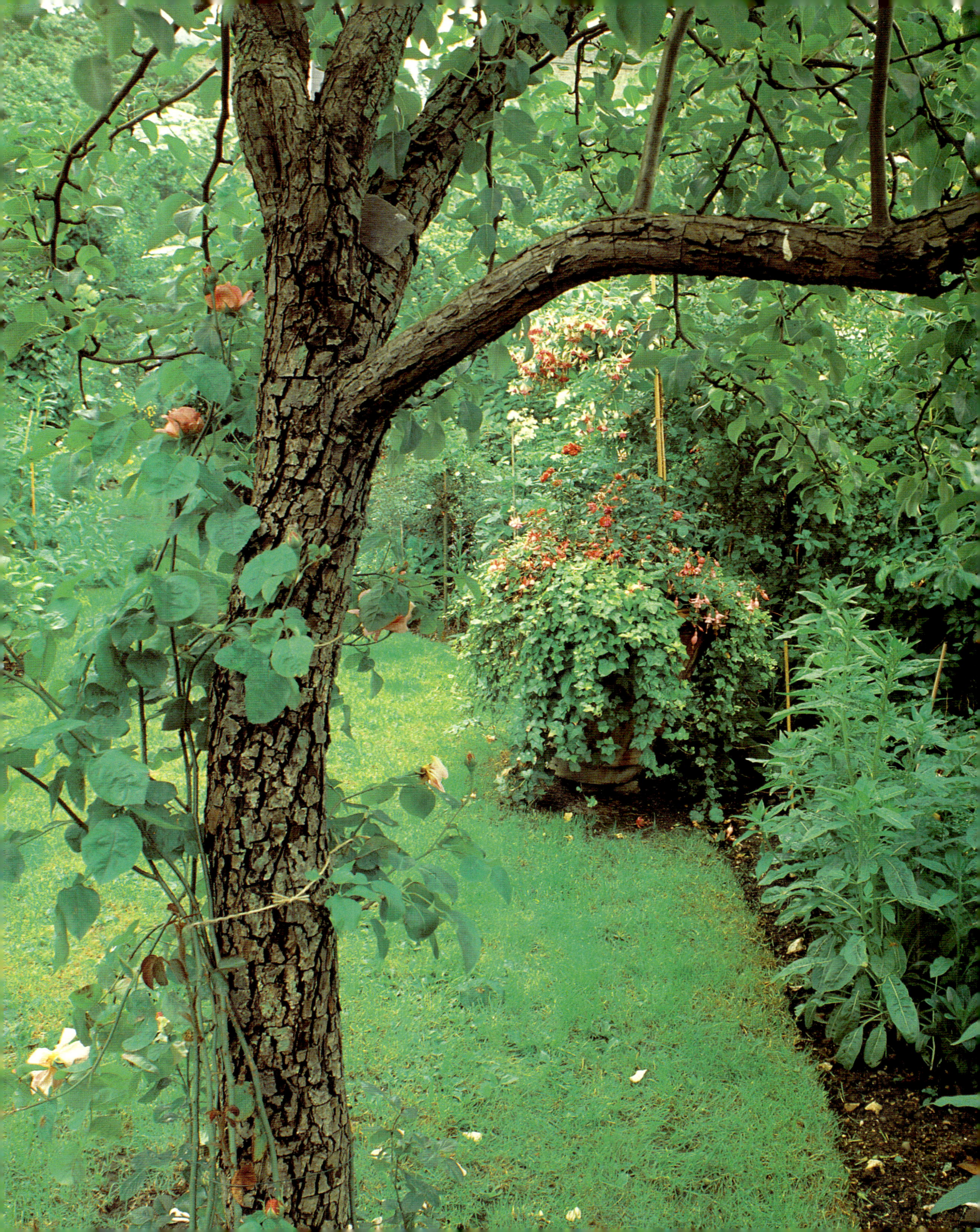

In the shrub garden the lawn narrows to create deeper borders, which are filled with a mass of shrubs chosen to provide colour, scent and foliage throughout the year. Behind the seat a dark hedge of × *Cupressocyparis leylandii* screens the greenhouse and kitchen garden.

mixes brilliant blues, reds and yellows to create audacious colour schemes at which others can only marvel – and his raw materials are startlingly eclectic. His extraordinarily fertile imagination is stimulated quite as much by a pile of cauliflowers and carrots, or cow parsley and chilli peppers, as by a collection of hothouse flowers. Nor is he daunted by grandeur of scale, for his arrangements are apt to encompass mature trees studded with oranges or apples like precious stones, topiary in all shapes and sizes, or great swags composed of camellia boughs in full bloom. Moreover he is able to combine such grand architectural statements with sprays of simple old-fashioned border favourites arranged with the casual looseness of a country bouquet. It is all accomplished with a tremendous flair and *brio* not generally associated with English flower arranging – and indeed his cornucopiae of fruit and vegetables, shells and bark, fresh flowers and dried have about them the voluptuous sensuality and the richness of texture and colour of an Italian Renaissance still life.

No one who knows his work, then, would be unprepared for the sheer romantic extravagance of Kenneth Turner's garden in Wandsworth. As you approach the graceful ivy-clad wrought-iron gate you cannot fail to notice the unusual quantity of plants growing happily over the railings, on to the pavement and in to each other, casually intertwining to form interesting tangles. A tunnel of narrow arches leads the way to the house; covered with roses, honeysuckles, vines and clematis it signals even to casual visitors that here they are entering a separate world. To either side lies a jungle of elegant bamboos, camellias, cotoneasters and more ivies, while a large *Magnolia grandiflora* threatens to engulf the house, aided and abetted by a honeysuckle and a golden hop. The magnolia adds a note of grandeur, picked up by terracotta pots of box topiary lining the path, an element of stylized formality which hints at the intriguing marriage of styles to be found within.

When he found this house six years ago Kenneth Turner was really looking for a cottage in the country, but something about the road appealed to him, and once he had seen the garden here the decision was made – it was love at first sight. Viewing the long (175 feet), narrow space with a designer's eye, he decided to make a virtue of necessity, and to play on the garden's length by creating a series of 'rooms'. He believed that 'the sort of garden where you can see from one end to the other, an uninterrupted expanse of green lawn with the odd tree, bordered on either side with beds, is desperately dull'. What was needed was a framed view wherever you looked, a new focus for the eye every thirty or so feet, so that 'because one has seen so much one is deceived into thinking the garden is enormous'. He also longed to recreate the excitement he had felt as a child in his grandfather's walled garden, where every door promised mystery and surprise. In a space which at the time contained only a few espalier trees, an apple, a damson and a couple of roses, the possibilities were almost infinite.

As you enter the garden from the conservatory, where Kenneth Turner delights to entertain friends among the plants and candlelight, the exuberance and profusion of the planting is almost overwhelming. Plants clam-

A FLORAL DECORATOR'S GARDEN

ber up and through and over one another before cascading down again in elegantly riotous profusion. Under an old apple tree, weighed down with 'New Dawn' and 'Albertine' roses, *Clematis montana* and a honeysuckle, stands a faded green wooden table. On a summer's evening, by the light of old-fashioned hurricane lamps, this is the perfect place for entertaining, and in this sylvan setting there is no need for a table decoration; instead Kenneth Turner may simply place a pot of night-scented stocks by each chair.

On the mossy York stone paving (laid to replace the biscuit-coloured crazy paving that was here before) stand quantities of terracotta pots, an echo of the gentle formality to be found in front of the house. Box topiary – which Kenneth Turner loves for its severity, its formality, and also its usefulness – and evergreens and ivies provide a framework of soft green architectural shapes, and look especially dramatic in snow. There are always hardy camellias, for use outside or inside the house, and masses of roses and lilies in summer. At this time of year the architecture is virtually submerged by drifts and cascades of blooms in white and every shade of pink: masses of nicotiana and night-scented stocks, petunias and pelargoniums, jasmine and geraniums. At night their perfume wafts through the open doors of the conservatory with every breeze.

Dotted among the pots are a quantity of urns and busts, Kenneth Turner's favourite props inside and out. Ivies, geraniums and fuchsias spill out of lichen-encrusted urns, their pedestals entwined by roses and jasmines, while the head of the Emperor Hadrian's lover Antinous rises from a sea of foliage and the fragile pink blooms of a miniature floribunda rose. One of the beauties of the pots is their versatility: at a moment's notice the roses or lilies may be massed on the table and surrounded by soft green moss or whisked into the house to throng another statue. Although Kenneth Turner does sometimes do set-piece arrangements for the house, he prefers 'the chaotic effect created by bringing things like terracotta pots and urns into the house'.

The area immediately to the rear of the house is the first of the garden 'rooms', of which there are five: the pot garden, the blue and white garden, the border garden, the shrub garden and the vegetable garden. The way through to the blue and white garden is crowded by a giant hogweed, *Heracleum mantegazzianum*, its great toothy leaves and lacy flower heads looming as much as ten feet overhead. Poisonous (too close a brush with the stem or foliage can produce a vicious skin rash) and invasive as it is, nothing else can match it for its spectacular shape, its

ON the terrace a bust of the Emperor Hadrian's lover Antinous emerges from a cloud of foliage and flowers, all growing in pots. Pots and urns are among Kenneth Turner's favourite props, and examples of all shapes and sizes stand on the mossy York stone terrace, to be arranged as the fancy takes him.

huge and beautiful golden seed heads, and the splendid shadows it casts. It is one of Kenneth Turner's favourites, dead or alive, inside or out.

The blue and white garden is a 'walk through' – there is nowhere to sit or loiter – and, like the border garden and the shrub garden, is full of plants suitable for fresh displays or for drying. Climbing 'Iceberg' roses scramble over *Viburnum plicatum* 'Mariesii', and *Clematis montana* and a ceanothus fall in white and pale blue cascades. Eucalyptus, artemisia and santolina foliage provide a silver setting, with a solitary rhododendron striking a sombre contrast. Two tall wooden pyramids clothed in ivy are tucked into the borders against a background of may trees on one side and a sorbus and walnut on the other, which together enclose the space and lend it privacy.

Another narrow entrance, this time marked by two huge bay trees, leads to the border garden. The constriction of entrances is a device often used to enhance the sense of space to either side, and to create a sense of expectancy. Here every 'room' feels like a secret garden, reached by means of a tunnel or low arch of greenery where you have literally to duck under, climb over or push aside stray branches. This sense of mystery is enhanced by an inescapable impression of exuberant growth all around; for plants which elsewhere would be trained, pruned, staked and tied here are simply given their head, and a helping hand only when needed.

The centrepiece of the border garden is a pretty and highly original seat made entirely of horseshoes, with a plump cushion made of moss. It stands in the shade of an old apple tree, and in spring the combination of blossom and the seat's delicate white-painted tracery is enchanting. The borders are filled with herbaceous perennials, many of them old cottage garden favourites: lilacs, peonies and hellebores give way in early summer to foxgloves, delphiniums and *Geranium philostemon*, underplanted with clouds of lower-growing lavender-blue *Nepeta mussinii* and bright green *Alchemilla mollis*. Roses climb up the apple tree and over the Gothic trellis, and the fragrant white blooms of *R.* 'Yvonne Rabier' are especially fine combined with hot pink penstemons. A froth of parsley and the

Two huge bay trees mark the narrow entrance to the border garden, from where, as you look back across the blue and white garden and the terrace or pot garden, the house and conservatory are virtually obscured by greenery.

A FLORAL DECORATOR'S GARDEN

scent of nicotianas surround them, and they are overhung by the boughs of a peach tree bearing deliciously perfumed fruit.

Another hogweed rises at the entrance to the shrub garden, where the lawn narrows to create more spacious borders. Here are forsythias and azaleas, camellias and rhododendrons, angelicas and pale mauve-flowered buddleias, a deutzia and a beautiful large onothera, hypericums and feathery-plumed macleayas. In dead of winter a *Viburnum farreri* scents the air with its clusters of white flowers tinged with pink, and in summer hollyhocks, sweet Williams and Canterbury bells jostle for space with masses of old-fashioned roses: blowsy cabbage roses and delicate damasks; bright pink 'Constance Spry' and silver-pink 'New Dawn' smothering old fruit trees.

At the far end a seat is backed by a row of dark × *Cupressocyparis leylandii*, which screens the working area of the garden and the greenhouse. Here lies the kitchen garden, where all manner of fruit and vegetables are to be found, including spinach, carrots, peas and broad beans, the peppery leaves of the Italian salad *rucola* (rocket), currants red and black, and blackberries on the boundary fence.

It seems fitting that this garden should begin and end with the pleasures of the table, starting with two exquisite dining rooms in the Gothic conservatory and the table under the apple tree, and finishing with the tender produce of the kitchen garden. As Kenneth Turner says, 'In this house you have drinks in the summer by the Edwardian seat, you can have dinner under the apple tree or have a barbecue, or you can eat in the conservatory.' Glorious to look at, to smell, to eat in, to stroll through, this is truly a garden of the senses.

THE idea of dividing this long narrow space into a series of 'rooms', each with a different character, has created a feeling of seclusion and intimacy. The entrance to each garden is narrow and shrouded with greenery, and only occasionally do you get a glimpse of the different gardens beyond.

211

A POST-MODERN GARDEN

When we think of gardens we tend to do so in terms of their design, their use of colour, their plant associations, their aesthetics, their atmosphere and perhaps a host of other things – but not, on the whole, their meaning. The habits of mind of previous centuries and other civilizations have by no means always been so literal in their approach; symbolism has a long and influential history in the development of gardens of both the East and the West. Every element of traditional Japanese and Chinese gardens has a higher or hidden meaning, and often more than one. Rocks in Chinese gardens, for instance, signified the landscape in general and mineral wealth in particular, and in their form could be taken to represent animals or monsters on the most mundane level, or at their most rarefied, if they

LOOKING back from the bottom of the garden, there is a view to the house with a double stairway made out of industrial material linking it with the garden. An American horse chestnut hangs its branches over the yew hedge; its flowers are greenish-white and the leaves are more delicate and smaller than its common relation.

AT the bottom of the garden is an 'eye-catcher'. The 'Future pavilion' has a forced perspective that converges on a mirrored window that looks as though it opens into the garden beyond. *Trompe l'oeil* is here used to suggest the theme of the future as shaped and distorted by the past; this play on time is recurrent throughout the garden.

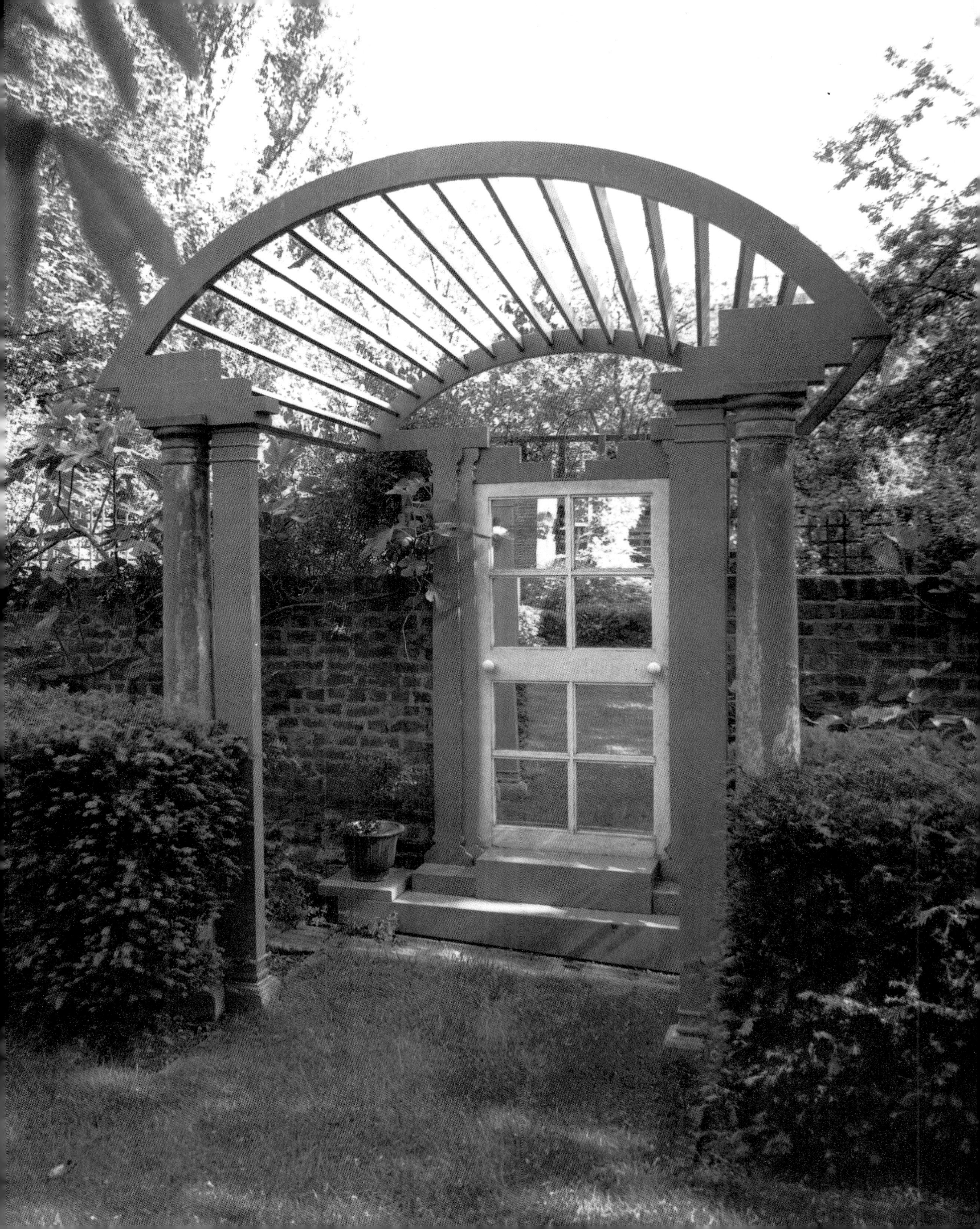

THE garden steps lead resolutely through the yew hedge and draw you into the central lawn which is enclosed by more yew planted in curve and stagger motifs. It creates a quiet space for chatting and picnicking.

could be construed as frozen clouds, they might be symbols of time.

From the gardens of Eden and the Hesperides to those of the Song of Solomon and the troubadours, Western gardens have lent themselves as metaphors for the summits of spiritual and emotional experience, becoming symbols of the state of divine grace or erotic bliss, or both. The compliment has been amply returned in subsequent centuries by those who have constructed real gardens in order to express a hidden meaning. Orders of battle, Christian's arduous journey in *The Pilgrim's Progress*, the Elysian fields, the garden of Venus (crafted in loving and explicit detail by Sir Francis Dashwood of Hell-Fire fame) and many other worlds have formed part of a gardening tradition which, with a few exceptions, has been virtually lost.

Charles Jencks, in the vanguard of post-Modernism and pioneer of symbolic architecture, had for many years set his face against such literalism when he embarked on this garden. Viewing the abandonment of symbolism in architecture as a great loss but not an irretrievable one, he struck a chord with the many people whose response to contemporary architecture tended to revolve around such epithets as 'soulless' and 'faceless'. According to Charles Jencks the lack of character in our environment is explained by the inherent scepticism of the age. The builders of Gothic cathedrals, for example, were aspiring to the expression of a sublime truth and a common and deeply held belief. Now, when there are few religious, social or metaphysical beliefs that are more than mere pieties, architects have little left to believe in except architecture itself: hence the inward-looking, literalistic and ultimately mundane nature of much contemporary building.

Charles Jencks' wholehearted application of his theories has resulted in an arresting addition to the sedate early Victorian brick-and-stucco landscape of Holland Park. Using as his basis a typical town house of the 1840s, he has created his Thematic House, of which every room, every corner and every feature down to the minutest detail is emblematic. The theme is time, and it is treated on two main levels: the cosmic (the seasons, the phases of the sun and moon and the galaxies) and the cultural (the civilizations of ancient Egypt, India, the Far East and the West). The entrance hall, the 'cosmic oval', expounds the themes, which are then expanded by rooms signifying the different seasons, by a 'solar stair' (with a 'black hole' mosaic), a 'moonwell' and a number of other rooms, all faithfully symbolic in all their aspects. There is no place here, sadly, for all the fascinating details, which are entertainingly described and explained by Charles Jencks himself in his book *Towards a Symbolic Architecture*.

Clearly when it came to the garden aesthetics were not to be the driving force, but might nevertheless be the happy consequence of the symbolic programme. In designing the 'garden of time' Charles Jencks was fortunate to have as his collaborator his wife Maggie Keswick, author of *The Chinese Garden*. The garden is a south-facing rectangle divided into quarters centred on the rear elevation of the house; each corner represents one of the points of the compass, one of the seasons, and one of four great civilizations: China, Egypt, America and Europe. A walk round the garden (in clockwise direction of course) thus progresses through the seasons, which are equated with the four civilizations, the four elements and the four ages of man. Walls of trellis and half-mirrored doors, signifying windows on the world, bound the two long sides, dividing the walk round the garden into twelve parts representing the twelve months of the year. The twelve sections also impose their own rhythm, and one day each will be defined by a plaque or sculpture. The doors are placed so that they are neither completely above nor completely below the brick wall, and the element of ambiguity is increased by the use of mirrors.

A walk round the garden with Maggie Keswick indicates that the stringency and rigour of their approach is mercifully not accompanied by high-minded seriousness. The overall shape of the garden evolved in response to the children's need for paths to cycle around, and the adults' need for a quiet space: hence the central lawn with a perimeter path of brick and a paved area near the house.

'THE future is behind you', reads an inscription on the door of the future pavilion – a teasing reference to the Post-Modern house reflected in the mirror. More cryptic inscriptions appear in mirror writing on the back of the piers: *E arriva dal passato troppo presto*' and '*A la recherche du temps qui vient*'.

PRIVATE GARDENS OF LONDON

SYMBOLIC features and ideas were the basis of the design for this garden. The four seasons; four great civilizations: China, Egypt, America, and Europe; the four elements; and four ages of man. Trellis and half-mirrored doors, signifying mirrors on the world, divide the wall round the garden into twelve sections representing the twelve months of the year.

The path starts in the east, with spring and China. All the plants and furniture here are of Chinese or eastern origin: peonies, cornus and Chinese pots and seats, to which they would like to add a huge rock. The path then leads south, under an old pear tree, to the Egyptian corner, where they commissioned a fountain with crocodiles in bas relief. At each corner the slope of the path changes and the bricks are laid to a different pattern, and virtually all along its length yew hedges give it a secret feel. The western corner is America, in the shade of a beautiful American horse chestnut which colours a gorgeous ochre in autumn. This is doubly appropriate, as not only is this the corner of autumn, but also the yellow matches the yellow of the wisteria leaves wreathing the handrail of the steps and of the summer (dining) room which overlooks the garden. The flowers are a greenish-white and the leaves, smaller and more delicate than those of the common variety, do not cast a heavy shade.

Europe, finally, in the corner nearest the house, has a large arbutus and the palace of the rabbits, a series of glass boxes at different heights, like a miniature modular building, and all in the shape of an E for Europe.

As the patterns of brick, sometimes laid with aluminium strips, echo the shapes of the windows, so the yew hedges are planted in the curve-and-staggers shape to be found all over the house, and when more established will be clipped lower near the house and taller at the bottom of the garden to give the illusion of greater depth. Planting was inevitably a problem, as it would have been sad only to have had one corner of the garden in bloom at a time. So instead they devised a symbolic colour scheme, muted for spring and winter, hot for summer and glowing for autumn.

At the bottom of the garden, on axis with the house, is an eye-catcher, the 'future pavilion', a mirrored door under a canopy of false perspective. It is flanked by two fig trees trained against the wall and chosen for their foliage, which contrasts with the dark yew hedge in front. As you approach, convinced that this door leads to another part of the garden, you begin to make out some lettering on the door: 'The future', it says; then you look down to the plinth which adds, 'is behind you'. This, a reference to the post-Modern house reflected in the mirror, was meant as a tease for the architectural world at a time before post-Modernism was taken seriously. As you glance up you read in the mirror two inscriptions written in mirror writing on the backs of the piers: '*E arriva dal passato troppo presto*', and, '*A la recherche du temps qui vient*'. The notion of *trompe l'oeil* is here used to suggest the theme of the future as shaped and distorted by the past: this play on the future and the past is a recurrent theme in the garden. One day a swallow, sadly unaware of the illusion, flew into the mirror with tragic results, whereupon it was decided that if ever it happened again they would paint a predatory bird, such as an eagle, on the glass.

Looking back from here you have the best view of the rear elevation of the house. Two tall conservatories, topped by the curve-and-stagger motif, overlook the garden. Between them (where a Palladian building would have a grotto, as Charles Jencks points out) is an imperial or double stairway made out of industrial materials, which seems to embrace the garden. Designing a structure of such elegance out of ready-made industrial materials gave Jencks great pleasure and it also allows for an easy and gracious descent to the lawn, where yew hedges seem to fold round you and draw you on further into the garden.

Overlooking the garden are the summer room, with sunshine-yellow table and chairs in the window alcove, and the sundial arcade, where a hemicyclium sundial designed by Mark Lennox-Boyd, with an obelisk as a gnomon, tells the time, date, altitude, direction and zodiac sign of the sun. It doubles as a window seat, and the whole window can be lowered electronically so that you are virtually sitting outside. White ceramic tiles cover the terrace outside, from where the view consists of modulations of green: pale lawn and dark yew.

As Charles Jencks observes, 'wherever the mind finds a system of meaning it is led on to seek, and thereby discover, more. Detective work, or playing the game of "Hunt the Symbol", is one of the great pleasures of looking at symbolic architecture.' This symbolic garden is full of invitations to hunt the symbol, but in the end it is the garden itself, full of growth and constant change, that tells us most about the passing of time.

A BRICK path with patterns changing at each corner surrounds the central lawn. A walk round it progresses through the seasons and through the four great civilizations. The walk starts here, in the East, with spring and China. Almost all the plants are of eastern origin. Peonies and cornus interspersed with lavender and other silver plants lighten the overall effect.

FURTHER READING

Jane Brown *Lanning Roper and his Gardens*, Weidenfeld & Nicolson 1987
Tom Carter *The Victorian Garden*, Bracken Books 1984
Myles Challis *The Exotic Garden*, Fourth Estate 1988
W. R. Dalzell *The Shell Guide to the History of London*, Michael Joseph 1981
A. K. Davidson, *The Art of Zen Gardening*, Hutchinson
Gardens of England & Wales, National Gardens Scheme, published annually
Sir George Gater & Walter H. Godfrey, eds *Survey of London*, London County Council 1936
David Goode *Wild in London*, Michael Joseph 1986
Trevor Griffiths *The Book of Old Roses*, Michael Joseph 1984
Miles Hadfield *Gardening in Britain*, Hutchinson 1960
Roy Hawkins *Green London*, Sidgwick & Jackson, 1987
Penelope Hobhouse *Colour in your Garden*, Collins 1985
Penelope Hobhouse *Private Gardens of England*, Weidenfeld & Nicolson, 1986

Hilliers' Manual of Trees & Shrubs, David & Charles 1975
Charles Jencks *Towards a Symbolic Architecture* Academy Editions, 1985
Edward Jones & Christopher Woodward *A Guide to the Architecture of London*, Weidenfeld & Nicolson 1983
Loraine Kuck *The Japanese Garden* Weatherhill, 1972
Michael Leapman, ed. *The Book of London*, Weidenfeld & Nicolson 1989
Teresa McLean *Medieval English Gardens*, Collins 1981
Betty Massingham *Town Gardens*, Pelham Books 1968
Thomas H. Mawson & E. Prentice Mawson *The Art and Craft of Garden Making*, Batsford 1926
Reader's Digest Encyclopaedia of Garden Plants and Flower, Reader's Digest 1978
Ann Saunders *The Art and Architecture of London*, Phaidon 1984
Michael J. Tooley *Gertrude Jekyll*, Michaelmas Books 1984
Edward Walford *Old and New London*, n.d.
Ben Weinreb & Christopher Hibbert, eds *The London Encyclopaedia*, Macmillan 1983

INDEX

Numbers in *italics* refer to illustrations

Aaron's rod 194
Abelia 154; *198*
  A. × *grandiflorum* 188
Abeliophyllum distichum 156
Abutilon 92, 135, 178
  A. 'Canary Bird' 178; *176*
  A. × *milleri* 200
  A. vitifolium 'Album' 40, 81, 205
Acaena microphylla 13
Acanthus 124, 191, 199; *21*
  A. mollis 27
  A. spinosus 21
Acer 87, 162; *44, 84*
  A. griseum 105; *95*
  A. japonicum 41; *198*
  A.j. 'Acontifolium' 100
  A.j. dissectum 142, *190*
  A. negundo 'Flamingo' 105
  A. palmatum dissectum 115
  A. palmatum 'Osak-azuki' 124
  A. pseudoplatanus
    'Brilliantissimum', 44
  A. shirosawanum 'Aureum' *190*
  snake-bark 100
Achillea 'Coronation Gold' 188
  A. 'Moonlight' *186*
  A. × *taygetea* 124
aconite, winter 156, 179
Actinidia deliciosa 104
Aesculus indica 166
Agapanthus 74, 163, 188; *159*
  A. 'Headbourne Hybrids' *189*
Ailanthus altissima 98, 166–7
Ajuga 41, 163
  A. reptans 178, 204
akebia 194
Albion Grove 18
Alchemilla 13, 69, 100, 155, 178
  A. mollis 20, 69, 74, 75, 162, 189, 199, 210; *70, 230*
Allium 199
  A. triquetrum 141; *141*
alstroemeria 115, 150, 178
alyssum 53, 92, 173
amelanchier 189
  A. canadensis 44
anagallis 115
Anaphalis triplinervis 124
Anchusa azurea 'Royal Blue' 124
Anderson, Mrs Ann 91, 92–3
Anemone 32
  A. blanda 162, 182

A. × *hybrida* 178
  Japanese 39, 100, 124; *36, 40*
angelica 211
Anisodoniea carpensis 15
Anthemis cupaniana 137
antirrhinum 173
Aponogeton distachyos 20
apple 33, 77, 80, 81, 109, 130, 151, 155, 162, 188, 196, 209, 210, 211; *13, 155, 192–3, 206*
  crab 39, 41, 92, 130, 196; *36, 40*
Aquilegia 64, 183, 204
  A. canadensis 33
Arabis ferdinandii-coburgii 204
Aralia elata 'Variegata' 40
Araucaria araucana 118
Arbutus 216
  A. unedo 22
arches 27, 28, 29, 75, 76, 77, 93, 105, 126, 182, 196, 208; *73, 104*
Artemisia 34, 40, 66, 163; *33*
  A. absinthium 34
  A. 'Powis Castle' 199, 210; *22*
  A. schmidtiana 'Nana' 204
  A. 'Silver Queen' 188
aruncus 75
arundinaria 186
Asarina erubescens 135
Asarum candatum 196
asparagus fern 93
Assinder, Marigold 24, 26, 28, 29; *27*
Assinder, Peter *27*
Astiboides tabularis 168
astilbe 66, 105, 124, 155
aubrieta 178
Aucuba 20, 189; *77*
  A. japonica 77
  A.j. 'Crotonifolia' 194
Austin, Alfred 150–1; *150*
Austin, David 163
Azalea 40, 46, 50, 75, 87, 88, 97, 104, 105, 115, 156, 200, 211; *42, 200*
  A. 'Kurume' *83, 94*
  A. mollis 178
  A. 'Palestrina' 68
Azara microphylla 28, 155

Bacon, Sir Francis 180, 183; *181*
bamboo 100, 105, 116, 140, 166, 167–8, 173, 208; *138*
  black 105, 106; *104*
  sacred 105
banana palm, Abyssinian 166, 167
Banks, Sir Joseph 121, 156

Barbirolli, Lady 112–17
Barnsbury 18, 190–1
Barnsbury Square 146–51
Barr, Robert 198
Battersea 132–7
bay 13, 58, 92, 105, 182, 202, 210; *210*
Beaverbrook, Lord 160–1
Beck, Mrs Thomasina 78, 80, 81
bee garden 161, 163; *162*
beech hedge 122, 124, 186, 187, 188, 198, 199, 201; *124, 125, 201*
Beerbohm Tree, Sir Herbert 96
Beeton, Mrs 150
Begonia pendula 176
Belgravia basement 49–50; *48*
Benson, Jeremy and Mrs 96, 97, 98, 100, 101
Benson, Robert and Mrs 96–7; *98*
Bentinck, Baron and Baroness 86
berberis 80, 183, 196; *199*
Bergenia 41, 76, 156, 196; *42, 157*
  B. cordifolia 77; *37, 38, 194*
betony 15
Billiardiera 15
Blake, William 70, 72
Bligh, Vice-Admiral William, sarcophagus of 34; *35*
Blomfield, Sir Reginald 144–5, 176
bluebells 63–4, 163, 173; *64*
bog garden 155
Bogod, Ann 49, 50
Bonar Law, Andrew 161
Boudicca, Queen 148
Bowen, Trevor 128
box 13, 39, 41, 58, 59, 67, 80, 192, 194, 195, 196, 202, 205; *14, 15, 40, 55, 58, 196, 203, 205*
  dwarf 34, 38, 58, 67, 82; *35*
  topiary 80, 208, 209; *180*
Brachyglottis 'Sunshine' 28, 41
broom, Moroccan 67
Brunel, I. K. 56
Brunnera 155; *200*
  B. macrophylla 'Dawson's White' 205
Bryan, Felicity 74
Buddleia 154, 182, 211
  B. alternifolia 27; *27*
  B. davidii 'Black Night' 124
  B. 'Harlequin' 196
  B. 'Lochinch' 188; *187*
  B. × *weyeriana* 27
Bupleurum fruticosum 21, 205; *202*
busy lizzie 49, 50, 53, 92, 182

Buxus sempervirens 'Augustifolia' 196
  B.s. 'Latifolia Maculata' 196
  B.s. Marginata' 192
  B.s. 'Suffruticosa' 15, 34; *35*

Calamintha nepeta nepeta 189
Caltha palustris 155, 182; *183*
Camellia 20, 26–8, 29, 36, 38, 40, 41, 50, 58, 59, 67, 68, 80, 92, 96, 97, 100, 104, 124, 125, 137, 140–1, 151, 154, 155, 156, 162, 173, 179, 182, 183, 194, 195, 202, 208, 209, 211; *58, 94, 138, 153, 154, 155, 156, 157, 197*
  C. reticulata 'Captain Rawes' 27
  C. × *r.* 'Crimson Robe' 28
  C. × *r.* 'Dr Clifford Parks' 28
  C. 'Cornish Snow' 22
  C.j. × *cuspidata* 'Cornish Spring' 27
  C. 'Francis Hanger' 20
  C. 'Leonard Messel' 20
  C. 'Marigold Assinder' 26
Camellia japonica × *williamsii* 27–8
  C.j. 'Adolphe Audusson' 21, 28, 176; *178*
  C.j. 'Akashi-gata' 156
  C.j. 'Alba Simplex' 27
  C.j. 'Are-jishi' 28
  C.j. 'C. M. Wilson' 28
  C.j. 'Contessa Lavinia Maggi' 28
  C.j. 'Devonia' 124
  C.j. 'Giulio Nuccio' 28
  C.j. 'J. C. Williams' 28
  C.j. 'Konkron koku' 28
  C.j. 'Kramer's Supreme' *28*
  C.j. 'Margaret Waterhouse' 28
  C.j. 'Mary Christian' 124
  C.j. 'Sylvia' 124
Campanula 28, 34, 75, 92, 117, 179, 182, 205; *29, 173*
  C. carpatica 179
  C. lactiflora 'Loddon Anna' 39
  C. persicifolia 100, 124
  C. portenschlagiana 78, 156, 182–3, 196, 199; *13, 157*
  C. poscharskyana 'Stella' 72
  C. pyramidalis 15
campion 15, 199
candytuft 137
Canna 166, 167, 169
  C. 'Firebird' 169; *168*
  C. × *generalis* 'Wyoming' 168, 169; *164*

219

INDEX

C. iridiflora 'Ehemannii' 169; *168*
Canonbury House 180–3
Canterbury bell 211
Cape figwort 155
Caplin, Charles 102, 104, 106; *102*
Capron, Mrs Deirdre 176–9
Cardamine pratensis 33
Caryopteris 201
  C. × *clandonensis* 124
Cassia obrusa 15
castor oil plant 50
catalpa 130, 186
Ceanothus 68, 75, 210; *73, 134*
  C. arboreus 'Trewithen Blue' 137
  C. 'Burkwoodii' 198
  C. × *delileanus* 'Gloire de Versailles' 117
  C. impressus 28
  C. thyrsiflorus 74
  C.t. 'Repens' 74, 163, 189
cedar of Lebanon 120
Centranthus 76; *77*
  C. ruber albus 163
cerastium 162
ceratostigma 75
Chaenomeles 100, 105; *104*
  C. × *superba* 'Nivalis' 155
  C. speciosa 'Apple blossom' 155
Challis, Myles 18, 164–9
chamaecyparis 154, 201; *122, 200*
Chambers, Ephraim 180
cheiranthus 34, 98
Chelsea: Lindsey House 54–9
  Physic Garden 118–21
  roof garden 42–8
cherry 32, 33, 40, 41, 76, 130, 151, 179, 189, 202
  Japanese *101*
  Korean 46
Chile pine (monkey puzzle) 118
Chinese gardens 82, 84, 86, 212, 216
Chiswick Mall:
  Strawberry House 152–7
  Walpole House 94–101
Choisya 92, 124
  C. ternata 75; *117*
Churchill, Winston 161
Cimifuga racemosa 68, 81
Cistus 14, 29, 75, 80, 121, 124, 163, 198, 202; *13*
  C. × *corbariensis* 198
  C. crispus 21
  C. ladanifer 198
Clapham Common 184–9
clarkia 150
clary 14
Claytonia 63
  C. sibirica 64
Clematis 27, 46, 50, 68, 75, 92, 93, 100, 104, 105, 114, 115–16, 137, 151, 191, 194, 195, 198, 208; *29, 104, 133, 137, 192–3, 197*

C. alpina 28, 124; *29, 100*
C.a. 'Colombina' 98
C.a. 'Frances Rivis' 29; *29*
C. armandii 20, 27, 36, 67, 109, 124, 162, 196, 204; *72, 74*
C. 'Comtesse de Bouchaud' 27, 137, 201
C. 'Contessa Lavinia Maggi' 20
C. × *durandii* 29, 106
C. 'Ernest Markham' 178
C. 'Etoile Rose' 115–16
C. florida 'Plena' 15
C.f. 'Sieboldii' 116
C. 'Gipsy Queen' 29
C. 'Hagley Hybrid' 78, 115, 116, 200
C. 'Henryi' 178, 205
herbacious 93, 124
C. × *jackmanii* 178
C. 'Kermesina' 137, 200
C. 'Lasurstern' 186
C. macropetala 196
C. 'Marie Boisselet' 65, 178; *66*
C. montana 28, 41, 64, 65, 66, 67, 72, 163, 201, 209, 210; *29, 66, 75, 163, 200*
C.m. 'Elizabeth' 81
C. 'Perle d'Azur' 65, 114, 137, 138; *66, 67*
C. redheriana 21
C. sibirica 'Ville de Lyon' 28; *29*
C. tangutica 93
C. viticella 'Purpurea Plena Elegans' 201
C.v. 'Royal Velours' 68
C.v. 'Vyvyan Pennell' 182
Clerodendron bungei 162
Coats, Peter 180
Cobaea scandens 162
Codrington, John 138–41
Coleridge, Samuel Taylor 47, 70
colonnades 57, 145, 195, 196; *57, 143, 194, 196*
comfrey 188
conservatories 13, 14, 15, 17, 46, 104, 105, 124, 134–5, 164, 208, 211, 216; *17, 137, 206, 210*
Convolvulus sabaticus 115
Cooke, Henry 166
cordateria 75
cornflower 64
Cornus 75, 199, 216; *217*
  C. alba 76
  C.a. 'Variegata' 76
  C.a. 'Elegantissima' 69, 77
  C. alternifolia 'Argentea' 22, 105, 114
  C. controversa 'Variegata' 116
  C. mas 156
  C. stolonifera 'Flaviramea' 194
corydalis 163, 195, 196; *196*
Corylus avellana 'Contorta' 105, 196

Cotinus 194
  C. coggygria 'Royal Purple' 44
Cotoneaster 22, 92, 117, 183, 186, 189, 196, 208; *117*
  C. horizontalis 74, 196; *72, 74*
  C. lacteus 151
  C. salicifolius 163
  C. thymifolium 15; *17*
cow parsley 15; *160*
Cowley, Abraham 130
Crambe cordifolia 14, 58
cranesbill 141; *38, 63, 141*
crassula 115
Crinum 106; *106*
  C. × *powellii* 100
Crocus 137
  C. tommasinianus 'Whitewell Purple' 81
Cubitt, Thomas 18, 148, 170
Cupressocyparis leylandii 211; *208*
Curtis, William 121
Cyclamen 20, 34, 100, 106, 178, 179, 189; *96*
  C. hederifolium 100
cymbidium 135
Cynara cardunculus 158
cyperus (umbrella grass) 105; *111*
cypress 32, 140, 194
  swamp 186
Cytisus battaudieri 67, 109

daffodil 114, 121, 137, 155, 179
  'Mountain Hood' 162
Daphne 124
  D. blagayana 27
  D. mezereum 34, 156
  D. odora 155, 156
Darmera peltata 169; *167*
Dashwood, Sir Francis 214
Datura 167, 169
  D. cornigera 169; *165, 167*
  D. 'Grand Marnier' 169
Davidia involucrata 105
Delamer, E. S. 146
delphinium 39, 40, 64, 124, 163, 173, 178, 183, 210; *64*
Derry & Toms roof garden 126–31
deutzia 41, 183, 211
Devonshire, Duke of 148
dianthus 14, 34, 69; *186*
Diascia 198; *199*
  D. elegans 14
Dicentra 28
  D. formosa 156; *157*
  D. spectabilis alba 205
Dicksonia squarrosa 168
dogwood 154
Donald, Duncan 121
Dufferin, Lady 122–5

East End tropical garden 164–9; *2–3*

Eccleston Square 170–3
Eccremocarpus scaber 17
  E.s. coccineus 189
Echinops 75
  Echinops ritro 75; *24*
edelweiss 204
Eleagnus 13, 17, 186
  E. pungens 'Maculata' 75, 178; *197*
Eliot, T. S. 184
Elizabeth, Queen Mother 186
Enkianthus campanulatus 106
Erica insitanica 22
Erigeron 199
  E. karvinskianus 22, 137, 198; *199*
erodium 78
Erysimum 124
  E. 'Bowles' 199
Erythronium dencansis 34
escallonia 137; *134, 201*
eschscholzia 150
Eucalyptus 92, 98, 100, 135, 196, 210
  E. gunnii 28, 80; *80*
  E. niphophila 167
Eucomis bicolor 135
Eucryphia 67, 77
  E. glutinosa 76
  E. × *nymansensis* 'Nymansay' 105
Euonymus 76, 186
  E. fortunei 'Silver Queen' 77
  E. japonicus 'Ovatus Aureus' 195
Euphorbia 92, 100, 137, 141, 196, 200; *21, 22, 175*
  E. amygdaloides 'Purpurea' 199
  E.a. robbiae 100, 183, 205
  E. characias wulfenii 21, 39, 178; *37, 194*
  E. mellifera 101
Ensete ventricosum 167
Evelyn, John 120

Fatsia 97, 141, 189
  F. japonica 20, 116, 135, 156, 168, 179, 183
Felicia amelloides 176
fennel 117, 201
ferns 20, 67, 68, 76, 81, 87, 88, 92, 93, 98, 116, 117, 121, 124, 149, 155, 156, 166, 167, 168, 178, 196, 200; *77, 157, 170, 198, 200*
Ferula communis 101
feverfew 121
fig tree 105, 130, 194, 216; *104*
Filipendula ulmaria 'Aurea' 80
Foreman, David 186
forget-me-not 64, 155; *63*
Forrest, George 26
Forsyth, William 121
Forsythia 211
  F. suspensa 20–1, 81, 178; *80*
Fortune, Robert 121
fountains 126, 128, 134, 145, 146,

220

INDEX

148, 149, 183, 216; *131, 132, 136, 146, 147, 178, 183*
foxglove 14, 81, 92, 93, 100, 124, 173, 179, 191, 200, 210; *11, 198*
Fremontodendron 196
  F. californicum 178
Fritillaria (fritillary) 32, 34, 137, 188; *33*
  F. meleagris 162
Fuchsia 15, 46, 49, 50, 53, 78, 80, 92, 93, 104, 173, 176, 200, 209; *21, 137, 178, 198*
  F. magellanica 199
  F.m. 'Alba' 20
  F.m. 'Versicolor' 29
Fulham: The Vineyard 158–63
  Zen garden 82–8
'Future pavilion' 216; *213, 215*

galtonia 124
Gape, William 120
Gardner, Mr and Mrs 148, 149, 151
Garrya elliptica 72, 156
Gaultheria procumbens 72
gazebos 148, 151; *146, 149*
Gentiana 115, 124, 179
  G. asclepiadea 34
George, Bernard 128
Geranium 21, 22, 28, 40, 64, 78, 92, 117, 124, 135, 151, 191, 195, 196, 209; *29, 42, 51, 64, 79, 178*
  G. endressii 75, 100, 196, 200; *41*
  G.e. 'Wargrave Pink' 178
  G. 'Johnson's Blue' 41
  G. macrorrhizum 41
  G. madurense 28
  G. philostemon 14, 188, 210
  G. platypetalum 124
  G. × *riversleaianum* 'Russell Prichard' 189
ginger 104, 167, 168
Gladiolus 53; *33*
  G. communis byzantinus 34
glasshouses 149–50, 166; *151*
Goffinet, François 73
Goldsmith, Oliver 180
greenhouses 17, 64, 77, 101, 109, 124, 134, 135, 148, 150, 199, 211; *64, 108, 122, 208*
Grevillea rosmarinifolia 137
grotto 148, 149; *146, 147*
The Grove, Highgate 70–7
Gunnera manicata 74, 169; *75, 167*

Hamamelis 'Pallida' 189
Hambury, Revd William 63
Hampstead 102–11, 142–5, 164
Hampstead Heath 72, 74, 75, 145, 192, 196; *76, 195*
Hancock, Ralph 130
Harlech, Pamela, Lady 38, 41

Harvey, Jacob 148
Hebe 201
  H. 'Blue Cloud' 21; *22*
  H. 'Midsummer Queen' 196
  H. subalpina 182
Hedera canariensis 'Gloire de Marengo' 67; *94*
  H. helix 'Buttercup' 195
  H.h. 'Hibernica' 41
Hedychium forrestii 168
  H. gardnerianum 168
Helianthemum 69, 199; *74*
  H. 'Wisley Primrose' 124
Helichrysum 13, 53
  H. bracteatum 107
  H. petiolatum 15
Helleborus 67, 81, 100, 117, 124, 155, 162, 173, 183, 199, 210; *96, 199*
  H. argutifolius 178
  H. orientalis 100, 156, 178; *95*
heliotrope, winter 156
Hemerocallis 124, 189
  H. 'Flore Pleno' 178
  H. 'Golden Chimes' 189
  H. 'Kwanso' 178
Heppell, Arthur 172, 173
Heracleum mantegazzianum 209–10
herbs, herb garden 15, 38, 53, 58, 67, 117, 121, 128, 130, 173, 205; *15*
herms, Venetian 122, 125; *4, 125*
Heuchera 178, 179
  H. 'Palace Purple' 178
Hibiscus 92, 105
  H. syriacus 137
Hieracium villosum 198
Highgate 70–7, 197–201
The Hill, Hampstead 142–5
Hillier, Malcolm 10
hogweed 192, 194, 209–10, 211
Holland Park 122–5, 212–17
holly 183, 205; *11*
hollyhock 92, 93, 151, 163, 182, 191, 211; *160, 182*
Holman, Nigel 24, 26
honeysuckle 49, 50, 72, 75, 92, 93, 191, 200, 208, 209; *89, 92*
hop, golden 80, 105, 208; *78, 80, 104*
horse chestnut 66, 78, 114, 130, 183, 186, 216; *66, 184, 185, 212*
  Indian 166; *165*
Hosta 20, 41, 50, 58, 66, 76, 77, 81, 97, 178, 204; *1, 21, 42, 55, 67, 170, 198, 200*
  H. fortunei aurea 189
  H.f. 'Marginata Alba' 67
  H. 'Honeybells' 189; *186*
  H. sieboldiana 189
  H.s. 'Elegans' 200
Hudson, William 121

Hydrangea 29, 46, 50, 75, 178, 179, 194; *13, 42, 45, 137, 142*
  H. aspera 168
  H.a. villosa 39, 124
  lacecap 50; *27*
  H. paniculata 'Grandiflora' 124
  H. petiolaris 125, 154, 178, 194
  H. sargentiana 20, 201
hypericum 100, 121, 189, 211; *119*

Iberis 178, 194; *51, 74, 175*
  I. sempervirens 137, 162
Ilex 196
  I. aquifolium 'Silver Queen' 34; *35*
Impatiens balsamina 92
indigofera 196
Iris 28, 39, 59, 100, 124, 173, 178, 182, 205; *59, 98, 200*
  I. ensata 155
  I. foetidissima 'Variegata' 201
  I. kaempferi 97
  I. laevigata 74, 155; *75*
  I. l. 'Alba' 97
  I. pallida 189
  I. pseudacorus 98
  I. p. 'Variegata' 81, 182 196; *183*
  I. reticulata 179
  I. sibirica 194
  I. unguicularis 156
  water 28, 74, 182, 196; *183*
Irving, Washington 180
Islington 180–3
Italian gardens 13, 145, 197, 198; *13, 14*
ivy 15, 41, 46, 49, 50, 53, 58, 66, 75, 76, 81, 92, 100, 114, 122, 124, 125, 137, 141, 148, 149, 151, 154, 155, 156, 163, 173, 178, 179, 182, 183, 192, 194, 195, 196, 205, 208, 209, 210; *21, 27, 42, 58, 59, 63, 74, 75, 77, 79, 94, 134, 145, 152, 170, 263*
  'Boston' 72
  'Goldheart' 49

Jacob's ladder 92
Japanese gardens 82, 84, 86–8, 212
Jasminum 28, 46, 50, 74, 81, 114, 151, 163, 191, 200, 209
  J. officinale affine 186
  J. polyanthum 15, 176
  J. sambac 17
  J. suavissimum 15
  winter-flowering 36, 156
Jekyll, Gertrude 22, 144, 150, 151, 155, 174, 176, 191; *56, 150*
Jencks, Charles 214
Jerome, Jerome K. 198
Juniperus 21, 192, 194; *194*
  J. 'Blue Carpet' 200
  J. sabina var. *tamariscifolia* 198
  J. scopulorum 'Skyrocket' 105

kale, purple 106, 109; *106*
Kan, J. 112
Kensington 174–9
Kerria japonica 155, 178
Keswick, Maggie 214, 215
Kew Gardens 156, 164, 169, 189; *155*
Kipling, Rudyard 64
knot garden 34, 38, 40; *33, 35*
Koelreuteria 130
  K. paniculata 121; *120*
Koustam, Gerald 116

laburnum 76, 130, 151; *71, 77*
Ladbroke Estate 60–9
Lady Venice garden 51–3
Lambeth 30–4, 118
Lamium 20, 40, 41, 141, 195, 196, 199; *141*
  L. galeobdolon 75, 96
  L. maculatum 'Album' 205
Lantana sellowiana 15
lanterns (*yuki-mi-doro*) 87; *83, 84, 87, 88*
Lapageria 104
  L. rosea 17; *120*
larkspur 173; *173*
Lathyrus latifolius 114
  L. sativus 'Azureus' 176
laurel 77, 92, 194; *134*
  Portuguese 163; *72*
Laurus nobilis 137
Lavandula (lavender) 13, 34, 58, 124, 126, 137, 155, 163, 188, 189, 191, 198, 204; *55, 180, 186, 187, 191, 199, 217*
  'Grappenhall' 10
  'Hidcote' 14, 69, 189; *186*
Lavatera 50, 173, 188
  L. thuringiaca 'Barnsley' 80, 109, 117, 163, 178; *105*
  L. t. 'Rosea' 107
lemon balm 92
Lennox-Boyd, Mark 217
Leverhulme, Lord 144, 145
Leycesteria formosa 105
Ligularia 100
  L. dentata 'Desdemona' 20; *23*
  L. wilsoniana 168
Ligustrum ovalifolium
  'Argenteum' 80, 196
  L.o. 'Aureum' 195
lilac 39, 63, 77, 151, 154, 163, 172, 182, 188, 200, 202, 210
Lilium (lily) 14, 15, 64, 67, 74, 75, 124, 135, 183, 198, 209; *11, 64, 133, 137, 150, 183*
  canna 92
  day 100, 156
  L. 'African Queen' 135
  L. 'Apollo' 178
  L. 'Green Magic' 178

INDEX

L. 'Mont Blanc' 178
L. 'Pink Perfection' 50, 135
L. regale 14, 50, 81, 135, 163, 178
L. speciosum 135
L.s. rubrum 178
madonna 34
martagon 34
water 74, 98, 155; *98, 154*
lily-of-the-valley 163
lily ponds 57, 98, 145, 146, 148; *98, 100, 146*
lime 78, 130, 176, 202; *175*
pleached 10, 41; *11, 41*
Limonium latifolium 'Violetta' 124
Lindsay, Lady Amabel 63
Lindsey House, Chelsea 54–9
Lippia citriodora 137
Liriodendron 114
L. tulipifera 33
Little Venice houseboat 51–3
Lloyd George, David 160–1
lobelia 49–50, 53, 92, 183, 201; *51*
Lonicera 194, 195; *71, 192–3*
L. japonica 'Aureoreticulata' 76
L.j. 'Halliana' 29, 67, 75, 78; *79*
L. periclymenum 'Belgica' 14
L.p. 'Serotina' 14
L. purpusii 156
loosestrife 15
Lotus hirsutus 117
Loudoun, John Claudius 60, 64
lovage 117
Luma apiculata 80
lupin 46, 173
Lutyens, Edwin 56–7, 59, 176; *56*
Lysichiton 169; *167*
L. americanus 154
lythrum *107*

McIntosh, C. 149
McKeon, John 18, 22
macleaya 211
Magnolia 19, 72, 87, 155, 156, 162, 167, 202; *84, 155, 156*
Himalayan 24
M. campbellii mollicomata 24, 26; *25*
M. delavayi 168
M. denutada 97
M. grandiflora 10, 38, 67, 74, 105, 183, 208; *70, 72*
M. × soulangeana 100, 106, 189
M. × s. 'Alba Superba' 39, 155, 192; *153*
M. × s. 'Lennei' 155; *153*
M. tripelata 168
Mahonia 41, 77, 92, 124, 155, 156, 183, 186, 205; *77, 84, 175*
M. japonica 21, 178
M. × media 'Charity' 106, 163
mallow 92, 104, 163
Malus floribunda 104

Malvern Terrace, Barnsbury 190–1
maple 35, 44, 130, 196; *95*
marguerite 64, 161; *63, 159, 162*
marigold 53, 182
marjoram *70*, 97
Marvell, Andrew 77
Masson, Christopher 132, 134
Mawson, Thomas 142, 144
Medhurst, John 186
Melianthus major 80, 168, 201; *80*
Mentha requienii 204; *203*
Metasequoia glyptostroboides 112, 114, 117; *112, 116*
Miller, Philip 120, 121
Mimulus longifolia 15
Moore, Dennis 53
More, Sir Thomas 54, 120
mosaiculture 150
mulberry 32, 57, 63, 64, 75, 77, 98, 105, 130, 155, 180, 182, 186, 189; *58, 63, 64, 94, 181, 182*
Muscari comosum 'Plumosum' 34
Myosotis scorpioides 'Mermaid' 74
Myrtus communis tarentina 80
myrtle 15, 32, 80

Nandina domestica 105; *117*
nasturtium 92, 106, 173; *106*
Nepeta 75, 188; *187*
N. mussinii 210
N. nervosa 14, 201
New Landscape School 144, 150
Nicholas, Tsar 148
Nicholson, Rosemary and John 30, 34
nicotiana 64, 81, 209, 211
Notting Hill Gate 36–41

Oldfield, Thomas Albion 18, 190
Olea europaea 121
onothera 211
orchid 166, 188
Osbeckia stellata 135
Osmanthus delavayi 186
O. heterophyllus 'Aureo-marginatus' 196
Osmunda regalis 20, 67
Osteosperum 162
O. jucundum 189

Pachysandra 77, 87; *77*
P. terminalis 41
palm 105, 126, 130, 166; *104, 131*
Abyssinian banana 166, 167
Chusan 166
pampas-grass 106
Pandorea jasminoides 17, 134
pansy 49, 53, 178
Parrotia persica 44
Parthenocissus 189; *160*
P. henryana 124; *123*

P. tricuspidata 'Veitchii' 72
Passiflora antioquiensis 134–5
Paulownia tomentosa (syn. P. imperialis) 100–1, 105, 166–7
Paxton, Joseph 148, 149
pear 33, 98, 109, 124, 216; *192–3, 216*
weeping 68
Peckham street 90–3
pelargonium 15, 49, 50, 53, 64, 78, 92, 93, 106, 121, 173, 176, 179, 182, 183, 209; *17, 107*
P. 'Frank Hedley' 198
penstemon 13, 14, 78, 155, 178, 201, 210
peony/*Paeonia* 64, 66, 80, 87, 100, 101, 121, 151, 163, 173, 178, 210, 216; *63, 64, 200, 217*
P. cambessedesii 100, 101
P. mascula arietana 101
P. mlokosewitshii 101
P. 'Souvenir de Maxime Cornu' 97–8
P. 'Superb' 100
P. tennuifolia 101
tree 97–8, 100, 104, 105, 106, 124, 182
Pepys, Samuel 186
pergolas 14, 64, 65–6, 88, 126, 135, 142, 145, 154, 155, 161, 162, 163, 187, 199; *43, 65, 131, 142, 155*
periwinkle 92, 194
Perovskia atriplicifolia 162
P.a. 'Blue Spire' 188
Petasites japonicus giganteus 169; *167*
petunia 49, 53, 150, 163, 176, 183, 209; *50, 159, 178*
Philadelphus 41, 66, 81, 93, 124, 137, 182, 183, 189, 200, 201; *41, 122*
dwarf 124
P. coronarius 77
P.c. 'Aureus' 44, 178
Phillips, Roger 172–3
Phlomis 124, 125
P. chrysophylla 21; *22*
P. fruticosa 39, 205
Phlox 75, 178
'Chattahoochee' 176
'White Admiral' 69
phormium 21
photinia 155
Phygelius 'Winchester Fanfare' 199
Phyllostachys nigra 105, 168
P. viridis 168
physic garden 33, 118–21
Pieris 29, 104, 115; *113*
P. 'Forest Flame' 22
P. japonica 80
P.j. 'Variegata' 29
pileostegia 163
pineapple 120
pinks 14, 34, 40, 98, 189, 196, 198; *97, 199*

'Laced Romeo' 14
'Margaret Curtis' 14
'Mrs Sinkins' 14, 40, 125
'Prudence' 14
Pitcairn, Dr William 148
Pittosporum 29
P. 'Irene Patterson' 29
P. tenuifolium 'Variegatum' 28
plane tree 33, 39, 40, 122, 125, 172, 183, 186, 189; *88, 170*
Platanus orientalis 20
Pleioblastus viridistriatus 168
plum tree 33, 130
plumbago 135
Polianthes tuberosa 135
Polygonum 53, 141, 178
P. sachalinense 22
pools and ponds 20, 28, 74, 87, 100, 101, 102, 105, 121, 134, 141, 149, 155, 164, 169, 182, 187, 188, 200; *20, 21, 23, 70, 75, 97, 128, 131, 132, 136, 141, 147, 152, 154, 155, 165, 183, 198*
goldfish pond 176
poppy 15, 64, 92, 125, 173; *63, 107*
Welsh 194
Populus lasiocarpa 167
post-modern garden 212–17
potentilla 21, 183
pot garden 209; *210*
Primula 28, 121, 178; *29, 33, 119*
candelabra 155
P. auricula 34
P. marginata 115
privet 10, 78; *11*
Prunus 104
P. 'Amanogawa' 65–6
P. cerasifera 'Pissardii' 77, 114, 201
P. laurocerasus 'Otto Luyken' 68, 75
P. × subhirtella 'Autumnalis Rosea' *179*
P. 'Tai Haku' 28, 39; *29, 101*
Pulmonaria 28; *200*
P. saccharata 'Alba' 205
pulsatilla 124
Putney, Cornish Combe in 24–9
Pyracantha 116, 124, 137, 163, 182, 194, 199, 201; *134, 197*
'Orange Glow' 75
Pyrus 200
P. salicifolia 199; *201*
P.s. 'Pendula' 68, 69, 75, 163; *22*

Quercus ilex 125
quince 32, 33, 105

Raworth, Mr and Mrs Richard 10, 15, 17; *16, 17*
redwood, dawn 112, 114, 117; *112, 116*
Regent's Canal 51–3

222

INDEX

Rhamnus alaternus 'Argenteo-
variegata' 28, 40
Rheum palmatum 58
Rhodochiton atrosanguineum 17
Rhododendron 26, 41, 66, 67, 72, 77,
92, 104, 105, 183, 200, 210, 211
   R. 'Cilpense' 28, 124, 155
   R. 'Grumpy' 137
   R. 'Lady Alice Fitzwilliam' 125
   R. 'Lady Chamberlain' 106; *110*
   R. *lindleyi* 134
   R. 'Pink Pearl' 178
   R. *yakushimanum* 113, 137; *115*
Rhus purpurea 20
Ribes 105; *104*
   R. *sanguineum* 155
   R.s. 'Brocklebankii' 200
Rickey, George 189; *189*
Robin, Jean 32
Robinia 68
   R. *pseudoacacia* 32, 68, 135, 199;
93
   R.p. 'Frisia' 93, 125
   R.p. 'Tortuosa' 92–3
Robinson, William 144–5, 150,
174, 176, 190, 191; *150*
rockery 102, 105, 121; *111*
rock rose 98
rocks 104–5, 149, 212, 216
   Zen use of 86–7; *82, 86*
rodgersia 58
roof gardens: Chelsea 42–8
   Derry & Toms 126–31
   Lady Venice 51–3
Roper, Lanning 132, 186, 188, 189;
184
Rosa, acicularis nipponensis 34
   R. *banksiae* 28, 191; *29*
   R.b. 'Lutea' 204
   R. *centifolia pomponia* (de
Meaux') 34
   R. *chinensis* (China rose) 14
   R. *gallica officinalis* 34
   R.g. 'Versicolor' 34, 74; *33*
   R. *glauca* 28, 80, 91, 178, 199,
200; *199*
   R. *laevigata* 'Cooperi' 74
   R. *moyesii* 125
   R. *multiflora* 76
rose/*Rosa* 26, 28, 29, 32, 34, 39, 46,
50, 59, 63, 64, 66, 75, 76, 91, 92,
98, 100, 104, 116, 117, 124, 126,
128, 137, 141, 142, 144, 149, 154,
156, 161, 162, 163, 176, 182, 188,
189, 191, 199, 201, 208, 209, 210,
211; *29, 55, 71, 77, 100, 104, 112,
138, 149, 180, 191, 197, 199, 205,
207*
   'Albéric Barbier' 39, 163; *38, 160*
   'Albertine' 178, 209
   'Aloha' 115; *63, 115*
   'Apple Dawn' 124

'Ballerina' 50, 137
'Blanc Double de Coubert' 27
'Bloomfield Abundance' 21
'Blue Moon' 149
'Bobbie James' 21; *22*
'Boule de Neige' 28; *29*
'Buff Beauty' 92, 116, 151, 171,
186
'Burgundia' 34
'Canary Bird' 199; *199*
'Cardinal Hume' 124
'Cécile Brunner' 21
'Céleste' 14
'Cérise Bouquet' 151
'Charles Austin' *186*
'Climbing Lady Hillingdon' 200
'Compassion' 116, 137
'Constance Spry' 211
'Crimson Glory' 149
'Duc de Guiche' 14
'Duchess d'Angoulême' 14
'Duchesse de Montebello' 14
'Elizabeth Arden' 149
'The Fairy' 67, 200
'Fantin-Latour' 28
'Félicia' 75
'Félicité Perpétue' 81; *80*
'Ferdinand Pichard' 200
'Fountain' 92
'Frühlingsgold' 189
'Gloire de Dijon' 116
'The Garland' 77
'Golden Showers' 29, 178
'Golden Wings' 189
'Graham Thomas' 189
'Iceberg' 28, 69, 100, 182, 191,
199, 205, 210; *36, 67, 69, 187, 199*
'Kathleen Harrop' 68
'Kiftsgate' 64, 188, 204
'Königin von Dänemark' 188
'Little White Pet' 21
'Magenta' 116
'Maiden's Blush' 11
'Mary Rose' 50
'de Meaux' 34, 137
'Mermaid' 202
'Mme Grégoire Staechelin' 36,
198
'Mme Hardy' 40, 188; *187*
'Mme Isaac Pereire' 137
'Mme Pierre Oger' 11
'Moonlight' 69
'Mousseline' 21
'Mrs Oakley Fisher' 200
'Nevada' 28, 106, 189
'New Dawn' 14, 28, 39, 59, 65,
209, 211; *29, 66*
'Old Blush' 20
'Paul's Himalayan Musk' 151
'Peace' 149
'Penelope' 163
'Pink Perpetue' 46

'Queen Elizabeth' 38, 116
'Rambling Rector' 14
'Roseraie de l'Haÿ' 28
'Sanders' White Rambler' 178,
188
'Sarah van Fleet' 28, 40
'Schneezwerg' 27
'Schoolgirl' 116
'Seagull' 15, 204
'Sophie's Perpetual' 14
'Super Star' 176
'Toby Tristram' 188
'Veilchenblau' 116
'Wedding Day' 72
'Yvonne Rabier' 40, 205, 216
'Zéphirine Drouhin' 21, 65
rosemary 10, 21, 34, 75, 80, 126;
22, 31, 205
Rubus 'Tridel' 183; *41*
Ruta 66; *199*
   R. *graveolens* 'Jackman's Blue'
162

sage 188
   pineapple 200
Salix babylonica pekinensii
'Tortuosa' 154
   S. *serpyllifolia* 115
salpiglossis 150
Salvia 34, 150, 201; *121, 187*
   S. *haematodes* 69
   S. *officinalis* 'tricolor' *33*
   S. *patens* 178
   S. *uliginosa* 14
Santolina 66, 69, 75, 124, 163, 204,
210; *203*
   S. *chamaecyparissus* 34
   S.c. *nana* 38
Sambucus nigra 'Laciniata' 183
   S. *racemosa* 'Plumosa Aurea' 186
Sasa palmata 168
Sauromatum venosum 200
Saxifraga 124, 200
   S. *cortusifolia* 125
Scabiosa 15
   S. 'Butterfly Blue' 188
schizanthus 150
seats (garden furniture) 66, 67–8,
91, 100, 146, 162, 163, 179, 182,
187, 188, 189, 196, 211; *32, 96, 185*
   wrought-iron 64, 81, 96, 100,
151; *63, 80*
'secret' gardens 76, 91, 93, 100,
138–41, 210; *77, 89, 96*
Semiarundinaria fastuosa 168
sempervivum 13, 98; *98*
Shika odoshi 88; *84*
shrubbery, shrub garden 76, 187,
192, 209, 211; *175, 208*
sink garden 10, 13
Sisyrinchium 198; *199*
   S. *striatum* 75, 98, 124, 204; *97*

Sitwell, Sir George 142, 144, 145
Sitwell, Osbert 145
skimmia 10, 72, 78, 100, 200; *200*
Sloane, Sir Hans 120–1
Smart, Christopher 180
smilacina 100
smoke tree 44
snowdrop 100, 117; *96*
Solanum crispum 163
   S. *jasminoides* 135
   S.j. 'Album' 14, 20, 182
Soleirolia soleirolii 20, 46, 88; *20, 21,
88*
Sollya heterophylla 116
Solomon's seal 100; *31*
Sophora tetraptera 125
Sorbus 210
   S. *aria* 182
Spanish garden 126, 128, 130; *127,
128, 131*
spiderwort 33
Spiraea × vanhouttei 205
Spry, Constance 206
Stachys byzantina 163, 178, 182;
162, 180
   S.b. 'Silver Carpet' 40
Stachyurus praecox 39, 156
stairs, steps 74, 75–6, 97, 98, 137,
145, 154, 198, 204, 216–17; *72, 73,
75, 79, 142, 155, 203, 212, 214*
   spiral 27, 46, 122
statuary, sculpture 13, 46, 76, 77,
78, 91–2, 116, 121, 122, 125, 154,
169, 179, 182, 188–9, 194, 195,
198, 201, 209; *14, 15, 27, 38, 42, 74,
77, 78, 113, 125, 152, 175, 189, 194,
201*
Stefanides, John 57
Stein, Mrs Mary 114
Stenham, Cob 74, 192
Stephanaudra incisa 194
Stewartia sinensis 125
stock, night-scented 209; *206*
Stokesia laevis 124
strawberries: alpine 109, 191; *191*
   wild 72, 194; *70*
Strawberry House, Chiswick
152–7
streptocarpus 15
Sturgis, R. Clipston 20
Sui Yang Ti, Emperor, Western
Park of 84
summerhouses 81, 145
Summers, Martin 42–7
sundials 117, 146, 217; *112*
sweet pea 46, 50, 189
sweet william 211; *173*
sycamore 104, 114, 151, 186
Symphoricarpos orbiculatus 'Foliis
Variegatis' 194, 195
symphytum 15, 28; *29*
Syringa meyeri 'Palibin' 151

223

INDEX

tamarisk 163
Taxus baccata 'Dovastonii Aurea' 194
tea house, Japanese 87–8; *84, 86*
terraces 18, 20, 28, 39, 58, 64, 74, 78, 80, 114–15, 134, 135, 145, 161, 163, 173, 183, 192, 204; *22, 64, 70, 72, 76, 122, 132, 133, 155, 163, 174, 200, 202, 203*
    York stone 66, 67, 96, 122, 124, 154, 182, 187, 198–9; *180, 199, 203, 206, 209*
Thematic House, Jencks' 214
teucrium 34
Thackeray, William 96
Thalictrum 11
    T. aquilegiifolium 124
thrift 34, 204
Thuja 194
    T. plicata 13, 14–15
Thymus (thyme) 34, 162, 192, 198; *162, 199*
    T. × citriodorus 'Silver Queen' 204
    T. serpyllum albus 204
toadflax, ivy-leaved 195; *196*
tombs 30, 34; *31, 35*
topiary 78, 80, 102, 105, 192, 196, 208, 209; *11, 180*
Trachelospermum jasminoides 15, 47
    T.j. 'Variegatum' 176
Trachycarpus fortunei 166
Trachystemon orientalis 20; *19*
Tradescant, John, the Elder 30, 32–3, 34, 118; *35*
Tradescant, John, the Younger 33, 172; *35*

Tradescant Garden, Lambeth 30–4
Tradescantia 34, 64; *64*
    T. fluminensis 33
    T. virginiana 33
tree of heaven 130, 166–7
trefoil, black 204
Trinity Hospice 184–9
Trollope, Anthony 170
tuberose 135
Tulipa 163; *33, 159*
    T. sylvestris 34
tulip tree 33, 98
    Himalayan 24, 26; *25*
Turner, Kenneth 206–11
Twickenham 10–17

verbena 176, 191; *178*
Verey, Charles 187; *185*
Veronica gentianoides 204; *203*
Viburnum 10, 39, 41, 46, 106, 200
    V. × bodnantse 106, 156
    V. × burkwoodii 155
    V. × carlesii 67, 205; *66*
    V. davidii 67, 124
    V. farreri 106, 211
    V. plicatum 'Lanarth' 125
    V.p. 'Mariesii' 44, 66, 199, 210; *199*
    V. tinus 75
    V. vitifolium 188
Victorian gardens 63–4, 146–51
vines 33, 128, 130, 135, 208; *126, 127*
The Vineyard, Fulham 158–63; *7*
Viola 28, 50, 67, 81, 92, 176, 191, 201; *50, 63, 97*

    V. cornuta 205
    V.c. alba 205
    V. septentrionalis 34
violet 117, 125, 156, 204
viper's bugloss 15
Virginia creeper 128, 189; *126*
Vitis 71
    V. 'Brant' 28; *29*
    V. coignetiae 76, 109, 135; *103, 135*
    V. pulchra 28
    V. solanum 133
    V. vinifera 'Purpurea' 194

Walford, Edward 72
wallflower 92
Walpole, Hon. Thomas 96
Walpole House, Chiswick 94–101
Walton, Izaak 32–3
Wandsworth 206–11
Ward Bagshaw, Dr Nathaniel 150
waterfalls 105, 149, 198; *111, 147, 198*
water gardens 121, 155, 195–6
water iris 28, 74, 182, 196; *183*
waterlily 74, 98, 155; *98, 154*
Watts, John 120
Weigela 29, 41, 44
    W. florida 'Variegata' 28, 29, 69; *44*
Whistler, James McNeill 56
whitebeam 28, 182
White Conduit House 18
white gardens 38, 39, 40, 67, 69, 202–5; *37*
Whittington, Mrs Sue 197–201
Wigandia urens 169

wild gardens 15, 78, 80–1, 100, 122, 124, 140, 161, 163, 188, 195, 196; *17, 96, 140, 160, 161, 196*
Wilkinson, Norman 154, 155
Williams, J. C. 28
willow, weeping 42, 68, 154; *128*
Wilson, Keith 42
Wisteria 10, 40, 64, 74, 78, 88, 92, 105, 106, 124, 125, 126, 128, 144, 151, 155, 162, 163, 173, 176, 179, 183, 186, 191, 194, 216; *10, 12, 16, 64, 79, 105, 145*
    W. floribunda 'Alba' 14, 204
    W.f. 'Multijuga' 58; *205*
    W. sinensis 162, 189
Wood, Anne 186
woodland gardens 34, 38, 40, 63–4, 67, 68, 100, 117, 121, 122, 125, 128, 130, 161, 162, 163, 173, 189, 195, 200; *40, 63, 96, 124, 125, 128, 129, 162, 170, 192–3, 197, 198*
wych elm 122

yew 13, 39–40, 69, 76, 77, 155, 186, 192, 194, 196; *142, 152, 155*
    hedges 13, 39, 41, 58, 76, 77, 100, 162, 196, 216, 217; *13, 17, 37, 59, 77, 96, 212, 214*
    Irish 74, 178; *190*
Yoshimura, Toshiyuki 86, 88; *87*
yucca 104, 105, 137, 166; *108, 111, 134*
    Y. filamentosa 33

Zantedeschia aethiopica 74, 92
Zen garden in Fulham 82–8

224